CONTRIBUTIONS *to the* HISTORY *of* ANCIENT FAMILIES *of* NEW AMSTERDAM *and* NEW YORK

CONTRIBUTIONS *to the* HISTORY *of* ANCIENT FAMILIES *of* NEW AMSTERDAM *and* NEW YORK

Edwin R. Purple

foreword by

Richard H. Benson

NEW ENGLAND HISTORIC
GENEALOGICAL SOCIETY

ISBN-13: 978-088082-308-1
Library of Congress Number: 2013948514

Cover design by Carolyn Sheppard Oakley and Ginevra Morse.
Cover image: "A Description of the Towne of Mannados or New Amsterdam," 1664;
used courtesy of D. Brenton Simons.

Printed in the United States of America

NEW ENGLAND HISTORIC GENEALOGICAL SOCIETY
Boston, Massachusetts
AmericanAncestors.org
2013

FOREWORD

Edwin R. Purple (1831–1879), author of *Contributions to the History of Ancient Families of New Amsterdam and New York*, published most of the contents of this book in *The New York Genealogical and Biographical Record* between 1875 and 1879. His work was based on original sources, and although infrequently footnoted, his wording often implied the sources of his information. His articles have stood the test of time, and some are still cited as the only compiled accounts of certain families, such as Sammans.

The key source Purple used was the records of the New York Dutch Reformed Church, which were published in the Record beginning in 1874. Early New York did not have vital records, and there were limited land and probate records. The church records are particularly valuable because they include wives' maiden names in marriage and baptismal records; the latter also include the names of sponsors, who were often relatives of the parents. However, the church records are sometimes difficult to use because spellings of names had not yet been standardized.

No doubt the manuscript records from the church were available to Purple, and he evidently studied them carefully to produce his section on Dutch aliases and variant spellings (pp. 115–120). He was cautious in his approach to stating relationships, which makes his work all the more valuable, especially when compared to the excessive statements of some of his contemporaries. For example, on p. 114 he says, "I suspect this Didlof Doren was the eldest son of Claes Ditelofszen . . . [and] . . . I suggest that it not improbable that Claes Ditlo, or Didlo, was identically the Claes Ditelofszen above mentioned."

Purple was one of several careful and capable late nineteenth-century genealogists researching New York families. Although many more sources are available today, the work of these genealogists is still valuable for their insights and well-considered theories, and frequently their work has not been superseded.

Richard H. Benson
Author of *The Barent Jacobsen Cool Family*

ANCIENT FAMILIES

OF

NEW YORK.

CONTRIBUTIONS

TO THE

HISTORY OF ANCIENT FAMILIES

OF

NEW AMSTERDAM AND NEW YORK.

By EDWIN R. PURPLE,

WITH A BIOGRAPHICAL SKETCH ON THE AUTHOR; AND ADDITIONS AND
EMENDATIONS TO THE WORK,

By SAMUEL S. PURPLE, M.D.

NEW YORK:
PRIVATELY PRINTED.
1881.

CONTENTS.

CONTENTS.

In Memoriam.*

EDWIN RUTHVEN PURPLE, the third son of Lyman Smith Purple and Minerva Sheffield his wife, was born in the town of Sherburne, Chenango Co., N. Y., on June 30, 1831. His maternal grandfather, James (Fones) Sheffield, was born in Charlestown, R. I., April 12, 1766, and was of the medical profession. His paternal grandfather was Ansel Purple, born in Middle Haddam, Ct., in 1773, and his earlier paternal ancestor Edward Purple, of Haddam, Ct., 1674, was of English descent.

After the death of his father, which occurred May 7, 1839, and before Edwin was eight years old, he was placed by his mother and elder brother at school in Earlville, Madison Co., N. Y., where he continued until the spring of 1846. In the summer of that and the following year he was employed at farm labor, living at home during the winter months, and attending the Earlville Academy—deemed at that time one of the best and most flourishing high schools in the county. In March, 1847, he came to the City of New York and secured employment as a clerk in a drygoods importing house. Here he remained about three years, until the spring of 1850. In 1848 he became a member of the Laight Street Baptist Church, to which his family belonged, and to which he remained attached while in the city.

In 1850 his employer arranged to close his business in New York, and established himself in San Francisco, Cal.—the land of great promise and of great attraction—and made such favorable overtures as to induce Edwin to follow him to that El Dorado; and accordingly, April 13, 1850, he embarked, on the steamship Cherokee, for Chagres, and went thence to Panama, where he took a sailing vessel (the bark Winthrop) for San Francisco, where he arrived on the 12th of July following, taking up three months, instead of a six months' passage around Cape Horn. On arrival he found that his employer, who had preceded him, had sold the stock of merchandise to arrive, and had abandoned the idea of setting up business for himself in California, having found that it was easier to sell goods at a profit than to secure a store at a moderate rent, or have any assurance against disaster. Remaining in San Francisco a few days, he went to Sacramento City, where, through the introduction of a friend, he hired an ox-team and wagon, loaded it with flour and other provisions, and started

* In part condensed from memorial sketches read before the New York Genealogical and Biographical Society, by Charles B. Moore, Esq. ; and the New York Academy of Medicine, by Laurence Johnson, M.D.

on a trading tour across the Sierra Nevada mountain range, to meet the incoming emigration across the plains. This expedition proved successful, and to him was both romantic and adventurous. Soon after his return to Sacramento, late in August, 1850, the cholera broke out there, and for days the principal business houses and public places of that city were closed, and the streets nearly deserted. On this calamitous account he left for San Francisco, and from thence went to Stockton, where, in December, 1850, he fell back to his former quiet position, and obtained a clerkship in the store of Seneca Dean, formerly of Orange Co., N. Y. There were many in that region from the Empire State.

In February, 1851, he commenced *mining* at Carson's Creek and Murphy's Camp, in Calaveras Co., and in October of that year formed a copartnership with Edwin T. Lake, an old trader in mining supplies, on the North Branch of the Calaveras River, and remained in this business two years. In the fall of 1853 he dissolved copartnership with Mr. Lake, designing to return to New York; but, being detained longer than he expected in the settlement of his business, he commenced the study of law in the office of William Jeff. Gatewood, Esq., of San Andreas, two miles from North Branch. His practical observance of rules as an accountant made the study of law as a science less difficult to him. In September, 1854, he was elected one of the justices in the Fifth Township, then one of the most populous in Calaveras Co. At that time the jurisdiction of justices of the peace extended to all actions, and in civil cases where the amount involved did not exceed five hundred dollars, and they had original jurisdiction in all actions to determine the right to mining claims. The business of the office, both civil and criminal, was large, and during his term was increased by disability, by reason of sickness of Judge Spencer, the other Township Justice. His mind and talents, to say nothing of his patience, were fully exercised. In the fall of 1855 he was elected one of the three supervisors of Calaveras County, and served in that capacity one year. In November, 1855, he was admitted to practise as an attorney at law in the county courts of Calaveras County. From 1855 to 1860 he was one of the nine proprietors, and was the secretary and treasurer of the San Antonio Ridge Ditch and Mining Company, which, in addition to supplying water for mining and agricultural purposes in the central portion of Calaveras Co., was also extensively engaged in the manufacture and sale of lumber in that region.

In May, 1860, he removed to Fort Yuma, California, where he was employed as Agent of the Butterfield Overland Mail Company, until the mail service between St. Louis and San Francisco on the southern route was discontinued in April, 1861. At that date, a contract having been made by the company with the government to carry a daily overland mail between St. Joseph's, Missouri, and Placerville, California, commencing July 1, 1861, the stock and stages of the company from Tucson in Arizona to Los Angelos in California were ordered to the new route between Placerville and Great Salt Lake City. On the 8th of May, 1861, in charge of one hundred and thirty horses and eighteen stages, with thirty men, he left Los Angelos for Salt Lake City, where he arrived, without the loss of an animal, on the 16th of June; the distance being about eight hundred miles, and half of which was through a desert country, inhabited only by roving bands of Indians. Here, as the Agent of the Overland Company, he remained until June, 1862, and then left there with a small company, principally old Californian acquaintances, for the Salmon River Gold Diggings in Oregon. Their heavy wagons loaded with supplies and drawn by oxen, were compelled to travel slowly, while the unusual falls of rain that season along the route greatly increased the difficulty and labor of crossing the mountain streams and very much retarded their progress. On the 30th of July they reached the Beaver Head, the main stream of the Jefferson Fork of the Missouri River, which they *prospected* for gold. Not finding the precious metal in paying quantities, they pushed on north to Gold Creek, in Deer Lodge Valley, where they arrived on the 7th of August. Here they concluded to abandon the idea of going to the Salmon River Mines, near Fort Walla Walla, 425 miles distant, and, owing to the shortness of the season, made preparations to go into winter quarters at Stuart's ranche, located at the mouth of Gold Creek, and owned by two brothers, James and Granville Stuart (afterward called American Fork). This was a favorite winter resort of the early trappers and pioneers. After leaving the Beaver Head they met a party of seven men, John White and others, on their way from Deer Lodge to Willard's Creek (a tributary of the Beaver Head) for the purpose of prospecting it for gold. These were undoubtedly the first white men that found gold in Willard's Creek (or Grasshopper, as it was called by them), the discovery of which peopled that country, till then a mountain wilderness, with at least fifteen thousand inhabitants in the spring and summer following. They contended with the rocks for subsistence and for wealth, and not with each other in arms, and, finding other rich placers in that region, fixed the status of Montana as one of the richest and most valuable of the western gold and silver producing Territories.

In December, 1862, Mr. Purple opened a store at Bannack City, where these new discoveries of gold were made, his stock in trade consisting principally of provisions and mining utensils, which had been brought with him from Salt Lake City. Having disposed of these, in December, 1863, he left the Territory of Montana for New York, where he arrived in February, 1864, after an absence from his native State of nearly fourteen years. Here he entered into a business connection with Gov. James Duane Doty, ex-Gov. of Wisconsin, and others, for the sale of mining property, in which they were mutually interested in Montana. In April, 1864, he left again for that territory, but was taken seriously sick, and returned in December following to New York. His many exposures had impaired his health.

In 1869 he became a member of the New York Genealogical and Biographical Society—the first year of the existence of the Society. On the 10th of December, 1870, he read before the Society his first paper, being extracts from the MS. autobiography of William Gowans, the antiquarian bookseller and publisher then but recently deceased. On the 13th of May, 1871, he read a paper on the Biography of Cadwallader Colden, a Colonial Governor, Physician, and Philosopher. He gradually acquired an interest in genealogical investigations and a taste for family history. He took up the Colden papers, in possession of his brother, and prepared for the New York Genealogical and Biographical Record the " *Notes Biographical and Genealogical of the Colden Family, and some of its Collateral Branches in America,*" which were published in the number for October,

1873. These notes were, perhaps, kept back too long, to give place to others less important and less attractive. An edition of fifty copies, in book form, of this article was privately printed in 1873.

The number of the RECORD for January, 1875, contained from his pen an elaborate *Biographical and Genealogical Sketch of David Provoost of New Amsterdam, and some of his Descendants.* An edition of one hundred copies of this article, in book form, was *privately printed* in 1875.

From early youth he exhibited a deep-rooted fondness for exact knowledge, particularly mathematics and history. This in after years led him, in genealogical pursuits, to examine carefully the source of New Netherland family history; and his attention was soon directed to the changing forms of Dutch family nomenclature. His careful and untiring application to this class of difficult investigations soon made him an expert in tracing with certainty the descendants of the first settlers of New Amsterdam.

The first instalment of his "*Contributions to the History of the Ancient Families of New York*" appeared in the RECORD for April, 1876, containing four generations of the Stillé, Woretendyk, Van Schaick, Somerendyk, Siecken, alias Dey family, Brevoort, Grevenraet, De Reimer, and Zyperus families. In the July number, Wouterszen Van Breestede, Peterzen Van Alcmaer, Santvoort, Echerson, Sammans, Stridles, Wanshaer, Tymens, and Van der Veen families. In the October number, the first three generations of the Leisler family, correcting many previous errors, and with a note embracing the De Kleyn family. An emended edition, consisting of seventy-five copies, in book form, was privately printed in 1877, with the following title: *Genealogical Notes Relating to Lieut. Gov. Jacob Leisler and his Family Connections in New York.* In the January number for 1877 appeared the Loockermans and Varicks; in the April and July numbers, the Kip family (much more full and exact than any we had before), with two corrections. An emended edition of seventy-five copies, in book form, was privately printed in 1877 with the following title: "*Contributions to the History of the Kip Family of New York and New Jersey.*"

In the numbers of the RECORD from January, 1878, to January, 1879, appeared the Meyer, De Meyer, and Varleth families, with various family connections, such as the Hermans, Brockholst, French, Philipse, Teller, Schuyler, Bayard, and others. There also appeared in the number for January, 1879, his very important and instructive list of "Dutch Aliases." To him are the readers of the RECORD indebted for the laborious indexes to names of several of the volumes of that work.

These varied and important contributions to the family history of New Amsterdam (or New Netherland) and New York, much of the material for which are derived from the unpublished as well as published records of the Reformed Dutch and other churches, are herewith reprinted, with extensive emendations and additions, as a memorial by his surviving brother.

It perhaps need not be said—nor is it to be supposed—that all he has written has been published. In the preparation of this personal history we have been permitted to consult the MS. history of the Purple Family, prepared, with much labor, by him and his only surviving brother,

He died at 47 years of age, and his travels and labors are ended. His style, like that of a truthful genealogist, was as free from surplusage, embellishment, or ornament, as that of an accountant's ledger. He had something biographical to say, but no one would discover by what he said that he had travelled far, or that he had ever visited California. His notes of travels, which are preserved, are both interesting and important. He wrote about such a notable character as Lieut.-Gov. JACOB LEISLER, so that few, whether friendly or hostile, had any reply or complaint; and in his writings there are exhibitions of depth and strength of thought and sentiment deserving of particular notice.

In 1876, the New York Academy of Medicine, having purchased a building for its use, and having received from his brother, who was then its President, a gift of over three thousand volumes of medical works, the value of which has been estimated at ten thousand dollars, Mr. Purple was selected to the important position of assistant or acting librarian, and, in the language of Dr. Laurence Johnson, his biographer before the Academy, he entered upon the duties of the office in the autumn of that year. He brought to the task before him not only a love for books, but an inexhaustible fund of patience. He began his work with the same painstaking care that characterized his labors as a genealogist, and of the work *he* here performed but little will ever have to be undone. He labored zealously and hopefully. He believed in a great and successful future for this library, and had an unbounded faith in its ultimate success. He continued to arduously labor in the library until February, 1878, when a sudden and alarming hemorrhage from the stomach suspended, for a time, his work. His progress toward recovery was slow. He visited the library from time to time, but his active labors were over. When satisfied that he would never be able to resume active duty as librarian, he tendered his resignation, and presented the sum due him as salary, which he had never drawn from the beginning of his work, to the library fund of the Academy, initiated by his brother. This generous and graceful act, on the part of one not a member, was without precedent in the history of the Academy. It deserved a special recognition. To provide for this and any future contingency of like character, the Academy created the honorary title of Benefactor, and Mr. Purple was the first elected to that title. His gift formed the nucleus of the Academy's present library endowment, which has grown, as the library has grown, to respectable dimensions. His death from pneumonia occurred on the 20th of January, 1879. To us of the New York Academy of Medicine, his life was full of promise and usefulness. He began here a work which is left to others to carry on toward completion. It is peculiarly fitting in this new Library Hall, which has just been dedicated under such brilliant auspices, that we pause for a moment from the usual labor which engages us to pay the tribute of respect to the memory of one whose last years were consecrated to its service.

He was the recipient of distinguished honors from various historical and other learned societies, none of which did he value more than that of honorary member of the Historical Society of Montana, located at Helena City, Montana.

On the 13th of February, 1868, he married MARY FRANCES, daughter of Charles HAWLEY and of Mary Van Antwerp (Lynch) Close of New York. Five children were born to them—three survive him, all daughters. His wife's descent was brought out briefly in the *History of the Kip Family*, and this was written when his little child was fatally sick. The dedication of it, as separately printed, was to the memory of this child as follows :

In Memoriam.

TO

SARAH SHEFFIELD PURPLE,

Born May 30, 1875, Died July 5, 1876,

In whose veins mingled the blood of some of the

FIRST

DUTCH HUGUENOT AND PURITAN SETTLERS

OF

NEW NETHERLAND AND NEW ENGLAND,

These Contributions,

to the preparation of which her brief life gave additional incentive,

Are Dedicated,

With Ardent Love for her Memory and Profound Sorrow for Her early Death,

By Her Father.

PEDIGREE.

Hendrick Hendrickszen Kip[1], Isaac Hendrickszen Kip[2], Isaac Kip[3], Abraham Kip[4], Gerrit Kip[5], Abraham Kip[6], Rachel Kip[7] (wife of James Lynch), Mary V. Lynch[8] (wife of Chas. H. Close), Mary Frances Close[9] (wife of Edwin R. Purple).

Issue :—Mary C. Purple[10], Frances M. Purple[10], Amelia G. Purple[10].

Adam Brower[1], Jacob Brower[2], Jacob Brower[3], Johannes Brower[4], Ellenor Brower[5] (wife of Gerrit Kip[5]), Abraham Kip[6], Rachel Kip[7] (wife of James Lynch), Mary V. Lynch[8] (wife of Chas. H. Close), Mary Frances Close[9] (wife of Edwin R. Purple).

Issue :—Mary C. Purple[10], Frances M. Purple[10], Amelia G. Purple[10].

Dr. Johannes De La Montagne[1], had by wife Rachel Defour, Jan De La Montagne[2], Jr., who had by wife Pieternella Picques, Jan De La Montagne[3], born in Amsterdam, who had by wife Annetie Waldron, Pieternella De La Montagne[4] (wife of Jacob Brower[3]), Johannes Brower[5], Ellenor Brower[6] (wife of Gerrit Kip[5]), Abraham Kip[7], Rachel Kip[8] (wife of James Lynch), Mary V. Lynch[9] (wife of Chas. H. Close), Mary Frances Close[10] (wife of Edwin R. Purple).

Issue :—Mary C. Purple[11], Frances M. Purple[11], Amelia G. Purple[11].

Gerrit Lansing[1], Hendrick Lansing[2], Maria Lansing[3] (wife of Huybert Gerritszen Van den Berg[2]), Maria Van den Berg[4] (wife of Abraham Kip[4]), Gerrit Kip[5], Abraham Kip[6], Rachel Kip[7] (wife of James Lynch), Mary V. Lynch[8] (wife of Chas. H. Close), Mary Frances Close[9] (wife of Edwin R. Purple).

Issue :—Mary C. Purple, Frances M. Purple, Amelia G. Purple.

ANCIENT FAMILIES

OF NEW YORK.

A proper respect for the memory of ancestors is not only laudable, but deeply implanted in the hearts of the good and wise of all civilized nations. To affect indifference to matters that pertain to family history is but to acknowledge the weakness of conceit, and to ignore the well-established law " that the past is the parent of the future." The founders of the new world, whatever may have been their ancestral origin in the old, joined hands and hearts in a common issue—the planting of a nation whose influence is now felt to the remotest parts of the earth. To trace the origin and disclose the somewhat obscure relations of some of the ancient families of the colony and State of New York is the purpose of the following pages.

STILLE. WOERTENDYK. SOMERENDYK.

(FIRST FOUR GENERATIONS.)

CORNELIS JACOBSEN, alias CORNELIS JACOBSEN VAN VREELANDT, alias CORNELIS JACOBSEN STILLE, the ancestor of the Somerendyck and Woertendyk families, was in New Amsterdam as early as May, 1639, and may have been the junior Cornelis Jacobsen, who, with Cornelis Jacobsen, Senior, of Mertensdyk, leased, on the 14th of May, 1638, from Barent Dircksen, baker, the bouwery or farm called Walenstyne. He and Jan Jacobsen Stille, probably his brother, were farmers and leased together 15th August, 1639, from Jonas Bronck, a lot of land with dwelling-house and stock. His brother was probably the Jan Jacobsen of Vrelant, who made a marriage contract, August 15, 1639, with Maritje Pieters, of Copenhagen, and who conveyed, July 29, 1644, to Lambert Valckenburgh, a house on the island of Manhatten with 25 morgens of land adjoining. He probably left the country soon after or died without issue.

On the 29th July, 1641, Cornelis Jacobsen Stille deeded to Lambert Huybertsen Mol a house and plantation next to Hans Hansen [Bergen] on Long Island, and May 13th, 1643, leased of Cornelis Van Tienhoven his bouwery in the Smiths Valley. On the 18th March, 1647, he obtained from Gov. Kieft a patent for bouwery No. 6, previously occupied by Wolfert Gerritsen [Van Couwenhoven], containing 28½ morgens of land.[1] This estate, says Mr. Valentine,[2] lay between Division Street and the East River, extending eastward nearly to Corlear's Hook, and on the south-west included Wolfert's Meadows, through which ran the stream which carried the waters of the Kalkhook, or Fresh Water pond, to the East River. The

1 Cal. of N. Y. Hist. MSS., Dutch, 1630, 1664, pp. 1, 10, 16, 22, 29, 67, 373.
2 Valentine's Manual, 1860, p. 556-8.

original Stille farm house was situated at the head of Chatham Square, on the north-west corner of the present East Broadway ; the kitchen stood on the opposite side of East Broadway.   Before 1668 Stille conveyed one-half of this farm to Augustine Hermans, which portion was again conveyed, January 10th, 1685, to Wolfert Webbers and Hendrick Cornelisen [Van Schaick] by Francisca Hermans, as attorney for her father.[1]   The premises were later known as the Rutgers farm, but have for many years comprised one of the most densely populated portions of the city.

1. CORNELIS JACOBSEN [Stille[1]], j. m., (young man or bachelor) from Vreelandt ; m. 1[rst], Aug. 24, 1642, Claesje Theunis, j. d., (young daughter or maid) from Amsterdam ; m. 2[d], July 26, 1659, Tryntje Walings, from Amsterdam.   He was living Jan. 20, 1683, and probably was the Cornelis Jacobse, of the city of New York, naturalized June 7, 1684.[2]   His widow, Teuntje [Tryntje] Walings, m. August 6, 1686. Simon Corneil, widower of Claesje Petit Mangin.—*Issue :*

2. i.   JACOB,[2] (10) bap. Sept. 27, 1643.
3. ii.   AEFJE,[2] bap. April 2, 1646; prob. m., Feb. 5, 1688, Jonas
          Liewens, [Lewis?] from England.
4. iii.   NEELTJE,[2] bap. Dec. 13, 1648 ; in the record of her marriage
          she is called Neeltje Hendricks, without doubt a clerical
          error ; at the baptism of her children Neeltje Cornelis and
          Neeltje Stille.   She m., May 19, 1669, Hendrick Cornelis-
          zen [Van Schaick].   See page 11.
5. iv.   JANNEKEN,[2] bap. June 30, 1652 ; m., March 31, 1675, Aer-
          nout Webbers, widower of Ariaentje Adriaens.   He had
          issue by 1[rst] wife, Wolfert, bap. Nov. 14, 1670 ; Marritie,
          bap. Oct. 19, 1672 ; Adriaen, bap. Nov. 18, 1674.   By his
          2[d] wife, Jannetie Cornelis, had Cornelis, bap. March 18,
          1676 ; Johannes, bap. June 26, 1678 ; Claesje, bap. Nov.
          17, 1680 ; Cornelis, bap. Aug. 28, 1683 ; Sara, bap. Aug. 9,
          1685 ; Rachel and Helena, twins, bap. Feb. 12, 1688 ; and
          Cornelis, bap. Feb. 19, 1693.
6. v.   TEUNIS,[2] (20) bap. March 19, 1656.
7. vi.   WALING,[2] bap. Oct. 6, 1660 ; no further account.
8. vii.   HENDRICK,[2] bap. March 3, 1666 ; no further account.
9. viii. THYMEN,[2] bap. Aug. 21, 1672 ; no further account.

10. JACOB CORNELISZEN STILLE,[2] (2) bap. Sept. 27, 1643.   It was a custom of great antiquity in Holland, and of common practice among the early settlers of New Netherland, to add to the name given to a male at his birth or baptism that of his father's first name with the addition thereto of zen, zoon, se, or sen, meaning son.   To the female's name was added her father's Christian name, with the addition usually of s, and sometimes (though paradoxical) zen or se.   His name appears more frequently in the records as Jacob Corneliszen, *i. e.,* Jacob son of Cornelis, than as Jacob Corneliszen Stille or Jacob Stille.   His sisters Neeltje and Janneken are called Neeltje Cornelis, Jannetie Cornelis, and rarely Neeltje and Jannetie Stille.   His sons took the surnames of Somerendyk and WOERTENDYK, finally retaining the latter as their family name.   He m. 1[rst], March 5, 1671, Aeltje Fredericks from Brasiel.   In the record of his 2[d] m., Feb. 6,

1 Hoffman's Estate and Rights of the Corp. of New York, 2d ed. Vol 2, p. 234.
2 Cal. N. V. Hist. MSS., English, p. 28.

1684, to Marritje Hendricx, widow of Hendrick Bastiaenzen, it appears that he was living at the Great Kill, which was in or near that section of the city on the North River side formerly called Greenwich. He died about the year 1711.—*Issue:*

11. i.   CLAESJE,[3] bap. Feb. 11, 1672; at the baptism of her children she is called Claesje Jacobs and Claesje Stille; m., Sept. 13, 1692, Reynier [Pieterse] Quackenbosch (from Oestgeest in Holland) widower of Lysbeth Masten. By his 1^{rst} wife, prob. a dau. of Jan Mast or Masten, of Flushing, L. I., bap. in N. Y., June 3, 1657, and whom he m., March 2, 1674, he had issue bap. in Albany, Livertje [Dievertje] and Claas, Dec. 9, 1685; Claas, Sept. 15, 1689.[1] By his 2^d wife Claesje Jacobs Stille, had issue bap. in N. Y.; Jacob, June 4, 1693; Marritje, Feb. 16, 1696; Johannes, Jan. 22, 1699; and Abraham, Feb. 25, 1705. His widow m. 2^d, Aug. 25, 1711, Jacob Koning or Coning, widower of Grietje Peters, and had Aaltje bap. Aug. 24, 1712; and Isaac, bap. Aug. 1, 1714.

12. ii.   GRIETIE,[3] bap. July 29, 1674; at the baptism of her children she is called Grietje Jacobs, Grietje Stille, and GRIETJE WOERTENDYK; m., Oct. 29, 1697, Wolfert Webbers, Jr., son of Aernout Webbers and Ariaentje Adriaens, before referred to.—*Issue:* Aernout, bap. May 22, 1698; Jacob, bap. Dec. 8, 1700; Ariaentie, bap. July 4, 1703; Frederick, bap. Sept. 23. 1705; Johannes, bap. Dec. 6, 1707; Cornelus, bap. April 10, 1710; Aaltje, bap. Dec. 10, 1712; Isaac, bap. July 24, 1715; and Lea, bap. March 23, 1718.

13. iii.   AEFJE,[3] bap. Aug. 4, 1677; her name appears in the records as Aefje [Eve] Jacobs, Stille, Woertendyk, and Somerendyk; m. 1st, Dec. 27, 1698, Thomas Shermer [Shearman?], widower of Frances Waerdt, and had Frederik, bap. July 1, 1705; m. 2^d, March 27, 1712, Samuel Jacobs, and had Samuel, bap. April 14, 1714. May 3, 1727, she was wife of Jacob Prys [Pryor?].

14. iv.   FREDERICK,[3] bap. Jan. 24, 1680; in the record of his marriage he is styled Frederick Jacobse Woertendyk; at the bap. of his first child Frederick Jacobse Somerendyk, and at the subsequent baptisms of his children FREDERICK WOERTENDYK; m. June 10, 1709, Dievertje, dau. of Reynier [Pieterse] Quackenbos, before mentioned; will dated Nov. 25, 1747; then of Tappan, Orange Co., N. Y.; proven July 19, 1771; names wife Dievertje; eldest son Reynier; Jacob; Aeltje, wife of Jan Vliereboom; Claesje, and Frederick. *Issue:* bap. in N. Y., Aaltje, Nov. 27, 1709; Reynier, Oct. 24, 1711, Reynier, March 14, 1714; Elizabeth, Sept. 9, 1716; Jacob, March 16, 1718; Frederick, April 10, 1720; Elizabeth, April 8, 1722; and bap. in Hackensack, N. J., Elizabeth, April 5, 1724.

15. v.   CORNELIA,[3] bap. April 26, 1682.

16. vi.   CORNELIS,[3] bap. March 15, 1685; he is called in the records Cornelis Jacobse and CORNELIS WOERTENDYK; m., April 13, 1710, Jenneke Peers, or Pearson, dau. of William Pearson

1 Pearson's First Settlers of Albany, p. 89.

and Grietje Kiersen ; she was bap. Nov, 14, 1686. Will
dated Nov. 18, 1768; then of the city of New York, merchant; proven April 29, 1775; names his only surviving
daughter, Mary Tucker, and his grandchildren, James, Robert,
and Thomas Tucker. *Issue:* bap. in N. Y.: Marytje, Jan.
17, 1711; m., July 31, 1728, James Tucker ; Jacob, April 6,
1712; and Elizabeth, Jan. 3, 1714.

17. vii.   JANNETJE,[3] bap. March 16, 1687 ; at the baptism of her children she is called Jannetje Somerendyk, Woertendyk and
Jannetje Jacobs; m. June 10, 1709, David Mandeviel.
Issue: Jacob, bap. Jan. 10, 1711 ; Antje, bap. Feb. 18,
1713; Hendrick, bap. Sept. 18, 1715; Davidt, bap. Oct. 30,
1717; Cornelis, bap. May 11, 1720; Maria, bap. Feb. 23,
1724; and Frans, bap. Feb. 1, 1727.

18. viii. FRANS, bap. July 24, 1689.

19. ix.   RACHEL, bap. April 17, 1692 ; m. in Hackensack, N. J., April
3, 1713, Jan Lefly (Leslie ?), of Barbadoes, and had, bap. in
New York, Marretje, Jan. 3, 1714.

20. TEUNIS CORNELISZEN STILLE,[2] (6) bap. March 19, 1656 ; his name
appears in the records as Teunis Corneliszen, Teunis Corneliszen Stille,
Teunis Stille, and TEUNIS SOMERENDYK ; the latter was finally adopted as
the surname of his family. In 1696 he is described as "of the Groot Kill,
husbandman"; in that year he purchased from Johannes Van Brugh and
Catherine his wife, a parcel of land lying north of the Great Kill, or Creek,
which ran along the present line of Gansevoort Street to the North River.
A few years prior to the Revolution, some of his descendants were living
at "Greenwich in the Outward of the city and county of New York," and
others at "Rumbouts Precinct, Dutchess County, N. Y." He was living
Sept. 2, 1724. He m. Jan. 10, 1682, Annetje Claes, j. d., from Groot
Schermer. *Issue:*

21. i.   CLAESJE,[3] bap. Jan. 4, 1683 ; died young.

22. ii.   NICOLAES,[3] bap. July 22, 1685; at his marriage he is styled
Nicolaes Woertendyk ; at the baptism of his children, Nicolaes Theunisse and NICOLAES SOMERENDYK, the latter becoming his own and the surname of his family. He ·m. March
19, 1708, Margrietje Heermans, prob. dau. of Egbert
Heermans, alias Egbert Fockenszen and Elsje Lucas ; she
bap. Sept. 2, 1687. *Issue:* Annetje, bap. March 13, 1709 ;
Annetje, bap. Feb. 4, 1711 ; Egbert, bap. Jan. 27, 1712 ;
Theunis, bap. Nov. 14, 1714; Annetje, bap. March 1, 1717;
Volkert, bap. April 18, 1720; and Elsje, bap. March 22,
1724.

23. iii.   GRIETIE,[3] bap. Sept. 18, 1687 ; at her marriage she is styled
Margrietje Teunis ; at the baptism of her children Grietie
Theunis and MARGRIETJE SOMERENDYK. She m. Dec. 23,
1703, Cosyn Andriesse, prob. son of Andries Jeuriaense and
Geertie Cosyns. *Issue:* Geertje, bap. April 18, 1705 ; An-
netje, bap. Sept. 24, 1707; Catlyntje, bap. April 10, 1710 ;
Claesje, bap. March 9, 1712 ; Margrietje bap. April 17,
1715; Theunis, bap. March 30, 1718; and Andries, bap.
April 10, 1721.

24. iv.   CORNELIS,[3] bap. Feb. 28, 1690 ; no further account.

25. v.   CLAESJE,[3] bap. March 2, 1692.
26. vi. Jacob,[3] bap. Aug. 9, 1694; in the record of his marriage and
at the baptism of his children is called JACOB SOMERENDYK;
m. 1st, Oct. 10, 1718, Sarah, dau. of Egbert Heermans and
Elsje Lucas; she was bap. Feb. 21, 1694. *Issue:* Theunis,
bap. March 15, 1719; Egbert, bap. Sept. 11, 1723. He
married 2d, Amerentia ——. He died in the Outward of the
city of New York, in 1750, leaving, besides children above-
named, Ann, Abigail, John, and Jacob.
27. vii. ABRAHAM,[3] twin, bap. March 28, 1697; no further account.
28. viii. ISAAC,[3] twin, bap. March 28, 1697; is called ISAAC SOMER-
ENDYK, in the record of his marriage and at the baptism of
his children. Married, March 14, 1724, Sarah, dau. of
Wessel (Pieterse) Van Norden and Jacquemyntje Van Couwenhoven; she bap. Aug. 17, 1701. *Issue:* Theunis,
bap. Sept. 2, 1724; Jacquemyntie, bap. Nov. 29, 1727.

VAN SCHAICK.

(FIRST FOUR GENERATIONS.)

Besides the two families of Goosen Gerritse and Claas Van Schaick, who
early settled on the upper Hudson, and are referred to by Prof. Pearson, in
the RECORD, vol. 2, p. 191, there was another of the same name, of which
Cornelis Aertszen, who settled in New Amsterdam prior to 1641, was the
head. In January, 1669-70, Ariaen Cornelissen, Hendrick Cornelissen, and
Lysbeth Cornelissen, described as the lawful heirs of Cornelis Aertsen, conveyed to Capt. John Berry, of Bergen, in New Jersey, two parcels of land
on the Island of Manhattan; "the first, lying and being on east end of Cornelis Jacobsen (Stille), and on the west end of Corlears plantation, &c;"
the second, "lying against land formerly belonging to Hans Kierstede, beginning from the first marsh, over against Augustine Hermans' land, from
thence to the fence of Bastiaen, the negroes land, and so to the fence of
Thomas Hall's land; which said two parcels of land were confirmed unto
the said heirs of Cornelis Aertsen, by a patent from Rt. Hon. Gov. Francois
Lovelace, bearing date, 16th Sept., 1669, &c."[1] Of his personal history but
little is known; Mr. Valentine in his History of the City of New York, says
he was at one time the tenant of Gov. Stuyvesant's farm, on the Bowery,
and long supplied the families of the city with country produce; he was
afterwards a tenant on the old Damen farm, east from Broadway, a short
distance above the city gate. He probably came to New Amsterdam with
his wife Belitje Hendricks, there being no record of their marriage here.
He was sponsor at the baptism of his gr-dau. Belitje, Oct. 1, 1663, and in
1665 was living without the land gate; he died between the year 1665, and
Sept. 1669. About the year 1680, his sons began to use the surname of
VAN SCHAICK. At his 2d marriage, July 10, 1662, to Weyntie Elberts,
widow of Aert Willemszen, he is called the widower of Belitje Hendricks.
By his 2d wife had no issue.

1.   CORNELIS AERTSZEN[1] and Belitje Hendricks had *issue.*
2. i.   HENDRICKJE,[2] bap. July 7, 1641; prob. died unmarried:

1 Hoffman's Estate and Rights of Corp. of N. Y.; Vol. 2, p. 239. N. Y. Conveyances; Liber A., p. 105.

3. ii.   Arie[2] [Adriaen] (6), bap. July 9, 1642.
4. iii. Hendrick (15), bap. Sept. 23, 1646.
5. iv.   Lysbeth, bap. Oct. 1, 1651; m. Jan. 14, 1672, Dirck Janszen
         Van Oosten, j. m., from Beest in Gelderland. *Issue:* Dirck,
         bap. Sept. 15, 1674; they prob. had Belitje, born March 24,
         1673, in Bergen, N. J.[1]

6. Arie [Adriaen] Cornelisen Van Schaick,[2] bap. July 9, 1642; He
was admitted a member of the Dutch Church in New York, May 29, 1673;
his wife joined, April 5, 1668; Commissioned Captain of foot, in the outward, Dec. 16, 1689.[2] In 1696, he held land lying above the Great Kill,
and North of land owned by Tunis Cornelisen Stille, comprising a portion
of the lower part of the present 16th ward. He married, Brooklyn, Feb.
27, 1662, Rebecca Idens of Nordingen. Will dated Aug. 2, 1694; proven
Jan. 11, 1700; names wife Rebecca; daughter Belitie, m. to Pieter de
Groot; son Yde m. to Ibel Gootbloet; daughters, Cornelia m. to Johannes
Pluvier; Elizabeth m. to Gerrit Onkelba; and Dina "ongetrout."
Issue:

7. i.   Belitje Adriaens Van Schaick,[3] bap. Oct. 1, 1663, at the
        General's (Stuyvesant) bowery; she joined the Church in
        New York, May 28, 1679, m. Dec. 10, 1681 (then living at
        the Fresh water), Pieter Janszen, j. m., from Amersfort. At
        the baptism of their first child, he is styled Pieter Janszen;
        at the subsequent baptisms, *Pieter Jacobszen* and *Pieter de
        Groot.* About 1695, he removed from New York to Hack-
        ensack, New Jersey. *Issue:* Rebecca, bap. Feb. 11, 1685;
        Lea, bap. Jan. 16, 1687; Jacob, bap. April 5, 1688; Rachel,
        bap. Aug. 10, 1690; Grietie, bap. Dec. 18, 1692; Lysbeth,
        bap. Feb. 20, 1695; and at Hackensack, Jacob and Arie,
        Sept. 20, 1696; Eegie, Nov. 15, 1698; Cornelia, Oct. 13,
        1700; Gritie, Nov. 1, 1702; Joannes, July 5, 1704, and
        Dina, Aug. 12, 1705.

8. ii. Iden [Ide] Adriaenszen Van Schaick,[3] bap. Nov. 28, 1665;
        m., Aug. 26, 1685 (then living, op. dit Eylt.), Ibel dau. of
        Frans Janszen Bloedgoedt and Lysbeth Jans; she bap. Sept.
        6, 1662, and joined the Church in N. Y., Nov. 30, 1683.
        Issue: Rebecca, bap. Sept. 19, 1686; Cornelis, Dec. 11,
        1687; Frans, bap. July 7, 1689; Lysbeth, bap. April 1, 1691,
        and Adriaen, bap. Dec. 25, 1692.

9. iii. Grietie Van Schaick,[3] bap. Nov. 6, 1667; m., Sept. 28, 1687,
         Johannes Van Imberg, from Albany. *Issue:* Rebecca, bap.
         Aug. 11, 1689.

10. iv. Cornelia Van Schaick,[3] bap. Jan. 9, 1670; m., Sept. 10,
         1690, Johannes, son of Cornelis Pluvier and Neeltie Van
         Couwanhoven; he, bap. Dec. 25, 1667. *Issue:* Rebecca,
         bap. April 23, 1693, and Margrietje, bap. Dec. 26, 1694.

11. v.   Lysbeth Van Schaick,[3] bap. Dec. 10, 1671; m., Sept. 10,
         1690, Gerrit, son of Adam Onckelbach and Neeltje Jans;
         he, bap. April 17, 1670. He joined the Dutch Church in
         New York, June 5, 1696; his wife joined March 2, 1698.
         Issue: Neeltie, bap. July 7th, 1691; Rebecca, bap. Jan. 8,

1693; Adam, bap. May 31, 1695; Maria, bap. May 23, 1697; Elizabeth, bap. Sept. 7, 1698; Adam, bap. Feb. 9, 1701; Adriaen and Elizabeth, twins, bap. Jan. 1, 1704; Gerrit, bap. Dec. 16, 1705, and Elizabeth, bap. March 7, 1708. Gerrit Onclebag, of the City of New York, distiller, made Will, July 10, 1732; proven May 21, 1733; names only his two daughters, Nelly, wife of John Van Gelder, and Rebecca, wife of Burger Sipkins.

12. vi. CORNELIS VAN SCHAICK,[3] bap. March 18, 1674; d. young.

13. vii. JACOB VAN SCHAICK,[3] bap. April 6, 1676; d. young.

14. viii. DINA VAN SCHAICK,[3] bap. April 10, 1678; m. Oct. 1, 1696, Hans, son of Dr. Hans Kierstede and Jannetje Loockermans; he, bap. Feb. 19, 1668. *Issue:* Johanna, bap. May 23, 1697; Rebecca, bap. Jan. 4, 1699; Hans, bap. April 17, 1700; Hans, bap. Aug. 13, 1704; and Adriaen, bap. Sept. 7, 1707.

15. HENDRICK CORNELISEN VAN SCHAICK[2] (4) bap. Sept. 23, 1646; he lived and probably died on that portion of the old Stille farm, before mentioned as having been purchased by him and Wolfert Webbers on the 10th Jan., 1685. Neeltje Van Schaick, his widow, with his other heirs, conveyed these premises, June 9, 1728, to Harmanus Rutgers. He died about 1709; m., May 19, 1669, Neeltje Hendricks [Cornelis], dau. of Cornelis Jacobsen Stille, both then living at the Fresh Water.—*Issue:*

16. i. BELITIE VAN SCHAICK,[3] bap. March 20, 1670; d. young.

17. ii. BELITIE VAN SCHAICK,[3] bap. April 2, 1672; m., June 28, 1695, Claes Janszen Bogaert, j. m., from Betfort. *Issue:* Jan, bap. May 5, 1697; Cornelis, bap. Jan. 14, 1700; Evert, bap. July 19, 1702; and Hendrick, bap. March 25, 1705. Claes Janse Bogaert was a baker in New York, and m. 2[d], Feb. 23, 1707, Grietje Jans, widow of Johannes Janse Van Tilburg, whose name appears in the baptismal record Grietje Concelje; she was probably dau. of Jan de Consielje and Fytie Schuts. He died early in 1727; by 2[d] wife had *issue:* Cornelia, bap. Dec. 28, 1707; Belitje, bap. Dec. 5, 1708; Cornelia, bap. Apr. 2, 1710; Johannes, bap. Sept. 9, 1711; Margrietje, bap. March 8, 1713; Elizabeth, bap. Sept. 19, 1714; Belitje, bap. June 13, 1716; Anneke, bap. April 20, 1718; and Petrus, bap. Sep 4, 1720.

18. iii. CORNELIS VAN SCHAICK,[3] bap. Feb. 27, 1675; d. young.

19. iv. ADRIAEN [Arien] VAN SCHAICK,[3] bap. Jan 26, 1678; m., May 5, 1702, Jannetje Jans, alias Sammans, dau. of Jan Thomaszen and Aefje Jacobs; she bap. Feb. 18, 1680. *Issue:* Neeltie, bap. March 14, 1703, and m., Aug. 20, 1721, Benjamin Herring, Shipwright, of the city of New York; Aegje [Eve], bap. Aug. 13, 1704, and m., Feb. 6, 1725, Isaac Van Hoek, Cordwainer, of New York; Jacob, bap. May 14, 1707, and Johannes, bap. Oct. 23, 1709.

20. v. CLAESJEN VAN SCHAICK,[3] bap. Dec. 29, 1680; m. 1st, June 16, 1700, Johannes Bogaert, of New Haerlem; he d. about 1711; m. 2[d], May 31, 1713, Johannes De Graaf, Cooper, of N. Y.; no issue bap. in the Dutch Church here.

21. vi. LYSBETH VAN SCHAICK,[3] bap. Jan. 23, 1684; m., Dec. 3, 1702,
Cornelus, son of Paulus Jacobsen Turck, and Aeltje Barents;
he bap. Sep. 20, 1679, and died in the spring of 1728. *Issue:* Cornelis, bap. Oct. 10, 1703; Aaltje, bap. Oct. 28,
1705; Neeltje, bap. April 13, 1707; Aaltje, bap. May 8,
1709; Belitje, bap. Nov. 18, 1711; Paulus, bap. July 4,
1714; Hendrik, bap. July 28, 1717; Neeltje, bap. Aug. 31,
1718; Aaltje, bap. March 26, 1721; Hendrik, bap. Jan.
15, 1724; Johannes, bap. March 2, 1726; and Klaasje,
bap. June 9, 1728.

In tracing the pedigree of this family, some facts in reference to Capt.
Goosen Gerritse Van Shaick's family have been gathered which deserve
notice. ANNATIE [Anna] LIEVENS, widow of GOOSEN GERRITSE VAN
SCHAICK removed from Albany, and joined, with her daughter Margareta,
the Dutch Church in New York, Sept. 4, 1691. Her will is dated April
27, 1702; proven Nov. 19, 1702; names son Levinus; daughters, Gerritje
Drayer; Catharina, wife of Mathew Clarkson; Anna Maria, wife of John
Van Cortlandt; and Margareta; also her granddaughter Margariet, wife
of Robert Livingstone, Jr.

GERRITJE [Goosense] VAN SCHAICK, m., Jan. 17, 1674, Capt. Andries
Drayer in Albany. On the 2[d] of March, 1699, with certificate (*met attes-
tatie*) from Copenhagen she joined the Dutch Church in New York; her
name is recorded, Juff[r] Gerritje Van Schaick, Wed[e] van de H[r] Andries
Draeyer, Rear Admiral of the King's fleet of Denmark and Norway. The
same day Capt. Andries Draeyer, j. m., joined with certificate from the
same place. He departed for Denmark April 29, 1700. Johanna Dorothea Drayer, j. d., perhaps her daughter, joined upon confession of faith
and belief, Feb. 28, 1700.

CATHARINA [Goosense] VAN SCHAICK, j. d., from New Albany; m., Jan.
19, 1692, Mathew Clarkson, Sect[t] Van't Gouvernment. *Issue:* Elisabeth,
bap. Jan. 8, 1693; David, bap. Aug. 19, 1694; Levinus, bap. Sep. 6,
1696; and Mathew, bap. April 9, 1699.

ANNA MARIA [Goosense] VAN SCHAICK, j. d., from New Albany; m.,
June 23, 1695, Mr. Johannes [Van] Cortlant, son of Stephanus Van
Cortlant[t] and Geertruyd Schuyler. *Issue:* Geertruyd, bap. July 4, 1697;
Johanna, bap. Aug. 25, 1702.

MARGARETA [Goosense] VAN SCHAICK, m., Aug. 25, 1705, Rev. Barnardus Freeman of Flatbush, L. I. She died Jan. 18, 1738, and he in 1741.[2]
Their only child, Anna Margareta, married her cousin David, son of Mathew Clarkson, above mentioned.

ENGELITIE [Goosense] VAN SCHAICK was the first wife of Col. Pieter
[Philipse] Schuyler, first mayor of Albany; their daughter Margariet
(the granddaughter referred to in the will) m., Aug. 26, 1697, in Albany,
Robert Livingstone, Jr., nephew of the first proprietor of the manor. He
was buried in the Dutch Church, Albany, April 21, 1725.[3]

ROBERT LIVINGSTONE, Jr., son of the first proprietor of the manor, m.,
Nov. 11, 1717, in New York, Margreta Howarding, and had Robert, bap.
Aug. 3, 1718.

1 Prior to 1685, this name is written Van Courtlant in the New York Dutch Church baptismal records.
2 Stiles' Hist. of Brooklyn, Vol. I., p. 183.
3 Munsell's Annals of Albany, Vol. I., p. 235.

SIECKEN. DEY. DYE.

(FIRST FOUR GENERATIONS.)

On the 25th March, 1758, Dirck Dey, of the city of New York, Gentle-man, conveyed to Trinity Church a lot of land lying west of Broadway near the present Canal Street. In the deed he is styled *the grandson and heir at law of Dirck Seicken, alias Dey.* Dirck Janszen, alias Siecken [Sichem, Sicken, Sycan, Zieken], alias Dirck Janse Dey, came from Am-sterdam at an early date, and settled in New Amsterdam, where he mar-ried 1st Dec. 28, 1641, Jannetje Theunis, j. d., from Amsterdam. He and Hans Reiger were soldiers in the service of the West India Com-pany, and for insolent behavior towards citizens on the Heeren Straat, and striking their superior officers, were sentenced to be shot, Feb. 21, 1647.[1] He afterwards was pardoned, and obtained from Gov. Stuyvesant, June 16, 1654, a patent for a plantation near Gamoenepaen (Communipaw, N. J.), at Mingackqua, which he sold to Enoch Michelse Vreeland, Feb. 13, 1679,[2] and a patent, May 12, 1668, for two parcels of land lying at Pem-brepogh. He was admitted to the rights of a small burgher in new Amster-dam April 26, 1657, and in 1665 was living *buyten de lant poort.* In 1677 Gov. Andross leased to him for thirty years the Duke's Bowery or farm, now belonging to Trinity Church, and after that date he lived upon the premises, and probably died there. He married 2d, Oct. 18, 1659, Geertie Jans (alias Langendyck), from St. Marten in North Holland. The will of Dirk Janse Dye, "living just without the city," is dated Dec. 5, 1683; proven July 11, 1693, some six or seven years after his decease; names his wife, Geertie Johnson, and his two children, Theunis and Jannetje Dye. His widow married, Nov. 11, 1687, Theunis [Gysbertse] Bogaert, widower of Sara Rapaille, living in the Walebocht (L. I.).

1. DIRCK JANSE SIECKEN, alias DEY,[1] had *issue* by 1st wife :

2. i.　　JAN[2] (Dircksen Seicken), bap. Sept. 22, 1652 ; a magistrate Aug. 31, 1674, at Minckaque and Pemrepoch (N. J.) ;[3] not named in his father's will, and probably died without issue.

3. ii.　　THEUNIS[2] (6), bap. Sep. 24, 1656.

By 2d wife had *issue :*

4. iii.　　JANNETIE[2] (Dircks), bap. Dec. 7, 1659 ; joined the church in New York Dec. 4, 1679 ; m., June 17, 1685, Frans Cornelis-zen, j. m., from Middelburg.—*Issue :* Geertie, bap. June 19, 1687; and Cornelis, bap. March 29, 1691.

5. iv.　　HENDRICK,[2] bap. July 24, 1661 ; d. young.

6. THEUNIS DIRCKSZEN DEY,[2] (3) bap. Sept. 24, 1656 ; m., Feb. 4, 1685, Anneken, dau. of Johannes Lucaszen Schouten (Schoute, Scholtes, Schol-tens) and Sara Jans ; she bap. March 17, 1666. Will dated Nov. 8, 1688 ; entered of record Jan. 15, 1688–9 ; his children not named. His widow m., Aug. 11, 1691, Joris Martenszen,[4] j. m., of the Walebocht.

1 Cal. of N. Y. Hist. MSS., Dutch, p. 107.
2 Winfield's Land Titles, Hud. Co., N. J., pp. 58, 65.
3 O'Callaghan's New Netherland Register, p. 101.
4 Joris Martenszen, alias George Ryerson, was the son of Marten Ryerszen and Anna Rapalje; bap. Sept. 19, 1666. By wife Annekin, widow of Theunis Dey, had issue : Johanna, bap. June 15, 1692 ; Mar-

Theunis Dey at his death owned the fee of a lot of land lying without the city land gate on the west side of the Highway, having to the north the farm of his Royal Highness, afterwards called the King's farm, on the south the land of Olof Stevenson (Van Courtlandt), *containing in breadth before and behind* eighteen rods and ⁷⁄₁₀ parts of a rod, and in length from the Highway to the water side. In 1750 Dey Street was laid out through these premises. He had issue :

7. i.   JANNETJE,³ bap. Nov. 24, 1685 ; m., 1707, Frans [Martense] Ryerson ; he bap. Aug. 2, 1685 ; after 1722 they removed from New York to Wegraw, Bergen Co., N. J., where he died prior to July, 1749. *Issue :* Marte, bap. March 10, 1708 ; Theunis, bap. March 13, 1709 ; Theunis, bap. July 15, 1711 ; Joris, bap. April 5, 1713 ; Antje, bap. Nov. 10, 1714, m. Andrew Denyke, of Bergen Co., N. J. ; Saratje, bap. June 24, 1716 ; Johannes, bap. April 27, 1718 ; Jenneke, bap. Aug. 21, 1720 ; Dirck, bap. Oct. 10, 1722 ; and Maritje, bap. in Hackensack, N. J., Dec. 25, 1726.

8. ii. DIRCK,³ bap. March 27, 1687 ; m. Jane ——. Will dated Aug. 4, 1761 ; proven May 29, 1764 ; had issue him surviving : Theunis Dey, of Saddle River, Bergen Co., N. J. ; Jane, who married John Varick, son of Jacobus Van Varick and Anna Maria Brestede ; they lived in New Barbadoes, N. J. ; she died there in 1811 ; Ann, who married, Dec. 12, 1764, William McAdam from Aireshire, North Britain ; he was a merchant, and died, s. p., in New York, 1779 ; Mary, who married, Nov. 24, 1761, David Shaw, merchant, of New York city.

9. iii. SARA,³ bap. June 10, 1688 ; m., at Hackensack, N. J., April 30, 1709, Hendrick Janse Spier, of "Pommerpogg," N. J. ; she died before 1730, and had issue her surviving : Theunis, Maritie, Hannah, Janneke, and Leah.

BREVOORT.

(FIRST FOUR GENERATIONS.)

The head of this family was probably HENDRICK JANSZEN VAN BREVOORT,¹ "aged about 60 years" on the 8th of June, 1690, on which day his deposition was taken before the Mayor of New York respecting an assault upon Lieut.-Gov. Jacob Leisler.¹ It is said that he came from the town of Bredevoort, in Guelderland, to New Amsterdam about 1700.² He was here earlier than this, and purchased, Feb. 24, 1679–80, of Egbert Wouterse, lands lying west of the New Streets, north of lands of Conradus Van der Beeck, and west of lands belonging to Hendrick Janse Van der Veen, and confirmed to him by Wouterse's heirs May 20, 1683. It is probable that he first settled in the vicinity of Mespath Kill (Newtown Creek,

---

ten, bap. Sept. 17, 1693 ; Johannes, bap. Aug. 8, 1694 ; Marritje, bap. July 29, 1696 ; Marten, bap. Oct. 9, 1698 ; Helena, bap. Feb. 2, 1701 ; all of whom were baptized as the children of *Joris Martenszen* and Anna Schouten ; they also had Jores, bap. Jan. 5, 1703 ; Luykas, bap. April 9, 1704 ; and Blandina, bap. May 8, 1706, who were baptized as the children of *Joris Reyerse* and Antje Schoute.
  1 Doc. Rel. to Col. Hist. of N. Y., Vol. 3, p. 740, and Cal. N. Y. Hist. MSS., English, p. 179.
  2 Todd Genealogy, p. 28.

L. I.), and may have been the Hendrick Jansen who was a resident, 1656, of Middleburg, afterwards Newtown.[1]   He probably had three children who lived to maturity, viz. :

1. i.   JAN HENDRICKSZEN,[2] (4).
2. ii.   FRANS HENDRICKSZEN,[2] (10).
3, iii.   MARRITJE HENDRICKS,[2] j. d., Van Brevoort, in't Sticht Van Uytrecht, op Stuyvesants bouwereye, who married 1st, July 2, 1673, Hendrick Bastiaenszen, j. m., Van Cuylenburg.   He was prob. a son of Bastiaen Ellisen.   Their children took the surname of Ellessen and Elles (Ellis ?).   She became a widow and married 2[d] Jacob Corneliszen Stille.   *Issue*, by 1st husband :   Hendrickje, bap. Aug. 23, 1673; m., Dec. 9, 1691, Dirck Zlyck (Slyck, Slyk, Slyke) ; Marritie, bap. Sept. 29, 1675; m., Sept. 26, 1706, Johannes Claesen Van Heyningen ; Hendrick, bap. Nov. 14, 1677 ; Jan, bap. Jan. 28, 1680 ; and Elias, bap. Jan. 14, 1682.

4. JAN HENDRICKSZEN[2] [BREVOORT], (1) j. m., Van Amersfoort, op Mispat, married, Jan. 29, 1668, Annetje Bastiaens, j. d., from Werckhoven. She was prob. the dau. of Bastiaen Ellisen, Wheelwright, afterwards a farmer, who purchased, May 20, 1683, from the heirs of Egbert Wouterse, a lot of land lying near Stuyvesant's Bowery.   This, with several other parcels, comprising the greater portion of the city bounded by 14th and 10th Streets, Bowery and 6th Avenue, was conveyed Nov. 13, 1701, by Bastiaen Ellisen to Jan Hendrickse Brevoort.[2]

Jan (Hendrickse) Brevoort was tutor (Guardian) of the children of Hendrick Bastiaense, whose widow, prob. his sister, married Jacob Cornelise Stille.   He began to use the surname of Brevoort about 1696 ; was a farmer and Assistant Alderman from the outward in 1702–3, and from 1707–8 to 1713–14, inclusive.   His will is dated Oct. 28, 1714 ; proven Dec. 21, 1714 ; names late wife Annetie, deceased ; eldest son Henry, of the outward, Weaver ; son Elias, of the city of New York, Carpenter ; daughters, Jannetie, wife of Thomas Seikelson, of the outward, Yeoman ; and Maria, wife of Zacharias Seikelson, of New Harlem, Blacksmith.   Appoints his sons Henry and Elias Executors.   Witnesses, Peter Arbell, Jan Willemse Rome (Romeyn ?), and John Conrad Codwise.   *Issue :*

5. i.   HENDRICKJE,[3] bap. Jan. 13, 1669 ; d. young.
6. ii.   HENDRICK BREVOORT,[3] bap. Dec. 17, 1670; m. 1st, Aug. 26, 1699, Maryken [Van] Couwenhoven, j. d., from Noortwyck,[3] dau. of Johannes Van Couwenhoven and Sara Frans ; she bap. April 2, 1679; m. 2[d], Oct. 5, 1705, Jaquemyntje Boke, dau. of Abraham Boke and Tannekin Andries, alias Tanneke Van Driese.   *Issue :* Johannes, bap. June 2, 1700 ; Maria, bap. Oct. 5, 1701 ; Abraham, bap. June 23, 1706 ; Abraham, bap. Sept. 24, 1707 ; Anneke, bap. Oct. 16, 1709 ; Hendrikus, bap. Dec. 9, 1711 ; Elias, bap. July 8, 1713 ; Elias, bap. May 1, 1715 ; and Jacob, bap. Oct. 2, 1717.

1 Riker's Annals of Newtown, p. 43.
2 Hoffmann's Estate and Rights of the Corp. of N. Y., Vol. 2, p. 191.
3 A settlement on the North River side of the Island, called the Bengoe Bowery, also by the Indian name of Sapponikan, otherwise North Wycke or North Witts, and afterwards Greenwich.—*Old Deed.*

He died about 1719, and his widow married, Oct. 21, 1721, Jacob Hassing, and had Tanneke, bap. Aug. 19, 1722.

7. iii.   MARRITJE JANS BREVOORT,[3] bap. Nov. 12, 1673; m., Aug. 23, 1693, Zacharias Sickelszen (Sickels), j. m., from New Albany. *Issue:* Johannes, bap. July 29, 1694; Jacobus, bap. Nov. 17, 1695; Sacharias, bap. Sept. 4, 1698; Sacharias, bap. June 12, 1700; and Thomas, bap. March 28, 1703.

8. iv.   ELIAS BREVOORT,[3] bap. June 21, 1676; m., May 16, 1701, Margrietje Jans, alias Sammans, dau. of Jan Thomaszen and Aefje Jacobs; she bap. Aug. 17, 1678. *Issue:* Aefje, bap. Aug. 27, 1701; Anneke, bap. Oct. 24, 1703; Hendrickje, bap. Nov. 21, 1705; Margrietje, bap. Feb. 18, 1708; Aegje [Aefje], bap. Jan. 17, 1711; Grietje, bap. Oct. 28, 1713; Johannes, bap. Sept. 18, 1715, and Elias, bap. March 30, 1718.

9. v.   JANNETJE JANS BREVOORT,[3] bap. April 9, 1679; m., April 5, 1702, Thomas Sickels. *Issue:* Sacharias, bap. Aug. 30, 1702; Sacharias, bap. Feb. 23, 1704; Hendrickje, bap. Oct. 7, 1705; Johannes, bap. March 16, 1707; Thomas, bap. March 6, 1709; Thomas, bap. Sept. 24, 1710; Wilhelmus, bap. April. 13, 1712; Marretje, bap. Sept. 13, 1713; Roberdt, bap. Nov. 2, 1715; Annetje, bap. June 2, 1717; Jannetje, bap. Nov. 30, 1718; Jannetje, bap. Sept. 18, 1720; and Elizabeth, bap. Oct. 10, 1725.

10. FRANS HENDRICKSZEN,[2] (2) j. m., Van Brevoort, married, Nov. 4, 1670, Beelitie Jacobs (Joris?), j. d., *Van Brugge in Vlaenderen, Wonende in Mitpats Kill.* At the baptism of her children she is called Belitie Joris, and probably was the dau. of Joris Stephenszen Van Alst and Geesie Harmans; bap. May 2, 1655. She became a widow, and m. 2[d], Dec. 5, 1684, George Atkins, j. m., from Virginia. *Issue:*

11. i.   HENDRICK,[3] bap. March 16, 1672.

12. ii.   HENDRICK,[3] bap. June 12, 1673.

13. iii.   GEESIE FRANS BREVOORT, bap. Nov. 10, 1675; m., about 1694, Benjamin Bill. At the baptism of her children she is called Geesie Frans, Geesie Van Alst, Geesie Brevoort and Geesje Atkins. *Issue:* Abigail, bap. Nov. 13, 1695; Benjamin, born Oct. 14, 1698, bap. June 27, 1705; Susanna, bap. Oct. 31, 1705; Marytje, bap. Jan. 3, 1711; Penelope, bap. May 25, 1712; Penelope, bap. April 17, 1715, and John, bap. Jan. 1, 1718.

GREVENRAET.

(FIRST THREE GENERATIONS.)

ISAAC GREVENRAET[1] (Greveraad, Greefraadt) came from Amsterdam and settled in New Amsterdam prior to 1652. Mr. Valentine says he was the son of Metje Grevenraet, from whom he inherited considerable real estate in this city. The earliest notice of him is found in the record of his first marriage, March 24th, 1652, to Elizabeth Jeuriaens j. d., also from

Amsterdam. He was a Schepen in 1662 and 1664, and enrolled a small Burgher, April 26, 1657.[1] On the 25th of October, 1673, he was appointed by Gov. Colve, Schont or Sheriff of the towns of Swaenburgh, Hurly, and Marbletown, in Esopus.[2] He married 2^d, June 2, 1663, Marritje Jans. j. d., from Amsterdam. *Issue:* Henricus, bap. Aug. 5, 1657; Andries, bap. July 16, 1659; Hendrick, bap. June 28, 1662; By 2^d wife: Lysbeth, bap. Feb. 27, 1664; Abraham, bap. March 22, 1665; Lysbeth, bap. May 26, 1666; Lysbeth, bap. Dec. 11, 1667; Anna Elizabeth, bap. June 9, 1669; Margariet, bap. July 11, 1670; and Johannes, bap. Aug. 28, 1678.

ANDRIES GREVENRAET[2] (s. of Isaac[1]), bap. July 16, 1659; m., July 2, 1684, Anna, dau. of Johannes Van Brug and Tryntie Roelofs; she bap. Sept. 10, 1662. He was captain and owner of a vessel, and engaged for many years in the coast trade between New York and Virginia. Will dated May 15, 1709; styled of the City of New York, mariner; proven June 17, 1710; names wife Anne; eldest son Isaac; appoints his cousin Abraham Gouverneur, Nicholas Rosevelt, and his cousin, Isaac Gouverneur, guardians of his children. *Issue:* Elizabeth, bap. Dec. 4, 1685; Isaac, bap. Nov. 16, 1687; Catharine, bap. Oct. 30, 1689; Elizabeth, bap. March 29, 1691; Lucretie, bap. Oct. 23, 1692; Johannes, bap. Jan. 21, 1694; Henricus, bap. April 26, 1696, and Lucretia, bap. Aug. 1, 1697.

HENDRICK GREVENRAET[2] (s. of Isaac[1]), bap. June 28, 1662; m., May 5, 1686, Sarah Sanders dau. of Robert Sanders and Elsje Barents of Albany. Like his brother Andries, he was a sea-faring man. Will dated March 11, 1699, at "Blewfield, Jamaica," prob. Bluefields Bay, on the southwest coast of Jamaica, near Savannah la mar; proven in 1699, the day and month not given; names wife Sarah; speaks of children, but names only his son Isaac, to whom he gives "a seal ring with a black stone in it marked H. G. M." *Issue:* Lysbeth, bap. in Albany, Dec. 25, 1686;[3] Elsje, bap. Feb. 16, 1690; Lysbeth, bap. July 11, 1692; Isaac, bap. July 29, 1694. Marytje, bap. July 25, 1697, and Henricus, bap. July 30, 1699.

DE RIEMER.

(FIRST FOUR GENERATIONS.)

LYSBETH GREVENRAET, probably an elder sister of Isaac Grevenraet[1], and the ancestress of the DE RIEMER family, of New York, was an early resident of New Amsterdam. She was thrice married, 1st to [Isaac?] de Riemer[1], prob. in Amsterdam, where some of her children (all by him) were born. She m. 2^d, Elbert Elbertszen, *Glasem* (Glasier). Elbert Eldertse, prob. the same as the agent of Isaac Grevenraet, conveyed May 21, 1655, lot 27, in the village of Gravesend, L. I., to Peter Ebel.[4] She m. 3rd, Feb. 14, 1659, Dominie Samuel Drisius, who was called to the church in New Amsterdam in 1652, as colleague pastor with Johannes Megapolensis, having previously been settled in the Dutch Church in London. He died in 1671.[5] She died Dec. 25, 1687, leaving issue named in her will as follows: Mrs. Margaret Steenwick; Machtelt Gouverneur, widow of Nicholas

1 O'Callaghan's Register of New Netherland, pp. 63-4, 184.
2 Doc. Rel. to Col. Hist. N. Y., vol. 2, p. 644.
3 Pearson's First Settlers of Albany, p. 56.
4 Cal. N. Y. Hist., MSS. Dutch, p. 59.
5 De Witt's Hist. Discourse, Aug., 1876.

Gouverneur, dec'd; Mr. Peter de Riemer and her deceased son, Hubart de Riemer. She also names Isaac and Elizabeth de Riemer, children of her deceased son, Hubart, gotten by Catharine —— *Issue:*

2. i. MARGARET DE RIEMER[2], from Amsterdam, m. 1st, June 5, 1658, Cornelis Steenwyck, from Haerlem. He was a Burgomaster in 1662, and Mayor of New York, 1682-3, an eminent merchant, and one of the most influential citizens of his time. A sketch of his life and character will be found in Valentine's Manual for 1864. He died in 1684. She m. 2[d], Oct. 20, 1686, Dominie Henricus Selyns,[1] widower of Machtelt Specht, by whom had no issue. She d. about 1712. *Issue* by 1st husband: Margariet, bap. Sept. 17, 1659; Jacob, bap. Nov. 13, 1661; Jacob, bap. Feb. 24, 1664; Isaacq, bap. Dec. 28, 1666; Cornelis, bap. April 7, 1669; Cornelis, bap. July 20, 1671; and Jacobus, bap. May 25, 1676.

3. ii. PIETER DE RIEMER[2], born in Amsterdam about 1643. In his deposition, June 8, 1690, respecting the riot at New York, he says he was "aged about 47 yeares."[2] He was a Glasier—a trade he probably learned with his step-father, Elbert Elbertszen. He m., Jan. 3, 1665, Susanna, dau. of Isaac de Foreest and Sara du Trieux. She bap. Jan. 22, 1645. His will is dated January 29, 1697; proven Oct. 5, 1702; names son Isaac and wife Susanna, who had deceased before Oct. 5, 1702. Their son Isaac bap. Jan. 10, 1666, m., Jan 10, 1689, Aeltje Wessels of New York, was a prominent merchant and an active partisan of Leisler. His brother-in-law, Jacob Teller, who was a sea-captain, was connected with him in various commercial enterprises. He was Mayor of the city in 1700, and was sometimes called Isaac de Riemer, sr., in contradistinction to his cousin, Isaac de Riemer, jr., son of Hubart[2]. *Issue:* Petrus, bap. Feb. 22, 1690; Isaac, bap. Sept. 6, 1691; Anna Elizabeth, bap. Sept. 10, 1693; Susanna, bap. July 21, 1695; Elizabeth, bap. Aug. 25, 1700; Margarita, bap. April 2, 1704; Isaac, bap. Jan. 25, 1708; and Steenwyck, bap. April 23, 1710.

4. iii. MR. HUYBERT DE RIEMER[2], so named in the list of church members, joined the Dutch Church in New York, Aug. 24, 1671. Opposite his name is written "Gestorven op Meeuwis." The place of his death here referred to was probably the town of Meaux or Meuse, in France, on the river of that name, and where his daughter Elizabeth was born. Mr. Valentine says he followed the profession of a Naval Surgeon, and married a respectable lady of this city.[3] He was probably married abroad, as there is no record of that event in the Dutch Church here. By wife Catharine he had *issue:* Isaac and Elizabeth. His son, Isaac, m., April 28, 1705, Antje Woertman, dau. of Dirck Janse, of the Ferry, alias Dirk Janse Woertman and Maritje Teunis; she was bap. in Brooklyn,

---

[1] Dom. Henricus Selyns, m. July 25, 1662, Machtilda Specht, j. d., from Uytrecht. They had one daughter, Agneta, bap. in New Amsterdam, July 1, 1663. Machtilda Specht d. Feb., 1686; Dom. Selyns d. July, 1701.
[2] Doc. Rei. to Col. Hist. of N. Y. vol. 3. p. 741.
[3] Valentine's Manual, 1853, p. 397.

June 15, 1684. They had *issue:* Isaac, bap. June 20, 1708; Hubertus, bap. Dec. 13, 1710; Marritje, bap. Jan. 27, 1714; Catharina, bap. Aug. 1, 1716; Elizabeth, bap. Feb. 11, 1719; Antje, bap. Oct. 4, 1721; Abraham, bap. June 17, 1724; and Dirk, bap. Oct. 5, 1726.

His daughter Elizabeth, j. d., Van Meeuwis, m., May 23, 1701, Henricus, son of Barent Hendrickse Courten (Coerten) and Styntie Wessels; he bap. Dec. 22, 1675. His will is dated Nov. 4, 1741; proven April 30, 1748. *Issue:* Margreta, bap. Dec. 13, 1704; m., Dec. 13, 1732, William Kingsland; Christina, bap. Feb. 10, 1708; Catharina, bap. June 21, 1710; Catharina, bap. Jan. 27, 1712; Elizabeth, bap. Oct. 7, 1713; Anna, bap. Jan. 25, 1716; Hendrikus, bap. Oct. 6, 1717; Barent, bap. Dec. 25, 1718, and Elizabeth, bap. Feb. 15, 1721. His wife was living at the date of his will, and only the following named children: Barent, Margareta, Christina, and Anna.

5. iv. MACHTELT DE RIEMER[2], the widow of Nicholas Gouverneur, joined the Dutch Church in New York, Nov. 29, 1682. He joined July 9, 1663. He was a prominent merchant in Amsterdam, engaged in trading to New Netherland. Though residing some time in New Amsterdam, it is believed that the greater portion of his life was spent in France and Holland, the former being his native country. He was living in Amsterdam, July 12, 1677,[1] and probably died there. His widow m. 2[d], Oct. 14, 1685, Jasper Nissepadt, Baker, of New York, and widower of Janneken Legende. She survived her 2[d] husband, and died about 1713; by him she had *issue:* Elizabeth, bap. Sept. 5, 1686; Elizabeth, bap. Jan. 1, 1688; and Margarietje, bap. Nov. 17, 1689. By her 1st husband she had two sons: Abraham and Isaac.

ABRAHAM GOUVERNEUR, son of Nicholas Gouverneur and Machtelt de Riemer,[2] born 1671. In 1689, then a youth of eighteen, he was made Clerk of Leisler's Committee of Safety and Town Clerk of New York.[2] He was attainted of high treason, April, 1691, with Leisler and Milborne, condemned to death, and his property confiscated. This judgment was reversed in 1695, and his estate restored.[3] He was elected to the Assembly in 1699, served until 1702, was Speaker in 1701, "and was regarded in his time as among the ablest and best of the Leislerian party." He married Mary Milborne, widow of Jacob Milborne, and dau. of Jacob Leisler, m. l., dated May 16, 1699. She was bap. Dec. 12, 1669, and died 1751. His will is dated Sept. 12, 1739; proven Oct. 8, 1470. *Issue:*

1. NICOLAAS GOUVERNEUR, bap. Feb. 25, 1700; m., about 1723, Geertruyt Reinders [Rynders], dau. of Barent Reinders and Hester Leisler. He died before Sept. 1739, leaving *issue:* Abraham, Esther, Barent, and Nicholas. His widow m. 2[d],

---

1 Doc. Rel. to Col. Hist. N. Y., Vol. 2, pp. 542-752.
2 Valentine's Manual, 1864, pp. 582.
3 Doc. Hist. N. Y., Vol. 2, pp. 542-752.

Oct. 14, 1741, David, son of William Provoost and Aefje
Van Exveen, and removed to Hackensack, N. J.
2. JACOBA GOUVERNEUR, bap. Dec. 5, 1701.
3. ELIZABETH GOUVERNEUR, bap. July 9, 1704; died 1751, unmarried.
4. JACOB GOUVERNEUR, bap. May 7, 1710; died young.
5. MARIA GOUVERNEUR, bap. July 13, 1712; m. 1st, Sep. 23, 1735,
Henry Myer, Jr., son of Hendrick Myer and Wyntje Rhee.
He was bap. July 26, 1713. She m. 2^d, Dec. 31, 1742,
Jasper Farmer, merchant, of New York.

ISAAC GOUVERNEUR, son of Nicholas Gouverneur and Machtelt de
Riemer,[2] was a merchant, in New York. He m., June 24,
1704, Sara, daughter of Dr. Samuel Staats and Johanna
Reynders [Rynders]. His will is dated May 16, 1728; date
of probate not given. He probably died in 1728; *Issue.*
1. JOHANNA GOUVERNEUR, bap. April 15, 1705; m., May 10, 1729,
Cornelis, son of Cornelis and Margaret (Van Borsum) Low.
He was bap. March 31, 1700.
2. MAGDALENA GOUVERNEUR, bap. Aug. 18, 1706; m. John Hall.
3. SAMUEL GOUVERNEUR, bap. Feb. 29, 1708; died young.
4. MARGARETA GOUVERNEUR, bap. Sept. 2, 1709; died Nov., 1758,
unmarried.
5. ALIDA GOUVERNEUR, bap. April 8, 1711; m., May 12, 1737, John
Broughton, and had *issue:* Shelton, John, Sara, and Mary.
6. NICOLAAS GOUVERNEUR, bap. April 19, 1713.
7. SARA GOUVERNEUR, bap. Oct. 17, 1714; m., Nov. 3, 1746, Lewis
Morris, jr. She was his second wife, and died at Morrisania,
Jan. 14, 1786. He died same place, July 3, 1762.[1]
8. GEERTRUV GOUVERNEUR, bap. March 9, 1716.
9. SAMUEL GOUVERNEUR, bap. Feb. 20, 1720.
10. ISAAC GOUVERNEUR, bap. Oct. 8, 1721.
11. ABRAHAM GOUVERNEUR, bap. Sept. 29, 1723.

ZYPERUS.

In August, 1659, Rev. Michiel Zyperus (Superius) left the island of
Curacao for New Netherland in the hope of receiving a call there to the
ministry.[2] He joined the church in New Amsterdam Jan., 1660, his name
appearing in the list of members, "Michiel Ziperius, Propenent," or Stu-
dent in Divinity. His wife, Anna Claes Duurcoop became a member
earlier, but in 1663 joined the church in Brooklyn.[3] They removed
to Virginia (Vertrocken na de Virginjes) probably in 1664. They had
issue: Cornelis, bap. Dec. 21, 1659, and Hillegond, bap. at Stuyvesant's
Bowery, Aug. 14, 1661.

1 N. V. G. and B. Record, Vol. 7, p. 18.
2 Cal. Hist. MSS., Dutch, p. 331.   3 Stiles' Hist. of Brooklyn, i. 426.

WOUTERSZEN—BREESTEDE.

EGBERT WOUTERSZEN from Yselstein, a town in Holland, was residing June 20th, 1640, at Jan de Lachers Hook, (at present Mill Creek Point, Jersey City,) at which date he gave a receipt for three imported milch cows and three mares hired from the West India Company. He took the lease of a bouwery, Dec. 1, 1646, on Manhattan Island, and May 10, 1647, obtained a patent for a tract of land called in Indian Apopcalyck, lying across the North River, west of the Manhattans.[1] He was enrolled a small burgher of New Amsterdam, April 17, 1657, and married, Sept. 1, 1641, Engel Jan Van Breestede, widow of Jan Janszen. He died about 1680, *without issue.* It appears that his wife had by her first husband the following named children, who are described in a deed dated May 20, 1683, as the children and co-heirs of Egbert Wouterse, late of the city of New York, deceased.[2]

1. JAN JANSZEN VAN BREESTEDE who m. Nov. 1, 1647, Marritje Lucas j. d. of New Amsterdam. In the New York D. C. Baptismal records she is called *Marritje Andries.* They had a large family of children who comprised the third generation of the BREESTEDE family of New York.

2. TRVNTJE JANSZEN VAN BREESTEDE who m. June 3, 1646, Ruth Jacobszer. of Renselaerswyck, (Rutger Jacobse Van Schoenderwoert or Van Woert), and whose descendants assumed the surname of RUTGERS.

3. DOROTHEA JANS VAN BREESTEDE who, m. April 19, 1650, Volckert Janszen from Fredrickstadt, and whose descendants comprise the DOUW family of New York.[3]

4. ELSJE JANS VAN BREESTEDE, who m. 1st, May 17, 1643, Adriaen Peterszen Van Alcmaer, widower of Grietje Pieters, of whom presently. She married 2d Hendrick Jochemse of Esopus.

ADRIAEN PIETERSZEN VAN ALCMAER.

On the 3d of Feb. 1640, Adriaen Petersen of Alcmaer, purchased of Hendrick Petersen of Wesel, a plantation near the reed valley, hard by *Sappokanican* (Greenwich) on the Island of Manhattan. This is the first notice found of him. On the 7th September, 1645, he obtained a patent for a lot of land north of the fort, and April 13, 1647, another for a tract near Sappokanican. He married May 17, 1643, ELSJE JANS VAN BREESTEDE, dau. of Jan Janszen and Engel Jans Van Breestede, and the stepdau. of Egbert Wouterszen. At the time of his marriage he was the widower of Grietje Pieters. Some incidents of the manner in which he wooed and won his second wife, have come down to us in the record of the Council Minutes of that period. It appears that Elsje was in the service of Cornelis Melyn, of Staten Island, who brought suit against Egbert Wouterszen, husband and guardian of Engel Jans, her mother, for damages on account of Elsje's marriage engagement before her term of service to him had expired. On the trial of the case Sept. 11, 1642, she testified

[1] Cal. of N. Y. Hist. MSS. Dutch, p. 13,36, 375.
[2] New York Conveyances. Liber 12, p. 126.
[3] Pearson's First Settlers of Albany.

that her mother and another woman had brought a young man to Staten Island whom she had never seen before, and desired her to marry him; she declined at first, as she did not know him, and had no inclination to marry, but finally consented. She concluded her testimony by returning in court the pocket-handkerchief she had received as a marriage present. On the 16th October following, she made a declaration that she sent for Adrian Pietersen, and that on his coming to Staten Island she accompanied him on board his yawl. A week later, Melyn and the Fiscal had Pietersen before the court charged with Elsje's abduction. Pietersen was ordered to bring her into court, deliver her to Melyn, and receive her again from him on giving security for the payment of any damages that Melyn may have suffered.

He died prior to July 3, 1664, on which day Jan Janse from Breeste, (Jan Janse Breestede) guardian of his orphan children, petitioned for compensation for part of a lot belonging to his estate at the Marketfield in New Amsterdam.* His widow married Hendrick Jochemse of the Esopus, prob. the Hendrick Jochemse of Beverwyck, 1654–1669. Adriaen Pieterszen Van Alcmaer and Elsje Jans Van Breestede had *issue* :

   1. i.   JANNETJE bap. Aug. 5, 1643.

   2. ii. SYTJE bap. April 17, 1645 ; m. Jan. 24, 1666, Jacob Abrahams (Santvoort).

   3. iii. LYSBETH bap. *March* 24, 1647.

SANTVOORT.

(FIRST THREE GENERATIONS.)

   1. JACOB ABRAHAMSEN SANTVOORT[1] the head of the New York family of Santfort or Santvoort as it is written in the early records, embarked May, 1661, in the St. Jean Baptist for New Netherland. He came from Vianen, a town of Holland, and married 1st in New York, Jan. 24, 1666, Sytie Ariens (Adriaens) dau. of Adriaen Pieterszen Van Alcmaer, before mentioned. He was a shoemaker, and when the forced loan was levied by Gov. Colve in 1674, on the inhabitants of New Orange, his property was valued at 2,500 guilders. He m. 2d, Dec. 26, 1677, Magdaleentje Van Vleck. j. d Van Bremen. On the 17th June, 1685, they conveyed land in New York to *Enoch Michaelsen* (Vreeland) of Pemripoe in East Jersey, which is the last notice found of him. His widow was living Aug. 13, 1699, at which date she was a sponsor at the bap. of Thomas son of William Walton. *Issue :*

   2. i.   ABRAHAM[2] bap. Jan. 11, 1667 ; m. 1st, Feb. 27, 1679, Vrouwtje, dau. of Cornelis Janse Van Horn and Anna Maria Jansen ; she was bap. July 25, 1666. He was a mariner, and for some years captain of the sloop Sea Flower, engaged in trade with the West Indies, and the latter portion of his life a merchant in New York. For a further account of him and his children see N. Y. G. and B. Record, vol. vii. p. 23.

   3. ii.   ADRIAEN,[2] bap. May 30, 1668 ; died young.

   4. iii. ADRIAEN,[2] bap. March 13, 1670.

   5. iv. ISACQ,[2] bap. Nov. 5, 1671 ; died young.

   6. v.   ISAAC,[2] bap. Dec. 29, 1672.

* Cal. of N. Y. Hist. MSS. Dutch, p. 12, 82, 83, 266, 369, 374.

7. vi. AELTJE,[2] bap. Oct. 7, 1674 ; m. Feb. 26, 1696, THOMAS SAND-
ERS, Bolter, of New York, son of Robert Sanders and Elsje
Barents, of Albany. *Issue:* Robert, bap. Oct. 4, 1696 ;
Styntje, bap. Dec. 26, 1697 ; Robert, bap. Jan. 1, 1700 ;
Jacob, bap. Oct. 19, 1701 ; Elsje, bap. Oct. 27, 1703 ;
Anneke, bap. Jan. 30, 1706 ; Maritje, bap. May 13, 1708 ;
Jacob, bap. June 9, 1712 ; and Beatrix, bap. Sept. 25, 1715.

8. vii. JACOB[2], bap. Sept. 13, 1676.

9. viii. MARYKEN,[2] bap. Nov. 27, 1678 ; m. Sept. 7, 1698, *Willem
Wallen*, j. m. Van N. Yorck. This name is thus incorrectly spelled
in the D. C. Marriage records. In the Baptismal records it rightly
appears WILLIAM WALTON. He was probably the son of Thomas Walton
and —— Lawrence, whose m. l. is dated Dec. 16, 1671. Thomas Walton
resided at Staten Island, and was arrested July 8, 1689, and confined in the
fort at New York for having said that he would retake the fort (from Leisler) with 200 men. He deceased prior to Dec. 12, 1689, at which date an
order was issued to Obadiah Holmes, justice of Richmond County, to
assist Capt. Thomas Lawrence in taking an inventory of his estate.*
Thomas Walton prob. another son of the above married Mary Stillwell; m.
l. dated Dec. 23, 1698 ; of him we have no further account. WILLIAM
WALTON, was an eminent merchant and ship builder in New York. He
died May 23, 1745. His wife died Sept. 3, 1768. *Issue* : Thomas, bap.
Aug. 12, 1699 : d. 1727, unmarried ; Maria, bap. Nov. 30, 1701 ; Jacob,
bap. July 7, 1703 ; m. May 14, 1726, Maria Beekman, and had numerous
children ; he died Oct. 17, 1749 ; William, bap. Oct. 20, 1706 ; m. Jan. 27,
1731, Cornelia Beekman ; he erected the Walton House in Franklin
Square and d. s. p. July 11, 1768 ; Jacobus, bap. Feb. 27, 1709 ; died
young ; James, bap. March 28, 1711, d. s. p.; and Abraham, bap. Feb. 24,
1714, d. s. p.

ECKERSON.

(FIRST THREE GENERATIONS.)

JAN THOMASZEN, j. m. Van de Manhattans, m. Nov. 8, 1665, Apollonia
Cornelis, dau. of Cornelis Claeszen Swits (Switsart, Wits) and Ariaentie
Cornelis ; she was bap. Oct. 25, 1648. About the year 1692, he assumed
the surname of Eckerson, which was retained by his children as their
family name. It is variously spelled in the N. Y. Dutch Church records
Echons, Eckens, Eckes, Eckeson, Ekkisse, and *Etkins,* with several other
slight modifications. At the baptism of his children he is invariably styled
Jan Thomaszen.—*Issue:*

1. i. ARIAENTIE ECKERSON,[2] bap. Feb. 16, 1667 ; m. March 5, 1684,
VINCENT DE LA MONTAGNE son of Jean (Jan) de la Montagne and Petronella Pikes (Pyckes, Picques, Pieces). He
was bap. April 22, 1657 ; his name appears at the baptism
of his children, de La Montagne and Montagne. He died
May 26, 1773, at the great age of One hundred and sixteen
years " ' He may be said to have been the connecting link
between the Dutch Directors and the American Revolution
—between Stuyvesant and Washington.' " * *Issue:* Pieternel, bap. April 11, 1685 ; Pieternel, bap. April 3, 1687 ;

---

* Cal. of N. Y. Hist. MSS., English, p. 185. Doc. Rel. to Col. Hist. N. Y. vol. iii. p. 597.

Jan. bap. Feb. 24, 1689; Thomas, bap. Feb. 15, 1691; Apollonia, bap. April 15, 1694; Jesse, bap. Nov. 8, 1696; Petronella, bap. Nov. 19, 1701; Annatje, bap. Oct. 3, 1703; Fincent, bap. Dec. 2, 1705; and Rachel, bap. May 4, 1707.

2. ii. THOMAS ECKERSON,[2] bap. Jan. 27, 1669; m. 1ˢᵗ Sept. 10, 1697, Rachel Van Slechtenhorst j. d. from Albany; m. 2ᵈ Nov. 29, 1700, Elizabeth Slingerlant, dau. of Teunis Cornelise Slingerlant of Albany. At his second marriage his name is recorded *Thomas Achtent. Issue :* Jan, bap. Aug. 27, 1701; Annatie, bap. Dec. 16, 1702; Appalonia, bap. Nov. 22, 1704; and Theunis, bap. May 14, 1707.

3. iii. CORNELIS ECKERSON,[2] bap. April 9, 1671; m. Aug. 24, 1693, Willemtje Vlierboom, j. d. of Albany, both living at Tappan. *Issue :* Jan, bap. June 26, 1695; Matthys, (?) bap. Nov. 8, 1696; Jan, bap. March 22, 1699; Cornelis, bap. Jan. 12, 1701; Jacob, bap. Feb. 28, 1703; and Thomas, bap. March 3, 1706.

4. iv. SARA ECKERSON,[2] bap. Oct. 4, 1673; m. Jan. 8, 1696, ABRAHAM JANSZEN (VAN AERNAM), j. m. Van Mitspadt Kill, son of Jan Dirckse Van Aernam and Sara Theunis; he was bap. April 9, 1673. *Issue :* Jan, bap. May 10, 1696; Abram, bap. Dec. 26, 1697; Sara, bap. Oct. 22, 1699; Apalonia, bap. Feb. 9, 1701; Isaac, bap. Dec. 5, 1703; and Isaac, bap. July 15, 1705.

5. v. JAN ECKERSON,[2] bap. Feb. 9, 1676; m. June 3, 1696, Maryken Jans, dau. of Jan Dirckse Van Aernam; she was bap. July 14, 1675. *Issue :* Jan, bap. Sept. 7, 1698; Thomas, bap. Oct. 13, 1703; Apolonia, bap. Aug. 22, 1705; and Thomas, bap. Jan. 7, 1708.

6. vi. LYSBETH ECKERSON,[2] bap. May 29, 1678; m. June 24, 1698, DIRCK UYTTEN BOGAERT,[†] j. m. Van N. Yorck. *Issue :* Gysbert, bap. Sept. 24, 1699; m. Nov. 26, 1720, Catharine, dau. of Joost Palding (Paulding) and Catharine Jans Duyts; Apalonia, bap. March 18, 1702; and Jan, bap. April 23, 1704. Elizabeth Ekkesse, widow, prob. the widow of Dirck Uytten Bogaert, m. May 26, 1713, Ralph Potter.

7. vii. MARGRIETJE ECKERSON,[2] bap. ——, 1680 (?); m. Nov. 29, 1700, Focco Heyrmans (VOLKERT HEERMANS), son of Egbert Fockenszen, alias Egbert Heermans, and his wife Elsje Lucas; he was bap. Feb. 7, 1679. *Issue :* Elsje, bap. Nov. 5, 1701; Egbert, bap. Jan. 30, 1704; Jan and Apalonia, twins, bap. May 2, 1706; Luykas, bap. April 10, 1709; Margrietje, bap. Nov. 22, 1710; Egbert, bap. Oct. 11, 1713; and Annatje, bap. Oct. 3, 1716.

---

[*] O'Callaghan's Hist. of New Netherlands, vol. ii. p. 21.

[†] He was probably a son of Gysbert Uyten Bogert and his wife Willemtje Klaas; the latter with Isaac Stoutenburg was sponsor at the baptism of Dirck's first son, Gysbert. It appears to have been a universal custom among the early Dutch settlers to give the eldest son his (paternal) grandfather's name, and this custom affords an almost unerring rule in tracing the line of descent. The father of Dirck Uytten Bogaert, was probably the Gysbert Uytden Bogaert who on the 26th of May, 1684, obtained an Indian Deed for a tract of land, lying on the north bank of the Catskill, extending from Boomties Hook, (at the mouth of the Catskill), up the Hudson River to a small Kill, opposite Vastrix Island, thence west to Dirck Tennissen's mill; thence south to the first little Kill that flows into Hans Vossen Kill; thence along the same to where it falls into the Catskill, and thence along the Catskill to Boomties Hook.—(Calendar of Land Papers, p. 28). Besides Dirck, he prob. had Aeltje, who m. 1st, Zacharias Zluys, and m. 2d, Nov. 14, 1695, Jacobus Van Duersen, j. m. from Albany; Neeltje, who m. July 2, 1690, Isaac Stoutenburg, j. m., of New York, each of whom had numerous children.

8. viii. CORNELIA ECKERSON,[2] bap. Nov. 15, 1682; m. Sept. 10, 1700, JEREMIAS BURROUGHS (Borry), j. m. Van Nieuw Thuyn, (Newtown, L. I.). *Issue:* Hannah, bap. May 24, 1701; Apolonia, bap. April 11, 1703; Elizabeth, bap. March 7, 1705; Jeremias, bap. Feb. 12, 1707; Jan, bap. March 30, 1709; Isaac, bap. Oct. 17, 1711; Maria, bap. Oct. 12, 1715; Abraham, bap. Oct. 29, 1718; Jeremias, bap. Feb. 15, 1721; and Abigail, bap. Dec. 16, 1724.

9. ix. RACHEL ECKERSON,[2] bap. April 11, 1685. By PETRUS STUYVESANT, son of Nicolaes Willem Stuyvesant and Elizabeth Van Slechtenhorst, had son Benoni, bap. May 2, 1706; Petrus Stuyvesant, bap. March 21, 1685, died (drowned,) in 1706; and she m. March 1, 1712, FRANS PIETERSE DE VRIES. *Issue:* Antje, bap. July 8, 1713; Jan, bap. March 25, 1716; Petrus, bap. Sept. 24, 1718; Thomas, bap. April 19, 1721; Symon, bap. Nov. 6, 1723; and Jan, bap. July 20, 1726.

10. x. JANNETJE ECKERSON,[2] bap. Nov. 2, 1687; m. June 1. 1710, BENJAMIN VAN VEGTE (Van Vechten). *Issue:* Cornelius, bap. Oct. 4, 1710; Jan, bap. April 1, 1713; and Ruben, bap. Dec. 21, 1715.

11. xi. MARIA ECKERSON,[2] twin, bap. Sep. 6, 1690; no further account.

12. xii. ANNA ECKERSON,[2] twin, bap. Sept. 6, 1690; no further account.

SAMMANS.

(FIRST THREE GENERATIONS.)

JOHANNES THOMASZEN, j. m. Van Amsterdam, m. Oct. 31, 1677, Aechtje Jacobs, j. d. Van N. Amersfort, both then living at *Sapponicam* (Greenwich, Manhattan Island). At the baptism of their first child, her name is written Aerhtie, at the others Aefje Jacobs, while his is given in each instance Johannes Thomaszen. Their children adopted the surname of SAMMANS (Samman, Sammons). *Issue:*

1. i. GRETIE SAMMANS,[2] bap. Aug. 17, 1678, m. May 16, 1701, ELIAS BREVOORT, see page 16.

2. ii. JANNETIE SAMMANS,[2] bap. Feb. 18, 1680; m. May 5, 1702, ADRIAEN VAN SCHAICK, see page 11.

3. iii. JACOB SAMMAN,[2] bap. June 11, 1683; m. May 27, 1706, CATLVNTJE BENSEN, prob. dau. of Johannes Bensen and Lysbeth Matheuse of Albany. *Issue:* Aegje, bap. Jan. 14, 1708; Aegje, bap. Feb. 12, 1710; Johannes, bap. March 9, 1712; Thomas, bap. June 13, 1716; Elizabeth, bap. Sep. 28, 1718; Samson, bap. Dec. 7, 1721; Dirk, bap. March 18, 1724; Margrietje, bap. May 4, 1726; Benjamin and Lena, twins, bap. Feb. 21, 1729; Rachel, bap. Aug. 16, 1730; and Mattheus, bap. June 1, 1733.

4. iv. THOMAS SAMMANS,[2] bap. Jan. 3, 1686. He was sponsor May 18, 1718, at the bap. of Margrietje dau. of Christoffel Van Nes, which is the last notice found of him. He prob. d. s. p.

5. v. RACHEL SAMMAN,[2] bap. July 11, 1691; m. June 24, 1717, STOFFEL (Christoffel) VAN NES, and had Margrietje bap. May 18, 1718. She m. 2d June, 17, 1726, Henricus, son of

Barnardus and Elsje (Meyer) Smith, and had Barnardus, bap.
May 22, 1727, and Aafje, bap. Feb. 16, 1729.

STRIDLES.

GABRIEL THOMASZEN, alias Striddles (Gabriel Tompson Strudles), and
wife Jannetje Dircx, joined the Dutch Church in New York, Dec. 1, 1692,
with certificate from Albany. He was there as early as 1662. A sketch
of his life appears in Pearson's First Settlers of Albany, page 107. His will
is dated Sept. 14, 1702, and Oct 19, 1703, an Inventory of his estate was
"recorded at the request of Jane Van Laer, Executrix of ye estate." He
names in his will son Thomas Stridles, and daughters Katharine, Jannetie,
and Neeltie. Appoints his dau. Jannetie Stridles, Executrix. Besides
those bap. in Albany, he had by wife Jannetje Dircx, the following named
children bap. in New York ; Johannes, bap. May 7, 1693 ; Fytje, bap.
Feb. 14, 1694 ; and Neeltje, bap. March 4, 1696.

His dau. Jannetje, bap. in Albany, Aug. 19, 1683, m. Nov. 8, 1702,
GERRIT VAN LAER, baker of New York, son of Stoffel Gerritse Van Laer
and Catharina Boots. She died 1717–18, and May 25, 1718, Gerrit Van
Laer petitioned for administration on his father-in-law's Estate. He m. 2d,
Jan. 3, 1719, Annatje Aertsen. Issue: Catharina, bap. Sept. 5, 1703 ;
Christoffel, bap. Oct. 25, 1704 ; Gabriel, bap. Oct. 3, 1705 ; Gabriel, bap.
Jan. 29, 1707 ; Gerardus, bap. Sept. 15, 1708 ; Sara, bap. Sept. 3, 1710 ;
Christoffel, bap. Oct. 24, 1711 ; Jannetje, bap. Dec. 10, 1712 ; Jannetje,
bap. July 14, 1714 ; Jannetje, bap. Jan. 25, 1716 ; Sara, bap. March 27,
1717 ; and by 2d wife : Eva, bap. Oct. 7, 1719 ; at the bap. of this child
his wife is named Annetje Ten Eyck. No other notice of the children of
Gabriel Thomaszen Stridles named in his will, has been found.

WANSHAER.

(FIRST THREE GENERATIONS.)

The head of this family was in New Amsterdam as early as 1644, following the vocation of Pilot. In the record of his marriage, Jan. 17,
1649, to Baertje Hendricks Kip, j. d. from Amsterdam, he is called Jan
Janszen, j. m. Van Tubingen, probably the town of that name in Suabia,
in Germany. At the baptism of his children his name is variously recorded, Jan Janszen Van St. Cubis, Van St. Ubus, Van St. Obyn, Jan
Van Sara, Jan Wanshaer Van St. Benen, JAN WANSHAER[1] (sometimes written Manshaer), and Jan de Caper, i. e. in English Jan the Sailor. He
was admitted to the rights of a small burgher April 18, 1657, and appears
to have been one of the substantial and respectable citizens of the city.
His name and that of his wife is recorded in the list of Old Members of
the Dutch Church, or of those who joined the church between 1649 and
1660. He resided on *Brouwer Straat*, now that part of Stone street
between Broad and Whitehall streets.

His widow married 2d, Dec. 12, 1677, Jan Dirckszen Meyer, widower of
Tryntje [Andriesse] Grevenraet.* She survived her second husband, by
whom she had no children, and was living July 12th, 1702. By her first
husband she had *issue*. 1. Abraham,[2] bap. Nov. 14, 1649 ; 2. Johannes,[2]
bap. Aug. 27, 1651 ; 3. Jacob,[2] bap. July 13, 1653 ; 4. Hendrick,[2] bap.
March 21, 1655 ; 5. ANTHONY WANSHAER,[2] bap. July 4, 1657 ; one of this
name, by wife Marritje Harperts, had Abraham,[3] bap. April 1, 1696. 6.

* She was probably a sister of Isaac Grevenraet.[1]

Robbert,[2] bap. Aug. 31, 1659 ; 7. Johannes,[2] bap. Sept. 30, 1661 ; 8. Johannes,[2] bap. Sept. 17, 1662.

9. JAN WANSHAER,[2] bap. Dec. 5, 1663 ; joined the Dutch Church in New York Feb. 26, 1696; m. Dec 8, 1698, Susanna de Nys, daughter of Pieter de Nys (Denyse) and Geesje Idens ; she was bap. Dec. 19, 1669. They had *issue* Johannes,[3] bap. Oct. 6, 1700 ; Abraham,[3] bap. July 12, 1702 ; Pieter,[3] bap. March 12, 1704 ; Pieter,[3] bap. March 21, 1705 ; and Johannes,[3] bap. Nov. 19, 1707, who m. Nov. 4, 1736, Christina Egberts ; 10, Carel.[3] bap. July 4, 1666.

11. JACOMYNTIE WANSHAER,[2] bap. July 13, 1667; joined the Dutch Church here Sept. 3, 1696 ; m. Feb. 16, 1698, Andries Abrahamse, j. m. of New York. *Issue*, Francyntje, bap. June 12, 1700 ; Sarah, bap. Dec. 21, 1701 ; Johanna, bap. Aug. 29, 1703 ; Abraham and Isaac, twins, bap. Aug 22, 1705 ; Andreas, bap. Dec. 14, 1707 ; and Sara, bap. Jan. 14, 1711.

TYMENS—VAN DER VEEN.

There is nothing more perplexing to one engaged in tracing the pedigrees of the early Dutch settlers, than the changes sometimes found in the name of the same individual. Among these will be noted those which occur in the children of a widow upon her remarriage, who frequently bear the name of their stepfather, as well as their proper Dutch patronymic. Thus the name of *Elsje Elberts*, daughter of Elbert Janszen and Elsje Jans, after her mother's second marriage to Otto Grim, is sometimes recorded *Elsje Grim*. So we find *Elsje Tymens*, after the third marriage of her widowed mother to Govert Loockermans, called *Elsje Loockermans*, as though she was his putative daughter instead of his step daughter.

ELSJE TYMENS (Thymens) wife of PIETER CORN. VAN DER VEEN and daughter of Thymen and Marritje Janszen, was born in New Amsterdam. Her father was a ship carpenter and must have come to New Netherland as early as 1633, perhaps with Director General Wouter Van Twiller in April of that year. On the 16th of April 1639, then aged 36 years, he made before Secretary Cornelis Van Tienhoven, with Jacob Hoffelsen (Stoffelsen ?), overseer, aged about 37 years, and Gillis Petersen Van der Gouw, house carpenter, aged 27 years, a deposition in regard to the dilapidated state of the Fort, and the bad condition of affairs generally at New Amsterdam, at the time of the arrival, March 28, 1638, of Director William Kieft in the ship Haring.* In 1642, he obtained a patent for land on Mespat Kill, L. I., and July 3, 1643, one for land on Manhattan Island, and another, July 13, the same year for land on Long Island. He died soon after. Her mother, Marritje Janszen, was a daughter of Tryn Jonas (Jansen ?) midwife at New Amsterdam, and a sister of Anneke Jans who married—first, Roelof Janszen, and second, the Rev. Everardus Bogardus. She married her second husband, Dirck Corneliszen j. m. van Wensveen, Aug. 28, 1646, by whom she had Cornelis (Dirckszen), baptized March 17, 1647; he married Nov. 17, 1672, Grietje Hendricks of New York, daughter of Hendrick Willemszen, and had son Dirck, baptized March 2, 1674. Cornelis Dirckszen, above named, deceased before May 1678, and his widow, Grietje Hendricks, married October, 1678, John Robinson, merchant of New York, and had Marie, baptized July 18, 1683, and Grietje baptized October 12, 1684. *Dirck Corneliszen*, the second

* Coll. N. Y. Hist. Society, vol. 1, New Series, p. 279.

husband of Marritje Janszen, was living in August, 1647, but had deceased before August, 29, 1648, at which date his widow gave a power of attorney to William Turck and Seth Verbrugge to receive certain accounts, &c., in the hands of Wouter Van Twiller at Amsterdam.[1] She married, third, Govert Loockermans,[2] by whom she had son Jacob, baptized March 17, 1652; he was a physician and settled in the county of St. Mary, Province of Maryland. For an account of his descendants see Vincent's History of Delaware, vol. 1, p. 474. Govert Loockermans died about 1670, and his widow was buried Nov. 20, 1677.[3] In her will, dated May 7, 1677, with codicil, dated Nov. 1, she is styled Mrs Mary Jansen, widow of Govert Lockermans, and names the three children of her daughter *Elsce Lysler* by Peter Cornelis Van der Veen deceased, as follows: Cornelius, Timothy, and Margaretta, to whom she gives the sum of one hundred guilders ($40) in beavers, at eight guilders a piece; to Anna, daughter of William Bogardus, the sum of fifty guilders in beavers. Names as *her universal heirs,* her children Elsie Tymans, married *with* Jacob Leysler; Cornelis Dirkse married *with* Grietie Hendrickse, and Jacob Lockermans *not married*. Makes a small bequest to Mary Van Brugh, daughter of Mr. Johannes Van Brugh, and to Susannah Leysler, her said daughter's daughter. Appoints her cousin, Mr. Johannes Van Brugh and Mr. Francis Rombouts Alderman, of this city, executors.

ELSJE TYMENS m. 1st Jan. 7, 1652, PIETER CORÑ. VAN DER VEEN j. m. from Amsterdam. The first notice of him is found in the record of his marriage. He was a merchant in New Amsterdam, admitted to the rights of a small burgher April 11, 1657, and in 1658 was appointed one of the Commissioners to treat with the Esopus Indians. Soon after his marriage he erected the first brick house built in this city, and situated on the present westerly side of Whitehall between Pearl and State Streets. He was the principal projector in company with Cornelius de Potter, of the first ship, the "New Love," known to have been built at this port.[4] He died in 1661, and his widow married Jacob Leisler, of whom hereafter. Pieter Cornelisen Van der Veen and Elsje Tymens had *issue*:

1. CORNELIS, bap. October 27, 1652; m. MAGDALENA WOLSUM and prob. d. s. p. His widow m. April 25, 1683, LEENDERT HUYGEN DE CLEYN (de Kleyn), of whom hereafter.

2. TIMOTHY, born 1654? There is no record found of his baptism; he was sponsor at the baptism of Johannes, son of Robert Walters, May 22 1687, which is is the last notice found of him.

   1. MARGARITA, bap. Feb. 18, 1657; m. May 15, 1682, ISAAC STEPHENSZEN, mariner of New York, and had—1. Margriet, bap. Feb. 9, 1684, who m. Sept. 12, 1700, Symon Pasco (Pasko), and had Symon, bap. July 7, 1703, and Elizabeth, bap. Sept. 8, 1706; 2. Pieter, bap. Dec. 25, 1685; 3. Elizabeth, bap. Nov. 20, 1687, d. young; 4. Elizabeth, bap. July 30, 1690, who married March 18, 1710, Jacobus Mauritz, and had Elizabeth, bap. June 29, 1712, and Elizabeth, bap. April 28, 1714, who m. June 26, 1738, James De Hart, and had Margrita, bap. May 2, 1739, and Jacoba, bap. Oct. 8, 1740.

4. CATHARYN, bap. June 29, 1659; not named in her grandmother's, will and prob. died young.

[1] Cal. N. Y. Hist. MSS. Dutch. p. 40, 42, 49.
[2] Govert Loockermans j. m. van Turnhout m. July 11, 1649, Marritje Jans j. d. Is it not probable that these are the persons above alluded to, and that j. d. after her name is an error in the marriage record?
[3] O'Callaghan's Hist. New Netherlands, vol. 2. p. 38.
[4] Valentine's Manual, 1860, p. 594.

LEISLER.

(FIRST THREE GENERATIONS.)

1. JACOB LEISLER[1] (Loyseler, Leysler, Leydsler, Leydser, Lysler), from Frankfort, came to New Netherland a soldier in the West India Company's service in 1660. He embarked in the ship Otter from Amsterdam, the 27th of April of that year. There was a tradition among his descendants that he came originally from France, and a vague report, a hundred years or so ago in New York, that he was a Swiss.[1] It is more likely that he was born in Frankfort, and was, therefore, a native of Germany. A Susanna Leydser was one of the sponsors at the baptism, Feb. 10, 1664, of Susanna, his eldest daughter. The conjecture is a fair one that she was his mother. He joined the Dutch Church in New Amsterdam Oct. 2, 1661, and married, April 11, 1663, Elsje Tymens, widow of Pieter (Cornelisen) Van der Veen, who was, in his day, a reputable and wealthy merchant of this city. He probably succeeded to the business left by Van der Veen, as a few years after his marriage we find him engaged in mercantile pursuits, through which, and by his marriage, he acquired a large estate, and was ranked among the wealthiest citizens of his time. In 1678, while on a voyage to Europe, he was taken prisoner by the Turks, to whom he paid a large ransom for his freedom. On the 10th of Sept., 1684, he was commissioned Captain of a Militia Company in New York. He purchased for the Huguenots, Sept. 20, 1689, of John Pell and Rachel his wife, six thousand acres of land within the manor of Pelham, now the township of New Rochelle, in Westchester Co., New York.[2]

Early in 1689 news reached New York of the overthrow of James the Second, and the accession of William, Prince of Orange, to the English throne. The people having determined to seize Fort James, in the interest of King William and Queen Mary, they selected Capt. Jacob Leisler to carry their design into effect. On the 3d of June, 1689, the day following its seizure, Lieut.-Governor Nicholson left New York for England. The same day Leisler issued a proclamation declaring that his intention in holding the fort was to preserve the Protestant religion, and that he should hold it only until the arrival of a Governor with orders from his Royal Highness, the Prince of Orange, then daily expected, into whose hands it would be immediately delivered up. But this expectation, unfortunately for him, and the peace of the Province, was not realized until the arrival of Gov. Sloughter, in March, 1691. In the meantime, Leisler, on the 16th of August, 1689, was commissioned Commander-in-Chief, by a Committee of Safety, who represented a majority of the community.

In Dec., 1689, a messenger arrived in New York, bearing a letter from the English Government, addressed "To Francis Nicholson, Esq., or in his absence, to such as for the time being, takes care for preserving the peace and administering the laws in His Majesties province of New York." This letter gave authority to the person addressed to take chief command as Lieutenant-Governor of the Province, and to appoint a Council to assist him in conducting the government. By the advice of the Committee of Safety Leisler, on the 11th Dec., 1689, assumed the style of Lieutenant-

---

[1] N. Y. Hist. Society Coll., 1868, p. 424.
[2] Bolton's Hist. of Westchester County, vol. 1, p. 376.

Governor, and selected as his Council, Pieter De La Noy, Samuel Staats, Hendrick Jansen (Van Feurden), Johannes Vermelje, for the city and county of New York ; Capt. Gerardus Beeckman, for Kings County ; Samuel Edsall, for Queens County ; Capt. Thomas Williams, for Westchester County ; and William Lawrence, for the County of Orange. They appointed Jacob Milborne Secretary of the Province and Clerk to the Lieutenant-Governor and Council. On the 28th Jan., 1691, Capt. Richard Ingoldsby arrived in New York, bearing their Majesties' Commission as Captain of Foot, and, without producing any legal authority, he demanded of Leisler the possession of the fort, which was refused. Henry Sloughter, who had been appointed Governor in Chief of the Province, arrived on the 19th of March following, late in the day, and Leisler, "having notice thereof, that same night (though very late) took care to deliver the fort to his order, which was done very early the next morning." Sloughter immediately ordered the arrest of Leisler, and his friends with him, and called a special Court of Oyer and Terminer, which was held for their trial in April following. By this court, composed of some of his most virulent enemies, and which from the first, had prejudged him and his associates,[1] Leisler, and Jacob Milborne, his son-in-law, were convicted and attainted of high treason, for not delivering the possession of the fort to Capt. Richard Ingoldsby, and sentenced to death. They were executed together near the site of the present Hall of Records,[2] on Saturday, May 16, 1691, while the populace was overawed by military force, and their enemies "were carousing in beastly triumph and drunkenness." After execution (by hanging), they were beheaded and their bodies buried in ground belonging to Leisler, east of the Commons, and near the corner of a street called George street, supposed to be in the rear of the present "Tribune Building," between Spruce and Frankfort streets. They were reburied, with great solemnity by a large concourse of citizens, in the Old Dutch Church, in Garden street, now Exchange Place, Oct. 20, 1698. The British Parliament, in 1695, passed an act reversing their attainder, and restoring their estates to their families, thus virtually censuring the illegality of their execution. (Dunlap's *History of New York, Vol.* 1 ; *Documentary History of New York, Vol.* 2 ; *The Administration of Jacob Leisler, by* Charles F. Hoffman, in Sparks' *American Biography, Vol.* 13 ; *Collections of the N. Y. Historical Society, for* 1868 ; Valentine's *History of New York.*)

Elsje Tymens, the widow of Jacob Leisler, survived him some 13 or 14 years. She was living Sept. 17, 1704, at which date she was a sponsor at the baptism of Elizabeth, dau. of Barent Reinders. *Issue.*

2. i. SUSANNAH[2], bap. Feb. 10, 1664 ; joined the Dutch Church in New York, Dec. 3, 1681, and removed *with certificate* some time after to Bergen (N. J.?). The date and place of her first marriage are not known. She m. 1st, *Michiel Vaughton* (called Farton in the Dutch Church Baptismal records), an Englishman and a *protégé* of Gov. Thomas Dongan, with whom he came to New York in August, 1683. He was a half-brother of John Spragg, Esq., who was a member of the Legislative Council in 1683, and subsequently Secretary of the Province of New York.

Governor Dongan describes Vaughton as having been " a volunteer two or three years on board ship with Captain Temple," etc., and "a pretty

[1] Gerardus Beekman, Johannes Vermelje, Thomas Williams, Meyndert Coerten, Abraham Brasher, and Abraham Gouverneur were convicted, with Leisler and Milborne, of high treason.
[2] Moulton's View of the City of New Orange in 1672, p. 22.

ingenious young man," who, happening to be in London when he came away, offered his services, which the Governor accepted and promised to aid him with money when in need of it "for to put him into some way." On the 11th of May, 1684, he was commissioned Clerk of the Market of New York, and in December following we find him Commander of the Sloop James, and authorized by warrant to proceed to the Sound and seize and send to the city all vessels that may seem to be engaged in unlawful traffic. Edward Antill was part owner of the vessel he commanded, Vaughton's share in it having been purchased with money loaned him by Gov. Dongan. In the spring of 1685, Hugh Riddle, a Scotchman and "poor Gentleman," coming into the Province from New Jersey, brought with him, without entry at the Custom House, a small parcel of linen of the value of three to five pounds. Some time after, Riddle and one of the Custom officers "drinking drunk together," fell to quarrelling, on which the officer went out, about one or two in the morning, and, meeting Vaughton, also a Custom House officer, compelled him to go with him to seize *uncustomed goods*, at Riddle's lodgings. Arrived there, they broke open the door, and Riddle, "still drunk," in endeavoring to keep them out, stabbed Vaughton, wounding him severely. For this offence he was thrown into prison, where he remained a long time awaiting Vaughton's recovery. Being in a starving condition, he was finally liberated upon the application of Mr. Vaughton, Mr. Spragg, and others, the Council ordering his goods to be released upon his paying the physicians their charges for attending Vaughton. These being more than the value of the goods, and Riddle a poor man, Mr. Spragg, in charity to him, paid the surgeons their demand, amounting to ten pounds.[1]

On the 24th of January, 1702, Susanna Vaughton, his widow, petitioned for a patent of 300 acres of land, lying in the vicinity of the Crom Elboogh (Crum Elbow Creek), in Dutchess County, "which she alleges to be part of a purchase made by Henry Pawling (Sheriff of Esopus in 1684), under a license granted to her husband, in company with said Pawling, and for which no patent has as yet been granted."

The last notice of Michiel Vaughton where his identity is certain is found in the record of the baptism of his son Michiel, September 9, 1688. The sponsors at this baptism were John Spragg, Robbert Walters, and Catharina Leydser. He probably died soon after. His widow m. 2d, March 12 1704, Leonard (Huygen) de Kleyn,* by whom she had no issue.

[1] Doc. Rel. to Col. Hist. of N. Y., vol. 3, p. 407-8-9, 493. Cal. N. V. Hist. Mss. English, p. 116-117, 128 134 and 306.

* LEENDERT (Leonard) HUYGEN OK KLEYN (de Cleyn, Cleyn) *Van Buuren*, was a son of Hugh Barentsen de Clein, who, with his wife and seven children, embarked from Amsterdam for New Netherland, in May, 1661, in the Beaver. Hugo Barents (de Kleyn) and his wife Mayken Bartels joined the Dutch Church in New Amsterdam, October 2, 1661. Leendert joined May 28, 1679, and m. 1st, April 26, 1683, Magdalena Wolsum (Wolsing, Wolsen), widow of Cornelis Van der Veen. He was a shop-keeper in New York for many years, but removed in the latter part of his life to New Rochelle, Westchester Co., N. V., where he died in 1735, having survived his second wife, Susannah Leisler, a number of years. The latter part of his name is frequently dropped in the Dutch Records, and he appears simply as Leendert Huygen or Huygens. *Issue:*

1. David, bap. May 24, 1684, d. s. p.
2. Maria, bap. March 7, 1686 ; m. February 28, 1708, Joseph Robinson, merchant, of New York, and had Leonard, bap. September 24, 1710 ; Richard, bap. September 17, 1712 ; Joseph, bap. January 2, 1715 ; and Maria, bap. January 14, 1719.
3. Elisabeth, bap. March 29, 1688 ; m. November 3, 1705, Anthony Lispenard, son of Anthony and wife Abeltie. At the baptism of his children his name is written Anthony Lippenard. In 1724 he removed to New Rochelle. *Issue :* Anthony, bap. July 27, 1709 ; Magdalena, bap. February 16, 1712 ; Leonard, bap. January 25, 1716 ; Johannes, bap. February 1, 1721 ; and Elisabeth, bap. February 5, 1724.
4. Barent, bap. February 28, 1690 ; m August 28, 1711, Cornelia, dau. of Rev. Rudolphus Varick and his wife Margareta Visboom, and had Leonard, bap. December 7, 1712. Barent de Kleyn died soon after, and his widow, Cornelia, m. 2d, July 22, 1715, Pieter Van Dyk.
5. Johannes, bap. February 4, 1694 ; d. s. p.
6. Magdalena, bap. January 26, 1696 ; d. s. p.
7. Catharina, bap. in Brooklyn, November 27, 1698 ; d. s. p.

MICHIEL VAUGHTON, son of Michiel Vaughton and Susannah Leisler, bap. September 9, 1688, m. May 15, 1712, Catharina dau. of John Donaldson (Danginson, Danillson, Dennissen, Dumelson) and Elizabeth Rodenburg.† In 1719 he was a merchant and afterwards a sail-maker in New York.

Will dated Dec. 28, 1732; proven Feb. 24, 1736; names wife, Catharin; eldest son, John; son, Jacob; daughters, Elizabeth, Susannah, Katherin and Mary. Appoints his wife and his cousins Paul Richard, and William Hamersly, of the city of New York, merchants, Executrix and Executors. *Issue:*

1. MICHIEL VAUGHTON, bap. Feb. 15, 1713; d. young.
2. ELIZABETH VAUGHTON, bap. Sept. 1, 1715.
3. JOHANNES VAUGHTON, bap. July 31, 1717; d. young.
4. JOHANNES VAUGHTON, bap. April 24, 1720.
5. JACOB VAUGHTON, bap. April 11, 1722.
6. SUSANNAH VAUGHTON, bap. Dec. 2, 1724; m. March 8, 1747, Maurits, son of Balthazer De Hart and Margrietje Maurits, of New York. They settled at Shrewsbury, N. J.
7. CATHARINA VAUGHTON, bap. Dec. 21, 1726.
8. MARY VAUGHTON, bap. Sept. 25, 1728; she prob. m. June 22, 1769, Pieter Wessels.

3. ii. CATHARINA,[2] bap. Nov. 8, 1665; m. Feb. 4, 1685, ROBERT WALTERS, j. m., from Plymouth, England. He was a merchant in New York, Alderman of the South Ward, 1688–9, member of the Assembly called under Leisler's authority in 1690, and member of the Colonial Council under Governors Bellomont and Nanfan, from 1698 to 1702, when he was suspended by Lord Cornbury. He was again a member of the Council under the administrations of Governors Hunter and Burnet, and Mayor of New York 1720–21–22–23. He died early in 1731. *Issue:*

1. ELISABETH WALTERS, bap. Nov. 1, 1685; m. Capt. Johannes Wendel, of Albany. See Pearson's First Settlers of Albany, p. 148.
2. JOHANNES WALTERS, bap. May 22, 1687.
3. MARIA WALTERS, bap. Nov. 24, 1689.
4. CATHARINA WALTERS, bap. ——, 1692?; m. Nov. 15, 1710, Johannes Van Hartsberge, and had Elizabeth, bap. Aug. 5, 1711; Johannes, bap. March 29, 1713; and Catharina, bap. Dec. 19, 1714. In 1719 he was a merchant at Surinam.

---

† Elizabeth Rodenburg, dau. of Lucas Rodenburg and Catrina Roelofs, was born on the Island of Curaçoa, her father being vice director there from about 1646 to 1657, the year of his death. Her mother was a dau. of Roelof Jansen and Anneke Jans, and after the death of her first husband married 2d, April 24, 1658, Johannes Pieterszen Ver Brugge [Van Brugh] from Haerlem, a prominent merchant and magistrate of New Amsterdam.

Elizabeth Rodenburg m. 1st, September 3, 1679, Ephraim, son of Augustyn Hermans and Janneken Verleth. He was bap. September 1, 1652. In August, 1673, when the Dutch fleet under command of Benckes and Evertsen captured New York, he was a Clerk in the Secretary of State's Office, and was commissioned with others, by the Dutch Council of war, to administer the oath of allegiance to the inhabitants on Long Island. Removing to the Delaware, he was appointed, in 1676, Clerk of the courts of New Castle and Upland, the court giving him in 1678 a certificate for his excellent conduct while in office. After his marriage in New York he returned to Delaware, and was appointed Surveyor (to which profession his father belonged) June 22, 1680, for the counties of New Castle and St. Jones. About this time he joined the Labadists, a short-lived religious sect, of which Jean de Labadie was the founder, and whose followers Dankers and Sluyter had with slight success sought to colonize on the Delaware. (Hazard's Annals of Penn., 426-51-72. Memoirs L. I. Hist. Soc., Vol. 1, xxxi., xxxiv., xxxv.) He died in 1689. His widow returned from New Castle and rejoined the Dutch Church in New York, September 1, 1689. They had issue bap. in New York: Augustinus, bap. July 7, 1680; Augustina, bap. June 1, 1684; Samuel, bap. April 20, 1687, and Ephraim, bap. October 7, 1688.

She m. 2d, March 24, 1692, John Donaldson, j. m. Van Galleway (Scotland?). He lived on the South or Delaware River where Catharina, their dau., named in the text, was probably born. They had another dau. Maria, bap. in New York, July 1, 1696, who married George Yates, merchant, of Philadelphia.

5. SARA WALTERS, bap. in Brooklyn, May 4, 1695; d. young.
6. JACOBA WALTERS, bap. ———. 1697.?
7. JACOB WALTERS, bap. March 20, 1700.
8. SARA WALTERS, born June 29, 9 o'clock in the evening; bap. July 2, 1704.
9. HESTER WALTERS, bap. Jan. 8, 1707

4. iii. JACOB,[2] bap. Nov. 13, 1667. He was active in procuring from Parliament the reversal of the attainder of his father and brother-in-law Jacob Milborne, and for this purpose visited England in 1694–5. After his return he resided in the South Ward of New York, where he was living in Nov., 1731. He died without issue.

5. iv. MARY,[2] bap. Dec. 12, 1669; joined the Dutch Church in New York, Sept. 2, 1688, and afterwards removed to Bergen. In Feb., 1690 (m. l. dated Feb. 3 of that year), she married JACOB MILBORNE (Milburne, Melborn), the active Secretary of her father, and one of the leading spirits of his administration. He was born in England about 1648, and was a brother of Rev. William Milborne, who settled as minister of the church at Saco, Maine, in May, 1685, and prob. died at Boston, August, 1699.[1]

It is alleged that he was convicted of clipping the Kings coin, and sold as a servant in the Barbadoes, and afterwards bought by a Hartford man.[2] If this story be true, he must have been a mere child at the time of the commission of the offence for which he was transported to Barbadoes. He was living in Hartford in 1663,[3] came to New York in 1668, being then twenty years old, and was employed by Thomas Delavall, a leading merchant, as clerk and bookkeeper, in whose service he remained until 1672. In October of that year he was admitted to plead with John Sharp and Samuel Edsal, Attorneys for the Plaintiff, in the trial of a suit in the Court of Assizes, at New York, on appeal from the Court on the Delaware, brought by Armigart Pappegoya (dau. of the Swedish Governor Printz) against Andrew Carr, for the recovery of Tinnicum Island.[4] He soon after engaged in trade as a merchant in New York, his commercial enterprises causing his frequent absence from the province. Returning from England on the 25th of August, 1689, he was appointed in December following Secretary of the Province and Clerk to Lieut.-Gov. Leisler, with whom his subsequent history and sad fate is identified.

It is probable that Mary Leisler[2] was the second wife of Jacob Milborne. In the list of members of the Dutch Church in New York, under date Nov. 29, 1688, appears the name of Johanna Edsal, h. v.[5] Jacob Melborn. Opposite her name, *Obyt* is written, but the date of her decease is not given. She was probably the dau. of Samuel Edsal and Jenneke Wessels, and bap. in Bergen, N. J., Sept. 4, 1667.

In the second preamble of the Act of Parliament in 1695, reversing the attainder of Jacob Leisler and others, the following is recited: "And whereas the said Jacob Leisler, also Jacob Milborne, Abraham Gouverneur, and several others, were arraigned in the Supreme Court of Judicature at New York aforesaid, and convicted and attainted of high treason and felony, for not delivering the possession of the said fort to the said Richard

1 Savage's Genealogical Dictionary, 3, p. 206. Folsom's Hist. Saco and Biddeford, p. 137.
2 Brodhead's Hist. of New York, 2, p. 196. Doc. Rel. to Col. Hist. N. Y., 3, 755.
3 Hinman's First Puritan Settlers of Conn. p. 54.
4 Hazard's Annals of Penn., p. 400.
5 Abbreviation of Huysvrow, the Dutch word for wife or housewife.

Ingoldsby, and the said Jacob Leisler and Jacob Milborne were executed for the same. May it therefore please your most excellent Majesty at the humble petition and request of Jacob Leisler, the son and heir of the said Jacob Leisler, deceased, *Jacob Milborne, the son and heir of the said* Jacob Milborne, deceased, and of the said Abraham Gouverneur, that it be declared and enacted," etc.[1]

The above is the only statement we have found, that Jacob Milborne left issue surviving him. This son (if the name is not an accidental interpolation in the above bill) was probably the fruit of Milborne's first marriage with Johanna Edsal, who, being in England at the time of his father's tragic death, afterwards remained there.

Mary Leisler,[2] widow of Jacob Milborne, m. 2ᵈ, in May, 1699, ABRAHAM GOUVERNEUR, for whose descendants, see pages 19 and 20.

6. v. JOHANNES,[2] bap. Dec. 20, 1671; d. young.

7. vi. HESTER,[2] bap. Oct. 8, 1673; m. BARENT RYNDERS (Reinders, Rynderts), of the city of New York, merchant, m. l. dated March 10, 1696. He was probably a son of Barent Reyndertse, smith, who was living at Albany as early as 1657, and died there in 1682.[2] His will is dated Feb. 5, 1725; proven Jan. 25, 1726-7. His widow, Hester, made will dated July 11, 1757; proven April 29, 1763. *Issue:*

1. GEERTRUYT RYNDERS, bap. Aug. 16, 1702; m. 1ˢᵗ, about 1728, Nicholas Gouverneur, and 2d David, son of William Provoost. By her first husband, Nicholas Gouverneur, she had Hester, bap. Sept. 7, 1729; died young; Abraham, bap. Nov. 22, 1730; Hester, bap. March 5, 1732; Barend, bap. Feb. 6, 1734; died young; Nicholaus, bap. June 15, 1735; died young; Barent, bap. May 29, 1737; and Nicholaus, bap. April 18, 1739. See pages 19 and 20.

2. ELIZABETH RYNDERS, bap. Sept. 17, 1704; m. July 3, 1729, Nicholas Bayard, son of Samuel Bayard and Margreta Van Cortlant, and had Hester, bap. July 29, 1730; Samuel, bap. March 22, 1732; Samuel, bap. June 13, 1733; Margareta, bap. Feb. 2, 1735; Nicolaas, bap. Nov. 14, 1736; Margareta, bap. Aug. 27, 1738; Judith, bap. Feb. 29, 1740; Barent Rynders, bap. March 31, 1742; and Elisabeth. bap. Oct. 15, 1746.

3. JOHANNA RYNDERS, bap. July 21, 1706; m. Dec. 12, 1723, David, son of David Provoost and Helena Byvanck. See vol. vi. p. 16, of the N. Y. G. AND B. RECORD. To the account of their family, there given, add that their dau. Helena, bap. May 24, 1728, m. 1ˢᵗ, —— Fresneau; m. 2ᵃ, June 19, 1760, Jacob Brewerton.

4. ESTER RYNDERS, bap. Oct. 31, 1708; d. unmarried.

5. BARENT RYNDERS, bap. Nov. 19, 1710; m. Feb. 3, 1740, Maria Cuyler. He died before July, 1757, leaving wife and dau. Hester surviving him.

6. JACOB RYNDERS, bap. Oct. 26, 1712; d. s. p.

7. ALIDA RYNDERS, bap. Oct. 31, 1716; m. March 10, 1743, Henry Cuyler, Jr., of the city of New York, merchant, son of Henry Cuyler and Maria Jacobs; he was bap. Sept. 25, 1715. They had issue: Barent Reynders, bap. March 20, 1745; Hester, bap.

[1] Documentary History of New York, vol. 2, p. 249.
[2] Pearson's First Settlers of Albany, p. 91.

Jan. 4, 1747; Maria, bap. June 15, 1748; and Alida, bap. Nov
12, 1749.

8. JOHANNES RYNDERS, bap. Jan. 14, 1719; d. s. p.

8. vii. FRANCINA,[2] bap. Dec. 16, 1676; m. 1st, THOMAS LEWIS; m. l.
dated Nov. 26, 1694. Will of Thomas Lewis, merchant, of New York,
"at this present time in good health but now bound out on a voyage," is
dated Jan. 10, 1699–1700; proven June 14, 1704; names: wife, Frances;
son, Thomas; "and the child with which his wife is big withall." Appoints
his wife and brothers, Leendart Lewis, and Barent Rynders, Executrix and
Executors. *Issue:*

1. THOMAS LEWIS, bap. ——, 1695.?
2. JAKOBA LEWIS, bap. in Brooklyn, Sept. 12, 1697; she m. 1st, May
   17, 1724, Jesse, son of Lucas Kierstede and Rachel Kip; he was
   a sea captain and prob. d. s. p.; his widow m. 2d, April 21,
   1734, Bartholomeus Schatts, by whom had *issue:* Reinier, bap.
   April 2, 1735; and Francina, bap. Sep. 12, 1739.
3. FRANCINA LEWIS, bap. in New York, April 9, 1699.
   Francina Leisler,[2] widow of Thomas Lewis, m. 2d, JOCHEM STAATS
   (prob. the widower of Antje Barentse Reyndertse, who died in
   1707[1]), by whom she had Elizabeth, bap. June 12, 1712, at
   which date Jochem Staats had deceased.

9. viii. MARGARET.[2] It is probably an error to place her name here as
the eighth child of Jacob Leisler. She is mentioned in the petition of her
mother, brother, and sisters to the Queen (1694?), praying for the reversal
of the Attainders pronounced against her father and Jacob Milborne.[2] No
other notice is found of her, and it is probable that she was the *step-daughter*
of Jacob Leisler, Margaret Van der Veen, who married Isaac Stephenszen.
See page 28.

LOOCKERMANS.

AMONG the early settlers of New Netherland were five* persons bearing
this name—Govert, Jacob and Pieter Janse Loockermans, and their sister Anneken, and a Balthus Loockermans. The modern form of the name
is Lockerman, but in the early records of the family it is spelt Loockermans.

BALTHUS or BALTHAZER LOOCKERMANS was perhaps a cousin of the
others, the exact relationship being difficult to determine, from the meagre
records that have come down to us concerning him. He and his wife
Engeltje Hendricks, had two children baptized in the Dutch Church in
New Amsterdam, viz., Jacob, May 28, 1662, and Jannetie, Oct. 14, 1663.

PIETER JANSE LOOCKERMANS was in New Amsterdam in January, 1642,
and we find traces of him here as late as Oct. 1648. In 1656 he was a
citizen of Beverwyck (Albany,) and purchased there, Nov. 16, of that year,
a house lot of Hendrik Gerritse (Van Wie or Verwey). In April, 1658,

---

[1] Pearson's First Settlers of Albany, p. 105.
[2] Coll. N. Y. Hist. Society for 1868, p. 335.
* Anthony Loockermans with his partners Messrs. (Paulus Leendertsen) Van der Grist, (Cornelis) Schutt
and (Cornelis) Steenwyck, on the 26th Nov., 1654, made an agreement with the Director (Stuyvesant) and
Council, for the charter of the ship Golden Shark, for a voyage to the West Indies. Of him we have no
other notice, and suppose that Govert Lookermans is the person alluded to. (Cal. N. Y. Hist. MSS, Dutch,
p. 143.)

he was a boatswain in the West India Company's service. He probably had the following children :

  i. PIETER LOOCKERMANS, who probably had two danghters, viz. : Marritje, married at Albany, Dec. 5, 1694, to Johannes Fonda, and Lammertje, married at the same place, Nov. 3, 1700, to Ariaen Oothout.

  ii. MARIA LOOCKERMANS, who married, 1st, Pieter Van Alen, of Kinderhook, widower of Maria Teller, and, 2d, in 1677, Gerrit Van Nes, of Greenbush.

  iii. HILLETJE LOOCKERMANS, who married, prior to 1682, Cornelis Stephense Muller, of Greenbush, 1663 ; of Claverack, 1720.

  iv. CAATJE LOOCKERMANS, who married, prior to 1683, Jan Salomonse Goewey, of Albany.

  v. ANNA LOOCKERMANS, who married, 1st, prior to 1684, Adam Winne, of Albany, and, 2d, Oct. 18, 1691, Jacob Teunise Van Woert, widower of Catryn Claas, of the same place.*

JACOB JANSE LOOCKERMANS also settled in Beverwyck, as early as 1657. On the 28th of July, in that year, the Sheriff brought a suit against him for having assaulted Meuwes Hogenboom, and split his face open from his forehead to his under lip with his knife ; he was find 300 guilders ($120), and ordered to pay for loss of time, board, and surgical attendance. In May, 1664, he and John Davits were Commissioners to negotiate a treaty of peace between the Mohawks and the Northern Indians, or Abenaquis, which they successfully concluded at Narrington, on the 24th of that month. In April, 1667, he purchased a house and lot in Albany, of Willem Jansen Schudt, and another July 25, 1684, of Laurence Van Alen. On the 24th of August, 1685, he obtained a license to travel, trade, and hunt among the Indians, as far as the Wagganasse and Attawaasse (Ottawas), with a company of thirty men. He was probably the Captain Loquerman, who, with Arian Abrahamse Schuyler and Jean Blaquerd, were detained as hostages in Canada by Gov. Denonville, while awaiting a reply to his letter to Gov. Dongan, dated Oct. 2, 1687, in which he complained of the infraction of the late treaty of peace by the English. He was living Aug. 18, 1700, at which date he was a sponsor at the baptism, in Albany, of his grandson Jacob, the son of Wessels Ten Broeck and Caatje Loockermans, who were married in Albany, April 2, 1684.†

ANNEKEN [ANN] LOOCKERMANS, j. d. Van Turnhout, married Feb. 26, 1642, OLOFT STEPHENSZEN [VAN CORTLANDT] j. m. Van Wyck in Duurstede. She probably came out with her brother Govert, on his return to New Netherland in Nov., 1641, her name first appearing in the records as one of the witnesses at the baptism, Dec. 1, 1641, of his eldest dau. Marritje. In the Members Book of the Dutch Church in New York, her husband's name is recorded Adolph Stephenszen Van Courtl, and at the baptism of their children, Olof Stephenszen Van Courtlant and Van Courtlandt. The name is now spelled, we believe, by the family, *Van Cortlandt.*

* Pearson's First Settlers of Albany, pp. 49, 54, 75, 85, 112, 128, 152, and Pearson's Early Records of Albany, p. 8. Cal. N. Y. Hist. MSS. Dutch, p. 195.
† Cal. N. Y. Hist. MSS. Dutch, p. 307–316. English, p. 139. Pearson's First Settlers of Albany, pp. 75, 109, and Doc. Rel. to Col. Hist. of N. Y., vol. 3, p. 513. Broadhead's Hist. of N. Y. vol. 1, p. 733.

Olof Stephenszen Van Cortlandt came to New Amsterdam in the ship Haring in 1637, a soldier in the West India Company's Service. He was promoted by Gov. Kieft, and in July, 1639, appointed Commissary of Cargoes, at a salary of thirty guilders ($12) per month. In 1645 was elected one of the Board of Eight men to adopt measures against the Indians, and in 1649, one of the Board of Nine men, of which body the following year he was President. He was elected Schepen of the City in 1654, and in 1655 was advanced to the higher position of Burgomaster, an office he held during the years 1656-58-59, 1662-63 and 1665. He was Alderman in 1666-67, 71, and succeeded Mr. Isaac Bedlow, upon the death of that gentleman, in the same office in 1673. His place of residence was in the Brouwer Straat, now Stone Street, where he was also engaged in business as a Brewer, in which occupation he became wealthy. "He had the character of being a worthy citizen and a man most liberal in his charities."* He died April 4, 1684, having survived his wife about a year. *Issue :* †

1. STEPHANUS VAN CORTLANDT, born May 7, 1643; bap. May 10, 1643; m. Sept. 10, 1671, Geertruyd Schuyler, j. d. Van Albania, dau. of Philip Pieterse Schuyler and Margareta Van Slechtenhorst.

2. MARRITIE [MARY] VAN CORTLANDT, born July 30, 1654; the records of the Dutch Church in N. Y. gives the date of her baptism July 23, 1645; m. April 27, 1662, JEREMIAS VAN RENSSELAER, j. m. Van Amsterdam, second son of Kilian Van Rensselaer, the first ancestor of the family in America.

3. JOHANNES [JOHN] VAN CORTLANDT, born Oct. 11, 1648; bap. Oct. 25, 1648; died unmarried.

4. FYTIE [SOPHIA] VAN CORTLANDT, born May 31, 1651; bap. June 4, 1651; m. May 6, 1671, ANDRIES TELLER, j. m. Van N. Albania, son of Willem Teller and Margariet Dunces (Donchesen).

5. CATHARINA VAN CORTLANDT, born Oct. 25, 1652; bap. Jan. 5, 1653; m. 1st Nov. 3, 1675, JOHANNES DERVALL, j. m. Van Amsterdam; he died Feb. 18, 1689, and his widow m. 2d Nov. 30, 1692, DE HR. FREDERICK PHILIPSZEN (Phillipse), wedr. of Margariet Hardens (Hardenbroeck), the first Lord of the Manor of Philipsburg.

6. CORNELIA VAN CORTLANDT, born Nov. 21, 1655; bap. Nov. 28, 1655; m. July 12, 1682, BRANDT SCHUYLER, j. m. Van N. Albania, son of Philip Pieterse Schuyler and Margareta Van Slechtenhurst. He was born Dec. 18, 1659. (Prof. Pearson, to whom we are indebted for the date of Brandt Schuyler's birth, says, in his "First Settlers of Albany," page 98, that he married 2d, April 16, 1741, Margareta Van Wyck. It was his grandson, Brandt, the son of Philip Brandtse Schuyler and Anna Elizabeth Staats, who married Margareta Van Wyck, and died Aug. 15, 1752. Their children were baptized in the Dutch Church in New York.)

7. JACOBUS [JAMES] VAN CORTLANDT, born July 7, 1658; his baptism is recorded the same day; m. May 7, 1691, Eva Phillipse, dau. of Frederick Phillipse and Margariet Hardenbroeck.

1. GOVERT LOOCKERMANS,[1] the most noted of his family, was born at Turnhout, a town in the Netherlands, and came to New Amsterdam in April, 1633. It appears he left Holland with Director General Wouter

---

* Doc. Rel. to Col. Hist. of N. Y., vol. i, p. 249. 431. O'Callaghan's Hist. of New Netherland, vol i, p. 211-12. Register of New Netherland. Valentine's Manual for 1849, p. 133-4-5.
† See N. Y. G. AND B. RECORD, vol. v., p. 71.

Van Twiller in the ship Soutberg, which captured on her voyage a Spanish caravel, the St. Martin, to which vessel he was transferred, and which was brought safely into port. With him came Jacob Wolfertsen (Van Couwenhoven), whose first wife, Hester Jans, was a sister of Loockerman's first wife. Upon his arrival he was taken into the service of the West India Company, as clerk, but he soon left this employment and engaged in business on his own account.

In 1640 he went back to Holland, where he married 1st, in Amsterdam, Feb. 26, 1641, Ariaentje Jans, with whom he returned to New Amsterdam in the ship King David, Job Arentsen, Master, arriving here Nov. 29, 1641.

On the 20th Jan., 1642, he purchased of Isaac Allerton the yacht Hope, in which he was engaged in trade between New Amsterdam and Fort Orange (Albany), and intervening points along the river, also to the South or Delaware River, and up the Sound to the mouth of the Connecticut. In July, 1644, while his vessel was passing Beeren Island, on the Upper Hudson, he was hailed by Nicholas Coorn, Commander at Rensselaer's Stein, and ordered to lower his colors. On being asked for whom, Coorn replied, "for the Staple right of Rensselaerswyck." But Loockermans refused with an oath to strike his flag "for any individual save the Prince of Orange and the Lords, his masters," whereupon Coorn fired several shots at his vessel, one of which "went through the sail, and broke the ropes and the ladder," and another "perforated the princely colors, about a foot above the head of Loockermans, who kept the colors constantly in his hands."

On the night of the 27th of Feb., 1643, Maryn Adriaensen and Govert Loockermans, by order of Gov. Kieft, led the attack of a company of citizens upon a party of Indians who had encamped with their women and children, at Corlears Hook. Thirty of the savages were killed while asleep and unsuspicious of danger from those they had deemed their friends. It is said that the recollection of this terrible and needless massacre, though approved by the general sentiment of that time, gave him much disquietude during the later years of his life.

His trading and shipping operations kept pace with the growth of New Amsterdam and the river towns, and before 1649 he had two or three times visited Holland, and established an extensive commercial correspondence with that country. He also carried on a large brewing business in Pearl Street, near the present Hanover Square, where he resided. In Sept., 1651, he was sentenced to be banished for three years on a charge of violating the revenue laws, but this sentence was not enforced, and he afterwards held some of the highest positions of honor in the Colony. He was one of the Board of Nine Men in 1647–9 and 1650, Schepen in 1657 and 1660, appointed one of the Orphan Masters Sept. 10, 1663, in place of Johannes Van Brugh, Indian Interpeter in 1658, and Commissioner in 1663, with Martin Cregier, to extinguish the Indian title to the lands from Barnegat to the Raritan. To the honor of the Dutch Settlers, be it said that they always pursued an honest course with the Indians in obtaining their lands by fair purchase. He was also a Commissioner, in May, 1653, with Johannes De La Montagne and David Provoost, appointed to attend the investigation of an alleged conspiracy of the Dutch and Indians against the English.

In 1666 he became a resident of Long Island in the vicinity of New Utrecht, his wife (by his second marriage) remaining in New York, where it appears she was engaged in shop-keeping, an occupation not uncommon for the thrifty Dutch women of that period. There is no doubt that he married his 2d wife Marritje Jans in the Dutch Church at New Amsterdam, July 11, 1649.

On the 13th of July, 1670, he was commissioned Lieutenant of a company of foot in New York, and probably died late in the autumn of that year.*

He possessed a superior education, for the times in which he lived. Bold, adventurous, enterprising, not much troubled with scruples, either in his trading intercourse with the Indians, or the more extensive traffic in which he afterwards engaged to the Netherlands, he amassed a large fortune, and was at his death probably the wealthiest citizen in New York. Dying intestate, it became a fruitful source of contention between his heirs for many years after. Like his friend, David Provoost, he was a thorn to the English, who hated him for the influence he wielded over the Indians, and his success among them as a trader, by what they termed a "crooked & pverse waye." It is recorded that Govert Aertsen, a small trader, was obliged to carry, in 1648, for his better protection when visiting the Connecticut Settlements, a certificate from the Magistrates of New Amsterdam that he was not Govert Loockermans. Our New England friends have since learned to discriminate better.

By his first wife Govert Loockermans' had *issue :*

2. i. MARRITJE² [MARIA or MARY], born Nov. 3, 1641, in the ship Coninck Davit (King David), on the voyage to St. Christopher and New Netherland ;† bap. Dec. 1, 1641; m. in New Amsterdam, Nov 12, 1664,‡ BALTHAZAR BAYARD, of Amsterdam, son of Samuel Bayard and Anna Stuyvesant.§ *Issue :*

1. SAMUEL BAYARD, born Sept. 20, 1665 ; died young.
2. ANAENTJE [ARIAENTIE] BAYARD, born Nov. 18, 1667 ; bap. Nov, 20, 1667 ; m. Oct. 26, 1691, SAMUEL VERPLANCK, son of Gelyn Verplanck and Hendrickje Wessels.
3. ANNA MARIA BAYARD, born March 6, 1670 ; bap. March 10, 1670 ; m. in New York, Oct. 28, 1697, AUGUSTUS JAY,‖ son of Pierre Jay, of La Rochelle in France, and Judith Francois.
4. SAMUEL BAYARD, born June 14, 1672 ; bap. June 16, 1672 ; no further account.
5. JUDITH BAYARD, born Jan. 31, 1677 ; bap. Feb. 7, 1677, and died on the 10th day after her birth.
6. JACOBUS BAYARD, bap. June 25, 1679 ; m. Dec. 22, 1703, Hillegond de Kay, dau. of Capt. Theunis de Kay and Helena Van Brugh.
7. GOVERT BAYARD, bap. Nov. 4, 1682 ; no further account.
8. JUDITH BAYARD, bap. May 23, 1685 ; m. March 5, 1722, GERARDUS STUYVESANT, son of Nicholas Stuyvesant and Elizabeth Van Slechtenhorst.

* Broadhead's Hist. of New York, vol. 1, p. 223, 401 ; O'Callaghan's Hist. of New Netherland, vol. 1, p. 142–344. vol. 2, p. 38 ; Doc. Rel. to Col. Hist. of N. Y., vol. 1, pp. 432–453, vol. 2, p. 472. O'Callaghan's Register of New Netherland ; Cal. N. V. Hist. MSS. Dutch, pp. 17, 18, 27, 28, 44, 46 ; Cal. N. Y. Hist. MSS. English, pp. 6, 7, 28, 102–3–8, 216, 248 ; Vincent's Hist. of Delaware, vol. 1. p. 472 ; N. V. G. AND B. RECORD, vol. 5; p. 69, vol 7. pp. 123–4 ; Valentine's Manual for 1852, p. 398.
† N. Y. G. and B. Record, vol. v., p. 69.
‡ From the family Bible. The Dutch Church records in New York give the date of their marriage Oct. 19, 1664.
§ She was a sister of Gov. Petrus Stuyvesant, and came with him to New Amsterdam—then a widow—with her three sons, Balthazar, Nicholas, and Petrus. She m. 2d, Oct. 14, 1656, Nicholas Verlet, widower of Susanna Gillis, and was again a widow before Jan. 19, 1683. Her son, Petrus Bayard, become a Labadist, and removed to the Delaware.
‖ This name is often disguised in the N. Y. Dutch Church Records as SJEE.

3. ii. JANNETIE,[2] born Sept. 23, 1643; bap. Sept. 27, 1643; m. Feb. 12, 1667, DR. HANS KIERSTEDE, son of Dr. Hans Kierstede and Sara Roelofs; he was bap. Sept. 21, 1644. *Issue:*

    1, HANS KIERSTEDE, bap. Feb. 19, 1668; m. Oct. 1, 1696, Dina Van Schaick, dau. of Arie Cornelisen Van Schaick and Rebecca Idens. See page 11.

    2. ADRIAENTIE KIERSTEDE, bap. April 8, 1670; m. Sept. 27, 1693, DIRCK ADOLPHSZEN [DE GROOF], of New York, son of Adolph Pieterszen Van der Groeft or De Groof and Aefje Dircks; he was bap. Nov. 3, 1669.

    3. CORNELIS KIERSTEDE, bap. Jan. 5, 1675; m. Sept. 9, 1703, Sarah Elswaert (Elsworth), dau. of Clement Elswaert and Anna Maria Engelbrecht; she was bap. March 27, 1683.

    4. JACOBUS KIERSTEDE, bap. April 14, 1677.

    5. ANNA ELIZABETH KIERSTEDE, bap. Dec. 17, 1679.

    6. SARA CATHARYN KIERSTEDE, bap. Nov. 5, 1681.

    7. ANNETIE KIERSTEDE, bap. May 24, 1684.

    8. MARRITJE [MARIA], bap. Oct. 3, 1686; m. March 18, 1711, PIETER DAVIDS.

By his second wife Govert Loockermans[1] had *issue:*

4. iii. JACÓB[2], bap. March 17, 1652. He was a Physician, joined the Dutch Church in New York Dec. 13, 1674, and in Oct., 1679, was a resident of the County of St. Mary, in Maryland. About the year 1681 he removed to Easton, Talbot County, Md., where he became a planter. He married, Jan 29, 167¾, Helena Ketin, and died August 17, 1730. *Issue:*

5. i. NICHOLAS[3], born Nov. 10, 1697; m. in 1721, Sally, dau. of Vincent Emerson, of the Grange near Dover, Del. *Issue:*

6. i. VINCENT[4], born at the Grange in 1722, m. 1st, Susannah ———, and 2d, in Feb., 1774, Elizabeth, dau. of John Pryor, of Dover, who survived him. He died at Dover, Aug. 26, 1785. By his first wife had *issue:*

7. i. VINCENT[6], who married ———, and had two daughters: Elizabeth[6], who m. THOMAS DAVY, of Philadelphia, and ———, who m. HON. NICHOLAS G. WILLIAMSON, of Wilmington, Del.

By his second wife, Vincent Loockermans[4] had issue:

8. ii. NICHOLAS[5], born Nov. 27, 1783; died March 20, 1850, unmarried.

9. iii. ELIZABETH[5], born Dec. 23, 1779; m. May 8, 1805, THOMAS BRADFORD, of Phila., son of Thomas Bradford and Mary Fisher. He was a descendant in the fifth generation of William Bradford, the first Printer in the Middle Colonies of British America.* He was born at Phila., Sept. 11, 1781, and died there Oct. 25, 1851. She died same place April 8, 1842.† *Issue:*

    1. VINCENT LOOCKERMANS BRADFORD, born Sept. 24, 1808. Lawyer in Phila. m. July 21, 1831, Juliet S. Rey, dau. of Emanuel Rey, Esq., planter, of the Island of St. Martin, West Indies.

    2. ELIZABETH LOOCKERMANS BRADFORD, born Sept. 19, 1810; m. Oct. 12, 1831, REV. WILLIAM T. DWIGHT, son of Timothy Dwight, D.D. See Hist. of the Descendants of John Dwight, vol. 1, p. 205.

* N. Y. G. AND B. RECORD, vol. iv., pp. 187-8.
† Simpson's Lives of Eminent Philadelphians, p. 131.

3. BENJAMIN RUSH BRADFORD, of New Brighton, Beaver Co., Penn. m. in 1860, Margaret Campbell, of Butler Co., Penn.
4. WILLIAM BRADFORD, born in 1815; a resident (1871) of Philadelphia.
5. THOMAS BUDD BRADFORD, born in 1816. He was a Minister of the Gospel at Dover, Del., and twice married. The name of his first wife we are unable to give. His second wife was Lucy H. Porter, dau. of Dr. Robert R. Porter, of Wilmington, Del. He died at Dover, March 25, 1871.

The account of Jacob Loockermans' and his descendants is mainly compiled from Vincent's History of the State of Delaware, vol. I., pp. 474 to 477.

VARICK.

THIS name appears indifferently in the Dutch Church Records as Varick and Van Varick, from 1687 down to about the beginning of the present century.* Mr. Valentine has asserted that the Rev. Rudolphus Van Varick, of Long Island, was the common ancestor of the Varick family in this State †—an obvious error. Jan Varick, of New York, 1687—1702-3, and Hackensack, N. J., 1720, probably his brother (if not the common ?), was the ancestor of the largest branch of the family bearing this name, both in New York and New Jersey.

REV. RUDOLPHUS VARICK came from Holland about 1685, in which year he succeeded the Rev. Casparus Van Zuren as minister of the Long Island churches, his residence being at Flatbush; he also occasionally ministered on Sunday in the Churches at Bergen and Hackensack, N. J. "During the Leislerian troubles, in 1689, Mr. Varick, as well as the other Dutch ministers, stood out against the authority of Leisler, and was treated with much harshness, being dragged from his home, cast into the jail, deposed from his ministerial functions, and fined heavily. These severities, which were heaped upon him for alleged treasonable utterances against Leisler, undoubtedly hastened his death.‡ His congregation also were divided, and many of them refused to pay his salary according to the terms upon which they called him from Holland—especially, as he says in a petition to the Governor, Sept. 11, 1691, for the six months of his imprisonment. The Court ordered the arrears of salary due him by his congregation to be collected, *by distress*, if necessary." §

His will is dated October 20, 1686; proven November 9, 1694. In it he styles himself Rev. Domine Rudolphus Van Varick, "Minister of the Reformed Dutch Congregacion on Long Island;" alludes to his children, but names only his wife, Margarita Visboom.'

His widow's will is dated October 29, 1695, with codicil, Nov. 15, 1695; proven January 2, 1695-6. She directs that her body be buried by the side of her husband, "if possible, in the Church of Midwout alias

---

* In the New York Marriage Licenses, Albany, 1860, it frequently appears as Varck and Van Varck.
† Valentine's Manual, 1861, p. 549.
‡ "This is Secretary Clarkson's statement (Doc. Hist. N. Y., 8vo., ii. 431, 432); but another party, not so favorably inclined, says that Varick was at first in favor of the revolution of Leisler, and influenced Kings County to act unanimously in its favor; but that, afterwards, he was won over to a contrary opinion, and created a diversion in the popular mind. The same authority says that he was suspected by the people of conspiring to seize the fort in New York, was arrested, and released, after a time, upon his submission to Leisler; that he favored the execution of the latter, ' made intolerable sermons' against him, and cherished animosity even to his dying day."—*Stiles' Hist. Brooklyn*, vol. i., foot-note, p. 169.
§ Stiles' Hist. Brooklyn, vol. 1, p. 169.

Flatbush;" names her daughters Joanna and Cornelia, and a deceased dau. Cornelia Hesther (?); sons Marinus and Rudolphus; her sister Engeltje; her niece Maritie (Maria), wife of Nicholas Tienhoven.* In the event of the death of all her children, she bequeaths to her sister Sarah, the wife of John Varick, and her niece Maritie, all her property equally. In the codicil she adds the name of her *eldest sister* Engeltje Visboom, to whom with her sister Sarah and *cousin* Maria, she gives, in case of the death of her children, to each one-third of her estate. Appoints Col. Nicholas Bayard, Lieut.-Col. Charles Lodwyck, and Mr. Jan Harbendinck, executors.

Of the children of Rev. Rudolphus Varick and his wife Margarita Visboom, we are unable to give any other account except of their daughters. Joanna married Albert Willet; m. 1. dated May 10, 1701. (RECORD, vol. iii., page 194.) Cornelia was twice married; first to Barent De Kleyn (see RECORD, vol. vii., page 148, foot-note), and second, July 22, 1715, to Pieter Van Dyck, Silver Smith in New York, the widower of Rachel Le Roux, and son of Dirck Franszen Van Dyck and Urseltie Jans Schepmoes. He was bap. Aug. 17, 1684.

PIETER VAN DYCK and Rachel Le Roux, dau. of Bartholemeus Le Roux and Geertruyd Van Rollegom,† m. Oct. 27, 1711, and had *issue :*

    1. RACHEL VAN DYCK, bap. Oct. 8, 1712.

By his second wife, Cornelia Varick, he had *issue :*

    2. MARGARETA VAN DYCK, bap. Feb. 22, 1716.
    3. DIRCK (RICHARD) VAN DYCK, bap. Dec. 4, 1717.
    4. ANNATJE (ANNA) VAN DYCK, bap. Jan. 13, 1720.
    5. CORNELIA VAN DYCK, bap. Nov. 15, 1721.
    6. RUDOLPHUS VAN DYCK, bap. Sept. 29, 1723.
    7. URSELINA VAN DYCK, bap. Sept. 29, 1725.
    8. SARA VAN DYCK, bap. Oct. 25, 1727.
    9. PETRUS VAN DYCK, bap. June 15, 1729.
    10. MARIA VAN DYCK, bap. Jan. 31, 1731; died young.
    11. MARIA VAN DYCK, bap. Aug. 13, 1732.

    1. JAN VARICK[1] and his wife Sarah Visboom, joined the Dutch Church in New York, June 1, 1687, with certificate from Rhenen—probably the small town of that name on the middle branch of the Rhine, in Holland. Two of their children, Jacobus and Margarita, were prob. born in Holland. About 1711-12, Jan Varick and his wife removed to Hackensack, N. J. He was living May 29, 1720, at which date he and his wife were sponsors at the baptism in Hackensack of Sara, dau. of Abram Varick. After his death his widow was engaged in selling merchandise, or Shop Keeping, at Hackensack. Her will is dated Sept. 8, 1731; proven May 12, 1736; names her sons Jacobus and Abraham Varick; daughters, Cornelia, wife of Thomas Jefferies; Mary; Margaretje, wife of Peter Stoutenburgh; her sister *Engeltje Visbooms*, and her grand dau. Catharin Magdannel (McDaniel). Jan Varick and Sarah Visboom had *issue :*

    2. i. JACOBUS[2] (8), probably born in Holland.
    3. ii. MARGARITA,[2] m. Dec. 24, 1719, PIETER STOUTENBURG, and had

---

* Nicholas Van Tienhoven, j. m. Van Midwout, m. Dec. 27, 1693. Maria Abrahams, j. d. Van Amsterdam, and had Debora bap. May 26, 1695.
† Jan Joosten, j. m. Van Haerlem, who m. June 4, 1660, Tryntje Jans Van Haerlem, was the ancestor of the Van Rollegom family.

issue: Isaac and Sara, twins, bap. Aug 7, 1720; and Johannes, bap. Sept. 23, 1722.

4 iii. CORNELIA,² bap. Jan 8, 1688; m. 1ˢᵗ, Aug. 10, 1712, RICHARD McDANIEL, and had Catharina, bap. March 15, 1713, who m. Sept. 28, 1736, John Schermer. She m. 2ᵈ, THOMAS JEFFRES, and had Annatje, bap. May 25, 1724, and Johannes, bap. Dec. 25, the same year.

5. iv. ABRAHAM² (17), bap. April 17, 1692.

6. v. MARIA,² bap. Nov. 14, 1697; m. Sept. 5, 1733, at Hackensack, N. J., JOHN McDOWELL of that place.*

7. vi. JOHANNES,² bap. May 4, 1701; not named in his mother's will, and prob. d. s. p.

8. JACOBUS² (2), probably born in Holland. He was a merchant in New York, but resided in Hackensack during the latter part of his life, where he died about 1745. He married Anna Maria, dau. of Andries Brestede and Anna Van Borsum; she was bap. May 25, 1681. They had *issue:*

9. i. JOHANNA,³ bap. Feb. 18, 1711; m. March 10, 1751, JOHN APPEL, of New York.

10. ii. SARA,³ bap. May 29, 1712; died young.

11. iii. JOHANNES,³ bap. Feb. 14, 1714; † m. 1ˢᵗ, May 6, 1739, Maria [Anna Maria] Brestede, dau. of Jan Brestede and Anna Maria Elsworth; she was bap. June 18, 1712; m. 2ᵈ, Nov. 28, 1747, Anna Schatts, dau. of Bartholomeus Schatts and Christina Kermer; she was bap. Feb. 27, 1715. He was a Baker in New York, and died in 1762, leaving wife Antie (Anna) and four children, viz., Mary,⁴ bap. Feb. 12, 1746; Lucretia⁴ (Christyntje?), bap. Aug. 28, 1748; Jacobus,⁴ bap. Aug. 15, 1750; and Johannes,⁴ bap. Jan. 16, 1754.

12. iv. ANDRIES,³ bap. Sept. 2, 1716; m. April 23, 1738, Aafje Ten Eyck, dau. of Andries Ten Eyck and Barendina Hardenburg; she was bap. Dec. 25, 1718. He was a Hatter in New York, and died in 1762, leaving son James,⁴ bap. April 15, 1739, who m. Nov. 16, 1760, Elisabeth Bogert; daughters Aafje,⁴ bap. Nov. 17, 1751, who m. Jan. 23, 1772, John B. Stout, Baker, of New York, and Barendina⁴ (Dinah), bap. April 3, 1754, who m. Aug. 19, 1773, Thomas P. Periam, Mariner, of New York. The widow of Andries Varick died in 1782.

13. v. ABRAHAM,³ bap. March 30, 1718; died young.

14. vi. DIRK³ (RICHARD), bap. Feb. 10, 1720; he was living in July, 1754, and probably d. s. p.

15. vii. SARA,³ bap. July 22, 1722; m. June 13, 1744, BALTUS VAN KLEECK. He married 2ᵈ, July 24, 1771, Ann Lawrens (Lawrence?). He was for some years a resident of New York city, but in the latter part of his life resided at Flushing, L. I., where he died in 1785. By his first wife Sara Varick, he had *issue:*

1. ANNA MARIA VAN KLEECK, bap. Oct. 8, 1746; d. s. p.
2. LOUWRENS (LAWRENCE) VAN KLEECK, bap. May 4, 1749; m. 1769 (m. l. dated Feb. 15, 1769), Cornelia, dau. of James and Judith (Newcomb) Livingston.‡ He was a Physician in New York, but resided last in Poughkeepsie, N. Y., where he died prior to 1783. His widow married Andrew Billings of the latter place.

---

* Marriage Records of Church at Hackensack.
† An error occurs on page 14, in line twenty-first from the top. For Jacobus Van Varick and Anna Maria Brestede, read *Abraham Varick and Anna Bertholf.*
‡ Holgate's American Genealogy. Mr. Holgate gives the name of her husband Dr. Balthus Van Kleeck, instead of Dr. Lawrence Van Kleeck.

This gentleman was appointed Captain by General Montgomery, and served with him at the siege of Quebec. He was subsequently Major in the Third Regiment of New York Continental Forces, commanded by Col. Rudolphus Ritzema.

3. JACOBA VAN KLEECK, bap. April 5, 1751; m. Feb. 19, 1769, Joshua Carman, of Dutchess Co., N. Y.

4. ELIZABETH VAN KLEECK, bap. July 7, 1754; m. Martin Wiltse, m. l. dated Nov. 13, 1775.

5. JOHANNA VAN KLEECK, bap. Aug. 22, 1756; d. s. p.

By his second wife, Ann Lawrens, he had *issue :*

6. BALTHUS VAN KLEECK, born 1772. ?

16. viii. ABRAHAM,[3] bap. Sep. 12, 1725; d. s. p.

17. ABRAHAM[2] (5), bap. April 17, 1692. He removed to Hackensack, N. J., where he m. July 12, 1718, Anna Bertholf, dau. of Rev. Guillaume Bertholf (pastor of the Churches of Hackensack and Aquackenonk, 1693–1724), and Martina Verwey; she was bap. at H., Feb. 27, 1698. They had issue baptized at Hackensack.

18. i. SARA,[3] bap. May 29, 1720; m. at H., Nov. 11, 1743, JACOB ZABRISKIE.

19. ii. MARTINA,[3] bap. April 22, 1722; m. at H., Oct. 25, 1747, PIETER ZABRISKIE, prob. a brother of Jacob, above named, and son of Jan Zabriskie and Margrita du Ry (Duryee?); he was bap. at H., Nov. 5, 1721.

20. iii. JOHANNIS[3] (JOHN) (26), bap. Dec. 25, 1723.

21. iv. GULIAN[3]* (JULIAN), bap. Feb. 13, 1726; m. Jan. 26, 1764, Mary Van Bueren. They had Ann,[4] bap. Dec. 9, 1764; Maria,[4] bap. Nov. 3, 1767, and prob. others.

22. v. RICHART,[3] bap. April 22, 1728.

23. vi. MARIA,[3] bap. Feb. 6, 1732; died young.

24. vii. JACOBUS,[3] bap. March 30, 1735.

25. viii. MARIA,[3] bap. Dec. 4, 1737.

26. JOHANNIS[3] (JOHN) (20), bap. Dec. 25, 1723; m. at Schraalenburgh, N. J., June, 1749, Jane Dye (Dey), dau. of Dirck Dey, of New York. Their children, baptized at Hackensack, were :

27. i. ABRAM,[4] bap. April 29, 1750; m. Trintie Vredenburgh, and had John Vredenburgh Varick,[5] born Oct. 24, 1780; and Abraham Varick, Jr.[5]

28. ii. DIRK,[4] bap. Jan. 12, 1752, died young.

29. iii. DIRK[4] (RICHARD), born March 25, 1753, bap. April, 1753. He was a lawyer in New York; Colonel in the Revolutionary war; Recorder of the city of New York from 1783 to 1789, and Mayor 1789 to 1800; for many years President of the Society of Cincinnati, and at the time of his decease President of the American Bible Society. He died at Jersey City, July 30, 1831, unmarried. He was buried in the rear of the Church at Hackensack, where a granite monument is erected to his memory.

30. iv. ANNE,[4] bap. Sept. 30, 1755, m. PETER ELTING, of New York; and had William, Anna Maria, and James Elting.

31. v. JENNEKE[4] (JANE), bap. June 1, 1760, m. 1st, —— HARDENBURGH; m. 2d, SIMEON DE WITT of Albany; she died there April 10, 1808,† leaving two sons, Richard Varick De Witt and George Washington De Witt.

---

* This name is so recorded in the Hackensack Church Baptismal Records.
† Munsell's Annals of Albany, vol. v., page 15.

32. vi. SARAH,[4] bap. Oct. 2, 1762; m. April 8, 1788, Rev. MOSES FRE-
LIGH, pastor of the Ref. Dutch Churches of Shawangunck, Ulster Co., and
Montgomery, Orange Co., N. Y. 1788–1817. He was the son of Petrus and
Maria (Wood) Freligh, and born (prob. in the town of Saugerties, N. Y.)
May 9, 1763, and died in Montgomery, Feb. 10. 1817. He was a brother
of the Rev. Dr. Solomon Frœligh, though unlike his brother he spelled his
name without the diphthong œ. His wife died Nov. 23, 1808.* They
had nine children, of whom the following seven were living in December,
1809, viz., Jane; Peter; Anna Maria; Catharina; Sarah; Rachel Hardenburgh; and John Varick Freligh.

33. vii. MARTYNTJE,[4] bap. August 20, 1767; died young.

34. viii. TEUNIS,[4] bap. May 14, 1769; died young.

35. ix. MARIA,[4] born Dec. 11, 1771; m. GARRIT GILBERT, and had
living in December, 1809, the following named children, viz., Jane; Richard Varick; John; Catharine; Henry; and Emma Gilbert.

36. x. JOHN Jr.,[4] born ——; m. Margareta Van Wyck, and had Theodorus Van Wyck Varick,[5] born May 15, 1790; Jane Dey Varick,[5] and
John Varick, Jr.[5]

☞ The statement that Col. Richard Varick (29) died unmarried is
not correct. He m. 1786, Maria Roosevelt, dau. of Isaac Roosevelt and
Cornelia Hoffman, of New York. She died July 19, 1841, aged 77 years
11 months and 17 days, and was buried by his side in the churchyard at
Hackensack. They had no children, or at least none surviving them.
Col. Varick's nephew, John Vredenburgh Varick, was admitted in the
Society of Cincinnati as a member in the right of. and shortly after the
death of his uncle. He died at his residence in Jersey City, May 18, 1835.

KIP.

IT is proposed in the following sketch to trace particularly the pedigree
of Gerrit Kip[5], son of Abraham Kip[4] and Maria Vanden Berg, who was
born in New York May 11, 1746, and married Feb. 12, 1768, Ellenor
or Nelletje Brouwer, and also to give some account of their descendants.
We shall, as far as our information enables us, notice as fully as possible
the first four generations of the Kips in this country; to extend our researches further, except in the instance above stated, would render this
sketch too voluminous, and therefore at variance with the original plan of
these contributions to the history of the ancient families of New York.

The transatlantic pedigree of the Kip family has appeared in various
American publications within the last thirty years, and while generally agree-
ing in the account given of Ruloff De Kype, the first known ancestor of the
family in Europe, the statements in reference to the immigrant ancestor to
America, Hendrick Hendrickszen Kip, have not always been in accord
with each other. It is impossible that the latter was the son of Ruloff De
Kype[2], anglicized to Kip, for had he been, his name would have appeared
in our early records as Hendrick Ruloffszen Kip, instead of as we now find
it, Hendrick Hendrickszen Kip. From this fact and for the reason that
no authority for the European pedigree has been given in the publications
referred to, it must with all such of like character, be regarded with suspi-

* Sprague's Annals of the American Reformed Dutch Pulpit, p. 83.

cion.* It has been the intention in these contributions, to confine our researches chiefly to the immigrant ancestors of old New York families and their immediate descendants, drawing the materials therefor, when not otherwise indicated, from the Records of the Reformed Dutch Church in New York, and from New York wills and conveyances.

1. HENDRICK HENDRICKSZEN KIP[1] (Kype), the ancestor of the Kip family of New York, came to New Amsterdam prior to 1643, with his wife, probably Tryntje † (anglicized Catharine), and five children who were born in Amsterdam. It is probable that his sixth child Femmetje was born here, *his* name appearing at her baptism, April 19, 1643, as Mr. Hendrick Hendricksz. He was perhaps of noble lineage, as it is related that the arms of the family were painted on the stained-glass windows of the first church erected in New Amsterdam. They were also carved in stone over the door of the Kip's Bay house, which is said to have been built in 1655 ‡, by his son Jacob.§ They are described as follows: "Azure, a chevron *or*, between two griffins sejant and a sinister gauntlet apaumé (tinctures not given). Crest, a demi-griffin holding a cross. Motto, 'Vestigia nulla retrorsum.'" Hendrick Hendrickszen Kip was a tailor, his name appearing sometimes in the records simply as Hendrick the tailor, and again as

---

* The following is the pedigree referred to. The first ancestor of the Kip family of New York, of whom there is any notice in history, was Ruloff De Kype of Bretagne, France, who was born about 1510-20. He was a warm partisan of Francis Duke of Guise, the furious and bigoted leader of the Catholic party against the Huguenots. On the triumph of the Protestants, which occurred soon after the general massacre of the inhabitants of Vassey in Champagne, in 1562, he fled to Holland with his three sons, where they lived for several years under an assumed name. In 1569, he returned to France with his son Henri, joined the army of the Duke of Anjou, and fell in battle near Jarnac, March 13, of that year. He was buried by his son Jean Baptiste, in a small church near Jarnac, where an altar tomb was erected to his memory. "The inscription on the tomb mentioned him as RULOFF DE KYPE, ÉCUYER (this title designating a gentleman who had a right to coat armor), and was surmounted by his arms, with two crests, one a game-cock, the other a demigriffin holding a cross, both of which crests have been used by different branches of the family in this country." He left *issue*

   i.   HENRI[2], who after his father's death entered the army of one of the Italian princes, and died unmarried.
   ii.   JEAN BAPTISTE[2] a priest in the Church of Rome.
   iii.   RULOFF[2], born 1544; he remained in Holland, became a Protestant, and settled at Amsterdam. He seems to have dropped from his name the French prefix De. He died in 1596, leaving *issue:*

   i.   HENDRICK[3] (in English Henry), born 1576. "On arriving at manhood, he took an active part in the 'Company of Foreign Countries,' an association formed for the purpose of obtaining access to the Indies, by a different route from that pursued by Spain and Portugal. They first attempted to sail round the northern seas of Europe and Asia, but their expedition, despatched in 1594, was obliged to return on account of the ice, in the same year. In 1609, they employed Henry Hudson to sail to the westward, in the little Half Moon, with happier results." He came to New Amsterdam in 1635, with his children, and some years after returned to Holland, where he died. [He did not return to Holland, but lived and died in New York.] His sons remained in New Amsterdam, and rose to important positions as citizens and landed proprietors. He m. Margaret de Marneil, and had *issue:*

   i.   HENDRICK[4], who married Anna, dau. of Nicasius De Sille.
   ii.   JACOBUS[4], born May 15, 1631; m. Feb. 14, 1654, Maria, dau. of Johannes De La Montagne.
   iii.   ISAAC[4], who married 1st Feb. 8, 1653, Catalina de Suyers; m. 2d Sept. 18, 1675, Maria Vermilye, widow of Johannes De La Montagne, Jr. (*Compiled from Holgate's American Genealogy; Lossing's Field Book of the Revolution; Duyckinck's Cyclopædia of American Literature, vol. 2, p. 551; Historical Notes of the Family of Kip of Kipsburg and Kip's Bay, New York. [By Rt. Rev. Dr. William Ingraham Kip.] Privately printed, 1871; Corwin Genealogy, p. 49.*)

† Bishop Kip gives her name Margaret de Marneil; Margaret was not a family name among the early Kips, and does not appear in the family before the first quarter of the last century. The name of Tryntie Kip is recorded in the list of old members of the Dutch Church of New Amsterdam, on the second line below that of Hendrick Kip, in the original record. As Tryntje, or Catharine, was a common name among the Kips, I have thought it probable that Tryntie Kip above alluded to, was the wife of Hendrick Kip[1], and that perhaps her family name was DROOGH, as Jacob Hendricksen Kip[2], son of Hendrick Hendricksen Kip[1], in 1647, gave to his *uncle* Harman Hendricksen Droogh, a power of attorney to receive money due him by the West India Compaoy at Amsterdam. (Calendar N. Y. Hist. MSS. Dutch, page 40.)

‡ Holgate and Lossing say it was built in 1641, but Jacob Kip, the Secretary of the Council of New Netherland, and reputed builder, was then a ten-year-old lad.

§ Hist. Notes of the Family of Kip of Kipsburg and Kip's Bay. New York. 1871; pp. 5-27.

Hendrick Snyder Kip. To a "resolution adopted by the Commonalty of the Manhattans" in 1643, he signs his name, Heindrick Heindricksen Kype. On the 28th April, 1643, he obtained a patent for a lot east of the fort, in the present Bridge Street near Whitehall, where he erected his dwelling-house and shop.* He appears to have been a man of marked individuality and to those he loved not, bitter and unrelenting, a quality of character his wife seems to have shared with him. The indiscriminate massacre of one hundred and ten defenceless Indians, men, women and children at Corlears hook, and Pavonia, on the night of February 25, 1643, instigated and ordered by Director-General Kieft, aroused in the breast of Hendrick Kip a feeling of extreme hatred for that official, and he boldly urged that he should be deposed and sent back to Holland.† On the 30th August, 1645, the Court Messenger (Philip de Truy) was ordered to notify the inhabitants to assemble in the fort when the colors are hoisted and the bell rung, to hear the proposals for a treaty of peace about to be concluded with the Indians. The Messenger reported that all the citizens on the Manhattans "from the highest to the lowest," would attend as they all had answered kindly, except one Hendrick Kip, the tailor.‡ While the entire community were willing to show some respect for Kieft on this public occasion, the sturdy old burgher alone exhibited contempt for the "man of blood," and refused to do him honor.

After the departure of Gov. Kieft for Holland, which he was destined never again to reach,§ Hendrick Kip became at once one of the leading men in New Netherland. He was appointed by Gov. Stuyvesant's Council, Sept. 25, 1647, one of the board of Nine Men, selected "from the most notable, reasonable, honest, and respectable" of the citizens of the commonalty, to assist the Director, or Governor, and Council; this office he also held in 1649, and 1650. He was a Schepen in 1656, appointed Feb. 2d, of that year, and was admitted to the rights of a great burgher April 11, 1657.‖ He was probably the Hendrick op Kippenburg who was a witness, March 24, 1664, in a suit between Govert Loockermans and Burger Joris, respecting the title to land in the Smith's Valley.¶ After the surrender of New York he took the oath of allegiance to the English in October, 1664. The name of Hendrick Kip, Senior, appears in the list of citizens who were assessed April 19, 1665, to pay the board and lodging of soldiers belonging to the city garrison.** This is the last mention found of him. The names of Hendrick and Tryntie Kip, probably his wife, are recorded in the list or register †† of old members of the Dutch Church of New Amsterdam. Opposite his name Domine Selyns has written "*obyt op Kippenburg*," but the date is not given. In what part of Manhattan Island, Kippenburg was located is not known; perhaps *Incleuburg*, or Fire Beacon Hill,

* Valentine's Manual, 1852, p. 389.
† May 6, 1643, Samuel Chandelaer made affidavit, that he heard Hendrick the tailor say: The Kivit (meaning the director), ought to be packed off to Holland in the Peacock, with a letter of recommendation to Master Gerrit (the public executioner), and a pound flemish, so that he may give him a nobleman's death. (Calendar N. Y. Hist. MSS. Dutch., p. 22; *see* also O'Callaghan's Hist. New Netherland, vol. 1., p. 272.)
‡ Cal. N. Y. Hist. MSS. Dutch, p. 97; O'Callaghan's Hist. New Netherland, vol. 1., p. 356.
§ He sailed from New Amsterdam in the Princess, August 16, 1647. On the 27th September following, the vessel was cast away on the coast of Wales near Swansea, and eighty-one persons, men, women, and children, perished, including Kieft, Fiscaal Cornelius Van der Huyghens, and the Rev. Everardus Bogardus. (O'Callaghan's Hist. New Netherland, vol. 2, p. 34.)
‖ O'Callaghan's Hist. New Netherland, vol. 2, p. 37, and New Netherland Register, pp. 55, 56, 62, 174.
¶ Cal. N. Y. Hist. MSS. Dutch, p. 263.
** Valentine's Manual for 1861, p. 616.
†† The following is the title-page of this register: 'T Ledematen Boeck Oft Register der Ledematen Alhier 't Sedert de Jare, 1649. (The Members' Book or the Register of the Members here at [and] since the year 1649.)

situated near 36th Street and Fourth Avenue, and in the vicinity of the old Kip farm, was so called at the period referred to.

Concerning his wife the following is taken from the Court proceedings at New Amsterdam, Sept. 29, 1644. William de Key *vs.* Hendrick Kip: action for slander; ordered that defendant's wife appear next Thursday, and acknowledge in court, that what she said to the prejudice of the plaintiff is false, and not to repeat the offence on pain of severe punishment.* She probably acknowledged her fault, whatever it may have been—as ordered by the court, as we find no further account of the matter. On Dec. 17, 1646, the Schout-Fiscal (Cornelius Van der Huyghens) charged her before the court with calling the Director (Kieft) and Council false judges, and the Fiscal a forsworn Fiscal. Hendrick Kip states that his wife has been so upset, and so out of health, ever since Maryn Adriaensen's attempt to murder the Director General (March 21, 1643), that when disturbed in the least she knows not what she does. Mrs. Kip denies the charge, and the parties are ordered to produce evidence on both sides.† What further proceedings, if any, in the case were taken, the records fail to disclose. She and her husband were sponsors, July 4, 1657, at the baptism of Anthony, son of Jan Janszen Van St. Obyn (*alias* Jan Wanshaer), which is the last notice found of her, where her identity can be clearly established. They probably had *issue.*

2. i. BAERTJE HENDRICKS KIP,[2] born in Amsterdam ; m. Jan. 17, 1649, Jan Janszen j. m. Van Tubingen, *alias* Jan Janszen Van St. Obyn, etc., *alias* JAN WANSHAER. In 1654 Jan Janszen Van St. Obyn is called the son-in-law of Hendrick Kip.‡ For a further account of him and his family, see Wanshaer, page 26.

3. ii. ISAAC HENDRICKSZEN KIP,[2] (8) born in Amsterdam.

4. iii. JACOB HENDRICKSZEN KIP,[2] (16) born in Amsterdam, May 16, 1631.

5. iv. TRYNTJE HENDRICKS KIP,[2] born in Amsterdam ; m. August 10, 1659, Abraham Janszèn, Van't Zuydtlandt in't landt Van de Briel. They were the ancestors of the VAN DER HEUL FAMILY of New York. At the baptism of their children her name is recorded, Tryntie Hendricks, Tryntje Kip, and Tryntie Hendricks Kips, while his appears at the bap. of their dau. Elizabeth, Aug. 15, 1660, as Abraham J. Van der Heul, and afterwards simply as Abraham Janszen. *Issue :*

    1. ELIZABETH VAN DER HEUL, bap. Aug. 15, 1660 ; m. May 16, 1682, Marten Abrahamszen Klock (Clock), of New York, son of Abraham Clock and Tryntie Alberts ; bap. Sept. 10, 1656. He was a merchant and Assistant Alderman from the Out Ward, 1695–97, and Alderman, 1698 to 1701. They had no children bap. in the Dutch Church in New York.

    2. TRYNTIE VAN DER HEUL, bap. March 19, 1662 ; m. June 17, 1685, Albert Clock of New York, son of Abraham Clock and Tryntie Alberts ; bap. Sept. 26, 1660. He was Captain of the sloop Elizabeth, and commissioned by Leisler, July 3, 1690, to act against the French. *Issue :* Abraham, bap. Nov. 28, 1686, died young ; Abraham, bap. Jan. 18, 1688 ; Tryntie, bap. Oct. 19, 1690 ; Marten, bap. May 7, 1693 ; Johannes, bap. Feb. 2, 1696 ; Sara, bap. Nov. 20, 1698 ;

---

* Cal. N. Y. Hist. MSS. Dutch, p. 91.   † Idem, p. 106. ⸜
‡ O'Callaghan's Index of Dutch MSS., Albany, 1870, p. 92.

Albartus, bap. Feb. 16, 1701; Pieternella, bap. Dec. 8, 1703; and Femmetje, bap. July 10, 1706.

3. MARRITIE VAN DER HEUL, bap. Nov. 19, 1664; m. August 4, 1687, Petrus de Mill of New York, son of Anthony de Mill and Elizabeth Van der Liphorst; bap. Oct. 12, 1661. He was Sheriff of the City of New York 1700-1. *Issue:* Anthony, bap. April 22, 1688, died young; Elizabeth, bap. Oct. 13, 1689; Catharina, bap. Sept. 24, 1693, died young; Catharina, bap. May 12, 1695; Anthony, bap. Sept. 22, 1697, died young; Petrus, bap. May 15, 1700; Antony, bap. Nov. 22, 1702; Johannes, bap. May 14, 1704; Maria, bap. Aug. 24, 1707; and Anna, bap. Nov. 13, 1709.

4. PETRONELLA VAN DER HEUL,* bap. Oct. 31, 1668; m. June 1, 1692, Carsten Leursen, Jr. of New York, son of Carsten Leursen and Geertie Theunis Quick; bap. July 10, 1672. *Issue:* Carsten, bap. March 12, 1693; Abraham, bap. Aug. 11, 1695; Geertje, bap. April, 1698; and Tryntje, bap. Oct. 27, 1700.

5. FEMMETIE VAN DER HEUL, bap. Aug. 6, 1671, m. Oct. 21, 1697, Benjamin Wynkoop, j. m. Van Kingstouwne. He was then living in New York, and was probably the son of Cornelius Wynkoop, an Elder of the Dutch Church at Esopus in 1671, and his wife, Marretje or Maria Jans. He followed the occupation of silversmith in New York. *Issue:* Cornelis, bap. Dec. 1, 1699, died young; Cornelis, bap. June 22, 1701; Abraham, bap. July 4, 1703; Benjamin, bap. May 23, 1705; m. (1731?) Eunice Burr; Catharina, bap. June 29, 1707; Johannes, bap. Sept. 14, 1712; and Maria, bap. August 29, 1714.

6. JOHANNES VAN DER HUEL, bap. Dec. 24, 1673; m. Nov. 11, 1699, Jannetje Rosenvelt (Roosevelt); she was probably the dau. of Nicolaes Roosevelt and Hilletje or Helena Jans. He was a merchant in New York, and in October, 1720, part owner of the Privateer Hunter. *Issue:* Abraham, bap. Sept. 8, 1700, died young; Abraham, bap. Nov. 9, 1701; Catharina, bap. Sept. 1, 1704; Nicolaas, bap. Nov. 6, 1706; Johannes, bap. Sept. 16, 1713; and Helena, bap. May 25, 1724.

7. HENDRICK VAN DER HEUL, bap. May 14, 1676; m. April 21, 1700, Maria Meyer, dau. of Hendrick Jilliszen Meyer and Elsje Claes Rosenvelt (Roosevelt); she was bap. June 25, 1679. *Issue:* Abraham, bap. July 6, 1701; m. (1727?) Maria Bound; Elizabeth, bap. March 21, 1703; Hendricus, bap. Nov. 1, 1704, died young; Tryntje, bap. Jan. 1, 1707; Johannes, bap. June 12, 1709; Hendricus, bap. Nov. 2, 1712; m. March 25, 1736, Anna Brestede.

6. v. HENDRICK KIP, JR.,[2] (27) born in Amsterdam.

7. vi. FEMMETJE KIP,[2] she was probably bap. April 19, 1643, her father's name being recorded at the baptism, as Mr. Hendrick Hendricksz. She joined the Church in New Amsterdam Jan. 2, 1661, and was a sponsor,

---

* One of this name, recorded as the wife of Johann Van Tilburg, joined the Dutch Church in New York Feb. 28, 1700, but we are unable to identify her.

July 13, 1667, at the baptism of Jacomyntie, dau. of Jan de Caper *alias* Wanshaer, which is the last notice found of her.

8. ISAAC HENDRICKSZEN KIP² (3), born in Amsterdam. He was admitted to the rights of a great burgher with his father, April 11, 1657. On the 21st June, 1656, he and his brother Jacob obtained each a patent for a lot of land in the sheep pasture at New Amsterdam. This locality, used for the purpose indicated during nearly the whole period of the Dutch possession, is described by Mr. Valentine * as lying south of the city ramparts (which stretched across the Island about forty feet above the present line of Wall Street), and "covering the present Wall Street and the block between Wall Street, Exchange Place, Hanover Square, and Broad Street." Nassau Street between Ann and Spruce was originally called Kip Street after one of the family.† Mr. Valentine says it was that part of Nassau Street below Maiden Lane, and so called in compliment to Jacob Kip the Secretary. Isaac Kip was a Yacht Captain, engaged in the river trade between New Amsterdam and the settlements at Esopus (Kingston) and Fort Orange (Albany).‡ In 1665 he was living in De Brouwer Straat, now Stone Street. He married first, Feb. 8, 1653, Catalyntje Hendrick Snyers (Snyder?). She was probably the dau of Hendrick Janszen Snyder, or Hendrick Janszen the tailor, and his wife Geertje Scheerburch. Mr. Valentine § says she was a daughter of Gillis Pietersen (Meyer), but he has mistaken the relationship. She was probably the sister-in-law of Jillis or Gillis Pietersen (Meyer) who married July 6, 1642, Elsje Hendricks, dau. of Hendrick Janszen Snyder above named. Isaac Kip married second, Sept. 26, 1675 at New Harlem, Maria Vervelje (Vermilye), widow of Joh. (Jean) de La Montagne. By his second wife he had no issue. He was living, in December, 1675, at New Harlem, and then belonged to the *first corporalship* of night watch in that place.‖ He died prior to October 6, 1686. *Issue:*

9. i. HENDRICK,³ bap. Feb. 8, 1654. Mr. Holgate in his American Genealogy, pages 110–112, says that he and Jacobus (Jacob) Kip, his brother, were co-patentees of the Manor of Kipsburg, a tract of land on the east side of Hudson river where Rhinebeck now stands, extending four miles along the river and several miles inland. This patent dated June 2, 1688, confirmed an Indian title to the land given July 28, 1686. He was probably the Lieut. Hendrick Kip of Capt. Baltus Van Kleeck's Company of Foot, in 1700, one of the eight Militia Companies in the counties of Ulster and Dutchess.¶ He married and had a number of children who settled in the vicinity of Rhinebeck.

10. ii. TRYNTIE,³ bap. Sept. 13, 1656; m. Jan. 5, 1676, PHILIP DE FOREEST, son of Isaac and Sarah (du Trieux) De Foreest; bap. July 28, 1652. He was a cooper, and removed from New York about 1680 to the Manor of Rensselaerswyck; he was buried in Albany, August 18, 1727.** *Issue:* Sarah, bap. Jan. 2, 1678; and the following baptized in Albany: Susanna, April 1, 1684; Metje, July 25, 1686; Isaac, Feb. 20, 1689; Jesse, Jan. 13, 1692; Catrina, Nov. 25, 1694; Johannes, Sept. 12, 1697; David, Sept. 8, 1700; and Abraham, Feb. 21, 1703.

11. iii. ABRAHAM,³ bap. Sept. 3, 1659. He removed from New York

* Valentine's Manual for 1860, pp. 527–8.
† O'Callaghan's Hist. of New Netherland, vol. 2, p. 213.
‡ Valentine's Manual for 1860, pp. 574, 608.
§ Valentine's History of New York, p. 119.
‖ Valentine's Manual for 1848, p. 387.
¶ Doc. Rel. to Col. Hist. of New York, vol. 4, p. 810.
** Pearson's First Settlers of Albany, p. 38.

to Albany where he married Oct. 16, 1687, Gessie Van der Heyden; in 1714, his house was on the south corner of Maiden Lane and Pearl Street, Albany. He was buried at Albany, June 28, 1731, and his wife, Feb. 9, 1748. They had *issue* baptized in Albany as follows: Isaac,[4] Nov. 18, 1688; Anna,[4] Dec. 20, 1691, died young; Anna,[4] June 17, 1694; m. at Albany, Nov. 29, 1716, Johannes Evertse Wendel; Catelyntie,[4] Aug. 8, 1697; m. 1719 (?) her cousin, Anthony Kip[4] (30); Jacob[4] and Cornelia,[4] twins, July 20, 1701. Cornelia[4] m. at Albany July 5, 1724, Teunis Arentse Slingerland, widower of Elizabeth Vanderzee, and was buried there March 16, 1745; Geertruy[4] and Catharina,[4] twins, Jan. 24, 1705; Geertruy, m. at Albany, Dec. 17, 1730, Simon Veeder, and was buried there, July 20, 1746.*

    12. iv. ISAAC[3] (28), bap. Jan. 15, 1662.

    13. v. JACOB[3] bap. Nov. 19, 1664; died young.

    14. vi. JACOB,[3] bap. Aug. 29, 1666. He is probably the *Jacobus Kip* born Aug. 25, 1666, mentioned by Holgate as the co-patentee with Hendrick[3] (9) of the Manor of Kipsburg, and who died Feb. 28, 1753. Mr. Holgate makes a mistake which is followed by Bishop Kip in saying that he was twice married, and first to Mrs. Henrietta (Hendrickje) Wessels, widow of Gulian Verplanck. It was his cousin Jacobus[3] (18) who married this lady. He married Rachel Swartwout, and though Bishop Kip calls her the daughter of John Swarthout (Swartwout), Esq., I think it more probable that she was the dau. of Roeloff Swartwout, first Sheriff of Wiltwyck, at the Esopus, and commissioned Dec. 24, 1689, a Justice of Ulster County. Both Bishop Kip and Mr. Holgate give the date of her birth April 10, 1669, and her death Sept. 16, 1717. She was living Oct. 2, 1726, and with her husband, then called Jacob Kip, Senior, was sponsor at the baptism of Rachel, daughter of their son Isaac.

    They had *issue:*

      i.   ISAAC,[4] born Jan. 8, 1696; m. Jan. 7, 1720, Cornelia, dau. of Leonard and Elizabeth (Hardenburg) Lewis; she was born Nov. 9, 1692; bap. Dec. 11, 1692, and died July 10, 1772; he died July 2, 1762.† They had the following named children bap. in the Dutch Church at New York: Elizabeth,[5] bap. April 9, 1721; Jacob,[5] bap. Oct. 17, 1722; Leonard,[5] bap. June 27, 1725; m. April 11, 1763, Elizabeth, dau. of Francis and Anneke (Lynsen) Marschalk, of New York; she was bap. July 30, 1732; through them Bishop Kip of California traces his ancestral line. Rachel,[5] bap. Oct. 2, 1726; and Elizabeth,[5] bap. Aug. 28, 1728. To these Bishop Kip adds Isaac, born 1732, and Abraham who m. Jan. 6, 1768, Dorothea Remsen.

      ii.   ROELOFF,[4] of Kipsburg, from whom that branch of the family descended. He died during the Revolution, aged 90 years.‡

      iii.   CATALYNTIE,[4] bap. at Albany, Feb. 18, 1705.

    15. vii. JOHANNES, bap. Jan. 20, 1669.

    16. JACOB HENDRICKSZEN KIP[2] (4) born in Amsterdam May 16, 1631. In August (?), 1647, he gave to Harman Hendricksen Droogh, his uncle, a

---

* Pearson's First Settlers of Albany, pp. 68, 102, 141, 149. Munsell's Annals of Albany, vol. 1, p. 237.
† Hist. Notes of the Family of Kip of Kipsburg and Kip's Bay, New York, 1871.
‡ Hist. Notes of the Family of Kip of Kipsburg and Kip's Bay, New York, 1871.

power of attorney to receive money due him from the West India Company at Amsterdam. The same year he was a clerk in the provincial Secretary's office at New Amsterdam, and, as early as Dec., 1649, was acting clerk to Director Stuyvesant's Council.* He was appointed, Jan. 27, 1653, the first Secretary of the Court of Burgomasters and Schepens of New Amsterdam. Upon his resignation of that office June 12, 1657, he engaged in Brewing, combining with this business that of a general trader or storekeeper.† He was a member of the board of Schepens in 1659, 1662, 1663, 1665, 1673, and president of the board in 1674. "On the 1st of March, 1660, Aert Anthonissen Middagh, Teunis Gysberts Bogart, Jean Le Clerc, Gerrit Hendrick Backer, Philip Barchstoel, Christina Cappoens, JACOB KIP, and Joris Rapalje, all residents of the Waal-boght neighborhood, petitioned the Director for permission to form a village 'on the margin of the river between the lands of said Bogart and KIP, so that,' as they expressed it, 'we may be in sight of the Manhatans, or Fort Amsterdam.' The position selected was probably the elevated point of land which jutted into the river about the foot of South Fourth Street, in the present Eastern District of Brooklyn, and which was known in the ancient time as the 'Keike' or 'Lookout.' "‡ There is no evidence, remarks the learned historian of Brooklyn, that Jacob Kip ever resided on the lands above referred to, and "it was probably owing to his desire to improve the value of his real estate, by securing the establishment of a village thereon, that this petition was made," and through his influence with the authorities, was granted.

In early times some member of the Kip family—was it Jacob or his father?—obtained a patent for a farm of 150 acres, on the East River, on what is still known as Kip's Bay. It is said that Jacob Kip in 1655, the year after his marriage, erected on this farm a house which was rebuilt in 1696, and was, for a short time during the Revolution, Washington's headquarters.§ It stood upon the line of [East] 35th Street, and was demolished in 1851. His house in the city was built in 1657, and situated in the present Exchange Place. He owned a number of city houses and lots, and in 1655 resided in the present Broad Street, near Exchange Place, and was there probably as late as 1674.‖ In 1686 he was living "Beyond the Fresh Water," the Kip's Bay farm doubtless being the place alluded to.¶ The following paper, dated 1657 (?), imperfect and unexecuted, gives an interesting description of a Dutch house at that period : "Conditions and terms on which Jacob Kip, proposes to sell publicly, to the highest bidder, his house, kitchen, hen or hog yard, and lot lying in the city of [New] Amsterdam, over against the house of Heer Oloff Stevense [Van Cortland], as the same is occupied by him. The house two and thirty feet long and twenty feet broad, inclosed with thick planks and a glazed pantile roof, has a garret and floor, cellar walled up three, four or five feet with stone, and has a brick chimney in the front room, also a shop, the partition walls of bricks, the inner room built up with brick all around (*rondtom*), bedstead,

* O'Callaghan's Register of New Netherland. Doc. Rel. to Col. Hist. of New York, vol. 1, p. 387.
† Cal. N. Y. Hist. MSS. Dutch, p. 130-186. Valentine's Manual for 1860. p. 608.
‡ Stiles' Hist. of Brooklyn, vol. 1, p. 113. Cal. of N. Y. Hist. MSS. Dutch, p. 221.
§ O'Callaghan's Hist. New Netherland, vol. 2, p. 213. Valentine's Manual for 1852, p. 390.
‖ Paulding's Affairs and Men of New Amsterdam, etc., p. 111. Valentine's Hist. of N. Y., p. 328.
¶ Coll. of the N. Y. Hist. Society, Second Series, vol. 1, p. 398.

counting house, and larder therein; besides the aforesaid house, there is a kitchen eight or nine feet wide and seventeen or eighteen feet long, on the side of the house, with a brick chimney, in use by him, together with a hen or hog yard in the rear, and the place paved with bricks, and an apple tree therein, also a common gangway on the west side of the house six feet wide, and a common well, and what more is thereon and fast in earth and nailed, except the andirons (*handizer*) and hearth stone. . . . . ." *
This house and lot was probably situated in the present Stone Street.

Jacob Kip married March 8, 1654, Maria dau. of Dr. Johannes De La Montagne and Rachel Monjour. The record of their marriage states that she was from Amsterdam. She was born Jan. 26, 1637, at sea off the island of Madeira, on the voyage of her parents to New Netherland.† Her father, born in 1592, was a Huguenot physician—a man of great and varied learning—who was, soon after his arrival here, appointed by Gov. Kieft a member of the Council, in which office he was continued by Gov. Stuyvesant, until the 28th of Sept., 1656, when he was appointed Vice-director at Fort Orange (Albany). Jacob Kip died about the year 1690, and the last notice found of his widow is on the 21st May, 1701, at which date she was a sponsor at the baptism of Maria dau. of Dirck Hooglant.

They had *issue :*

17. i. JOHANNES,[3] bap. Feb. 21, 1655. He was a Brewer in the city of New York, and m. Sept. 4, 1681, Catharina, dau. of Dr. Hans Kierstede ‡ and Sara Roelofs. He died in 1704, leaving his wife surviving him. They had *issue .*

    1. Jacob,[4] bap. Nov. 4, 1682 ; m. 1704 (m. l. dated Dec. 4, 1704), Cathalina de Hart, dau. of Jacobus de Hart and Cornelia Pieters ; 2. Hans,[4] bap. Sept. 5, 1684 ; 3. Maria,[4] bap. Sept. 19, 1686 ; m. June 24, 1710, Abraham Van Vleck ; 4. Sara,[4] bap. Nov. 11, 1688 ; 5. Hans,[4] bap. Oct. 5, 1690 ; 6. Blandina,[4] bap. Feb. 3, 1692 ; 7. Johannes,[4] bap. Jan. 31, 1694 ; 8. Blandina,[4] bap. April 26, 1696 ; 9. Catharina,[4] bap. July 7, 1697 ; 10. Catharina,[4] bap. Oct. 16, 1698 ; 11. Henricus,[4] bap. Oct. 20, 1700 ; 12 and 13. Benjamin,[4] and Blandina,[4] twins, bap. March 21, 1703. For an account of Benjamin Kip,[4] *see* Bolton's Hist. of Westchester, Vol. 2, 527.

* Pearson's Early Records of the City and County of Albany, etc. (1656-1675), p. 53.
† O'Callaghan's Hist. New Netherland, vol. 2, p. 21.
‡ DR. HANS KIERSTEDE from Maegdenburg (perhaps Magdeburg, the capital of the province of Saxony) was one of the earliest practising physicians and surgeons settled in New Amsterdam, and came here with Gov. William Kieft in March, 1638. He m. June 29, 1642, Sara Roelofs, born in Amsterdam, dau. of Roelof Jansen and Anneke Jans of Trinity Church celebrity. His wife is said to have been more proficient in the Indian language than any other person in the colony, and in May, 1664, acted as interpreter in the great treaty made at New Amsterdam between Gov. Stuyvesant and the neighboring Indian tribes. Having often acted in that capacity, she was presented with a large tract of land on the west side of the North River, by Oritany, the chief of the Hackinsack and Tappan Indians (Broadhead's Hist. N. V., 1, p. 731.)
Dr. Kierstede died about 1667, and his widow m. Sept. 1, 1669, Cornelius Van Borsum, of the Brooklyn Ferry, and removed to New Amersfort. She m. again at the latter place, July 21, 1683, Elbert Elbertszen [Stoothoof] widower of Aeltje Cornelis. She survived her last husband and died in New York about 1693, having on the 2d Sept., 1692, rejoined the Ref. Dutch Church here, with certificate from the church at Midwout. She had no children by her third husband, and probably none by her second. Dr. Hans Kierstede and Sara Roelofs had *issue :* 1. Jans, alias Hans, bap. Sept. 21, 1644 ; m. Feb. 12, 1667, Jannetie Lookermans ; 2. Roelof, bap. Jan. 1, 1647 ; m. 1670 (?) Ytje Jans or Ytje Alberts (perhaps Ytje, dau. of Albert Jans), both names being given at the bap. of their children ; 3. Anna, bap. April 23, 1651 ; 4. Blandina, bap. June 8 ; 1653 ; m. Nov. 28, 1674, Petrus Bayard ; 5. Jochem, bap. Oct. 24, 1655 ; 6. Lucas, bap. Sept. 23, 1657 ; m. July 18, 1683, Rachel Kip ; 7. Catharyn, bap. Jan. 4, 1660 ; m. Sept. 4, 1681. Johannes Kip ; 8. Jacob, bap. June 4, 1662 ; 9. Jacobus, bap. Nov. 28, 1663 ; m. 1693 (?), Anna Hooms (Homes ?) ; 10. Rachel, bap. Sept. 13. 1665 ; m. Nov. 19, 1686, William Teller, Jr., of Albany, then living in New York.

18. ii. JACOBUS,[3] bap. Oct. 15, 1656; m. May 28, 1685, Hendrickje Wessels, widow of Gelyn Verplanck.* His will is dated Sept. 19, 1702; proved at Jamaica, Queens Co., L. I., Oct. 31, 1702, and of record in liber Wills, 7, p. 38, New York Surrogate's office. In March, 1695, he was a merchant, engaged in trade in New York. He survived his wife, and died without issue, leaving his estate to his brothers and sisters, and to the heirs of his deceased wife. He is described in his will as "of the *county* of New Town"—a clerical error—Newtown, L. I., being the place referred to, and where he probably resided at the time of his death.

19. iii. ABRAHAM,[3] bap. Dec. 22, 1658. He was a Brewer in New York, and m. Jan. 26, 1697, Catalina de Lanoy, dau. of Abraham de Lanoy and Marritie Lubberts, and the widow of Isaac Van Vleck. They had no children bap. in the Dutch Church at New York, and it is probable he died without issue. He died before Nov. 30, 1720, leaving his wife surviving.

20. iv. JESSE,[3] bap. Dec. 19, 1660; m. Maria Stevens (Stephens, Stevenson), m. l. dated Sept. 30, 1695. About the year 1710 he removed from New York to Newtown, L. I. He owned there a grist-mill at Fish's Point, bequeathed to him by his brother Jacobus. Oct. 16, 1711, he purchased of Thomas and John Stevenson a fulling-mill, located near his grist-mill, and on the stream that empties at Fish's Point. He died at Newtown in April, 1722. His children, baptized in the Dutch Church at New York, were: 1. Maria,[4] bap. Dec. 16, 1696; d. young. 2. Elizabeth,[4] bap. Dec. 2, 1698; m. 1717, Thomas Fish, son of Nathan Fish, of Newtown, born May 28, 1693; 3. Jacobus,[4] bap. April 6, 1701; Abraham,[4] born July 22, bap. Aug. 29, 1703; m. Sarah, dau. of Nathan Fish, of Newtown; she was born March 28, 1699; † Thomas,[4] bap. Jan. 20, 1706; Jesse,[4] born Jan. 30, 1708, bap. May 9, 1708; Johannes,[4] born Oct. 11, bap. Dec. 11, 1709; Jesse Kip[3] had besides the children above named, two sons, Benjamin[4] and William,[4] born prob. at Newtown.

21. v. RACHEL,[3] bap. Jan. 11, 1664, m. July 18, 1683, LUCAS KIERSTEDE of New York, son of Dr. Hans Kierstede and Sara Roelofs; he was bap. Sept. 23, 1657. They had *issue*:

    1. HANS KIERSTEDE, bap. Aug. 3, 1684; m. March 3, 1710, Maria Van Vleck, dau. of Isaac Van Vleck and Catalina de Lanoy; she was bap. May 3, 1685. They had eight children bap. in the Dutch Church at New York.

    2. MARIA KIERSTEDE, bap. Aug. 29, 1686; m. 1709 (?) Cornelus Romme (Romeyn?), of New York, son of Jan Janszen Van Langestraat, *alias* Romme or Rommen, and his wife Marritie Arents; he was bap. Oct. 31, 1686. They had ten children bap. in the Dutch Church at New York.

    3. SARA KIERSTEDE, bap. Jan 16, 1689; m. 1713 (?) Pieter Van Ranst, of New York. They had ten children bap. in the Dutch Church at New York.

    4. JACOBUS KIERSTEDE, bap. March 20, 1692; m. Nov. 1, 1718, Sara dau. of Johannes Nerbery (Narbury?) and Aginetje Pro-

---

* For an account of the Verplanck family, *see* Pearson's First Settlers of Albany. p. 142 and N. Y. G. & B. RECORD, vol. i., p. 35.
† Riker's Hist. of Newtown, pp. 123, 366.

voost; she was bap. May 5, 1700. They had three children bap. in the Dutch Church at New York. He probably became a widower and m. second, Elizabeth dau. of Rip Van Dam and Sara Van der Spiegel.

5. JESSE KIERSTEDE, bap. May 31, 1695; m. May 17, 1724, Jakoba Lewis dau. of Thomas Lewis, and Francina Leisler; he was a sea captain and prob. d. s. p. *See* GENEALOGICAL MEMORIALS OF LIEUT.-GOV. JACOB LEISLER, p. 15.

6. RACHEL KIERSTEDE, bap. Jan. 9, 1698.

7. LUCÚS KIERSTEDE, bap. Oct. 22, 1699; m. Aug. 4, 1734, Maria Ryckman dau. of Johannes Ryckman and Catharina Kip; she was bap. Feb. 29, 1708. They had seven children bap. in the Dutch Church at New York.

8. BENJAMIN KIERSTEDE, bap. April 12, 1702; m. Sept. 22, 1722, Jenneke (Jane) Blom, dau. of Jacob Blom and Mayke Bosch; she was bap. March 7, 1705. They had six children bap. in the Dutch Church at New York.

22. vi. MARYKEN[3] (MARIA), bap. Dec. 5, 1666; m. August 4, 1687, DIRCK HOOGLANT, of New York, son of Christoffel Hooglant and Tryntie Cregiers; he was bap. Nov. 1, 1662. They had *issue:*

1. CATHARINA HOOGLANT, bap. April 13, 1698.
2. MARIA HOOGLANT, bap. May 21, 1701; died young.
3. MARIA HOOGLANT, bap. July 7, 1703.

23. vii. HENDRICK,[3] bap. Feb. 14, 1669; m. June 10, 1697, Magdalena Van Vleck. He died about 1698, without issue, and his widow married April 24, 1700, Alexander Baird,* a young man from Scotland.

24. viii. CATHARINA,[3] born 1672 (?). Her baptism is not recorded in the Ref. Dutch Church of New York. She is named in her brother Jacobus Kip's will, *Chatrin Rickman.* She m. July 11, 1697, JOHANNES RYCKMAN, son of Capt. Albert Janse Ryckman, Brewer, of Albany, and Neeltie Quackenbos. Johannes Ryckman joined the Dutch Church in New York, by letter or certificate from Albany, Sept. 4, 1697, and died before Dec. 23, 1736.† It is probable that he became a widower and married second, June 17, 1717, Cornelia, dau. of Isaac Van Vleck and Catalina de Lanoy; she was bap. Jan. 3, 1692. By his first wife had *issue:*

1. ALBERT RYCKMAN, bap. July 24, 1698; m. Catharina Christoffels, and had Catharina bap. Jan. 3, 1725.
2. JACOBUS RYCKMAN, bap. Jan. 19, 1701; m. Sept. 1, 1723, Geertruy Adrianse. They had five children bap. in the Dutch Church at New York.
3. NELLETJE RYCKMAN, bap. Nov. 8, 1702; died young.
4. JOHANNIS RYCKMAN, bap. April 18, 1705.
5. MARIA RYCKMAN, bap. Feb. 29, 1708; m. Aug. 4, 1734, Lucas, son of Lucas Kierstede and Rachel Kip.
6. TOBIAS RYCKMAN, bap. Feb. 1, 1710; died young.
7. TOBIAS RYCKMAN, bap. July 8, 1711; m. Maria Van Eps, and had Abraham bap. March 12, 1746.

* ALEXANDER BAIRD and Magdalena Van Vleck, widow of Hendrick Kip, had two sons bap. in the Dutch Church at New York, viz.: Wilhelmus, bap. April 12, 1704; and Robberd, bap. Nov. 13, 1706.
† Pearson's First Settlers of Albany, p. 94.

By his second wife Johannes Ryckman had *issue :*

8. ISAAC RYCKMAN, bap. July 27, 1718 ; m. Engeltje Niewkerk, dau. of Jan Cornelise Niewkerk and Jenneke Breestede, and had Johannes bap. Jan. 4, 1741 ; Isaak, bap. April 17, 1743 ; and Johannes, bap. Nov. 9, 1746.

9. and 10. NELLETJE and CATALYNTJE RYCKMAN, twins, bap. Nov. 30, 1720.

11. ABRAHAM RYCKMAN, bap. March 10, 1723.

12. SAMUEL RYCKMAN, bap. Feb. 13, 1726.

25. ix. BENJAMIN,[3] bap. Aug. 28, 1678. He was living Sept. 19, 1702, but probably died soon after, unmarried.

26. x. SALOMON,[3] bap. Nov. 15, 1682. His name is so entered in the baptismal records, but he is called SAMUEL in his brother Jacobus's will. Samuel Kip married about 1705, Margrietje Ryckman, dau. of Capt. Albert Janse Ryckman, of Albany. He probably removed from New York about 1721-2. They had bap. in the Dutch Church at New York : 1. Jacobus,[4] bap. Aug. 18, 1706 ; 2. Albartus,[4] bap. May 30, 1708 ; 3. Maria,[4] bap. June 7, 1710 ; 4. Albert,[4] bap. Jan. 24, 1714 ; 5. Johannes,[4] bap. Feb. 8, 1717 ; 6. Samuel,[4] bap. April 30, 1718 ; 7. Rachel,[4] bap. Feb. 12, 1721.

27. HENDRICK KIP, Jr.[2] (6.), born in Amsterdam ; m. Feb. 29, 1660, Anna de Sillen (De Sille) from Wyck, dau. of Nicasius De Sille,* First Counsellor to Director General Stuyvesant. He was admitted to the rights

---

* NICASIUS DE SILLE was the son of Laurens De Sille, the latter being described in December, 1654, as the late Advocate Fiscal of the States General, or United Netherlands. Laurens was probably the son of Nicasius De Sille, who was originally from Mechlin, in Belgium, and came to Amsterdam soon after the revolt of the United Provinces against Spain, was chosen Pensionary of that city, and sent in 1587, with others, on an Embassy to Queen Elizabeth of England : was Ambassador to Denmark, and afterwards to Germany, and was repeatedly sent a Deputy to the States General, and was twice Commissioner to the army whilst in the field ; he died Aug. 22, 1600, aged 57 years, and was buried in the choir of the Red church at Amsterdam. Nicasius of New Netherland was a native of Arnhem, the chief town of Guelderland, and came to New Amsterdam in the summer of 1653. In his commission as First Councillor to Director General Stuyvesant, he is described as a "man well versed in the law and not unacquainted with military affairs, of good character and satisfactory acquirements." He was directed to reside at Fort Amsterdam, and to deliberate with the Governor "on all affairs relating to war, police, and national force ; " to keep inviolate and increase all alliances of friendship and commerce : to assist in the administration of justice, criminal and civil, and to advise the Governor in all events and occurrences that might transpire in the Colony. He superintended the preparation of the Fleet and accompanied it with Gov. Stuyvesant in the expedition to the South or Delaware river, against the Swedes in 1655. In May, 1656, he was appointed Schout-fiscal in place of Cornelis Van Tienhoven, who had been ignominiously dismissed from the public service. In June following, he was commissioned city Schout of New Amsterdam, in which office he was succeeded by Pieter Tonneman in April, 1660. In the meantime he had become one of the proprietors of New Utrecht, L. I., where, in 1657, he built the first house erected in that town, which was demolished in 1850. The first records of the town are still preserved, in his handwriting. He resided at New Utrecht as late as 1674, and probably until his death, of which event we have found no mention. (*Doc. Rel. to Col. Hist. of New York, vol.* 2, *p.* 440; *Cal. of N. Y. Hist. Dutch ; O'Callaghan's Hist. of New Netherland, vol.* 2, *p.* 236 ; *Brodhead's Hist. of N. Y., vol.* 1 ; *Anthology of New Netherland.*) NICASIUS DE SILLE was twice married. The name of his first wife, who probably died before he came to New Amsterdam, is not known. In the record of his second marriage, the fact of his being a widower, is not entered, as was usual in such cases. He married second, May 26, 1655, Tryntje Crougers (Cregier) from the Hague, an alliance which proved the source of great unhappiness to both parties. By his second wife, from whom he separated by mutual agreement in 1668-9, he had no family. By his first wife he had *issue :*

    i.   LAURENCE DE SILLE, who married a dau. of Capt. Martin Cregier. "From Laurence De Sille," says Dr. O'Callaghan, "proceed all the branches of that family now in this country. They reside chiefly in the neighborhood of New York and Albany, having dropped the *de* before the name. The Rev. G. W. Sill, one of the descendants, is at present a clergyman in the State of Missouri." There is, however, another branch of the Sill family, descendants of John Sill who settled in Cambridge, Mass., in 1637, among whom, singularly, there was a Rev. G. W. Sill, an Episcopal Clergyman, who resided some years ago in Missouri. (*See* Sill Family Genealogy.)

    ii.   GERDIENTJE DE SILLE, m. Jan Gerretse Van Couwenhoven, of Brooklyn ferry ; he was born in 1639. (*See* Bergen Genealogy.)

    iii.   ANNA DE SILLE, m. Hendrick Kip, Jr.,[2] as noticed in the text.

There was a Walbrug De Sille who if not a daughter, was a near relative of Nicasius De Sille. She married first, Feb. 29, 1660, Frans Kregier (Cregier) from Borcken, son of Capt. Martin Cregier, and had Elisabeth bap. July 5, 1662. She married second about 1668, William, son of Rev. Everardus Bogardus and

of a great burgher in New Amsterdam, April 17, 1657,[*] and soon after removed to New Amstel on the Delaware. In a letter[†] dated at Amsterdam, 22d April, 1659, the Commissioners of the Colony on the Delaware, inform Vice Director Alrichs that "the brewers Kettle for Hendrick Kip, will be sent you by the first opportunity," from which we infer that he was engaged in business there, as a Brewer. In Sept., 1659, he was one of the Council, and June 29, 1660, was appointed by D'Hinoyossa one of the Commissaries at New Amstel.[‡] In a deed of Augustine Heerman, conveying to him a house and lot in New Amsterdam, dated Sept. 17th, 1662, he is described as "Mr. Hendrick Hendricksen Kip, the younger, residing on the South [Delaware] River in New Netherland." How long he remained there is not known, but it is probable he had two sons, Nicasius and Petrus, born on the Delaware. It is supposed that he afterwards settled at Pollifly, near Hackensack, N. J.[§] Hendrick Kip and Anna de Sille, were sponsors at the baptism in New York, March 21, 1703, of Henderikus, son of Petrus Kip. This is the last notice found of Anna De Sille, and if the Hendrick Kip, who was sponsor, with her, was her husband—which is probable—it is also the last notice of him.

They had two daughters bap. in the Dutch Church at New York, Cornelia,[3] June 12, 1661, and Catharina,[3] Nov. 9, 1664. Cornelia Kip (prob. dau. of Hendrick[2]), wife of Mathys Lyster, was a sponsor at the baptism in New York, of Petrus, son of Petrus Kip and Immetie Van Dyck, Dec. 26, 1709. Nicasius [Nicholas] Kip,[3] probably a son || of Hendrick[2] and Anna (De Sille) Kip, with his wife Antie Breyant[¶] (Bryant), joined the First Reformed (Dutch) Church at Hackensack, Sept. 22, 1694.[**] He died about 1711. They had *issue*, all bap. at Hackensack : 1. Hendrick,[4] born 1693 (?,) m. at H. July 24, 1714, Geertruy Van Dien ; 2. Pieter,[4] born 1695 (?), m. at H., March 5, 1720, Elsie Van der Beek ; 3. Isaac,[4] bap. 1697, m. at H. March 30, 1723, Willemintie Berdan, dau. of Jan Berdan and Eva Van Sickelen ; she was bap. at H., June 5, 1704 ; 4. Cornelis,[4] bap. Jan. 1, 1700, m. at H., Sept. 17, 1720, Eva, dau. of Jan Berdan ; she was bap. at H., Oct. 1697 ; 5. Jacob,[4] bap. Dec. 14, 1702, m. at H., April 6, 1728, Helena, dau. of Jan Berdan ; she was bap. at H., April 14, 1708 ; 6. Annatie,[4] bap. Jan 3, 1706, m. at

Anneke Jans, by whom she had bap. in New York : Cornelia, Aug. 25, 1669 ; Everhardus, Dec. 4, 1675 ; Maria and Lucretia, twins, Sept. 14, 1678 ; and Blandina, Sept. 13, 1680.

Daniel De Sille who gave Oct. 13, 1654, a Power of Attorney to Nicasius De Sille, to manage his affairs in New Netherland, was perhaps a brother of Nicasius. (*See* Cal. of N. Y. Hist. MSS. Dutch, p. 57.)

[*] O'Callaghan's Register of New Netherland, p. 174.

[†] Doc. Rel. to Col. Hist. of New York, vol. 2, pp. 61-75.

[‡] Hazard's Annals of Pennsylvania, p. 316.

[§] Corwin Genealogy, p. 49.

[||] Since writing the above we have been favored by Teunis G. Bergen, Esq., with the following, translated by him from the Flatbush town records. "January 29, 1678. Anna Kip (daughter of Nicasius De Sille) bound out her son Nicholas to Jan La Montangie, Master Cooper of New York, to learn said trade of Cooper, for six years, his time to commence May, 1678."

[¶] In 1687—the day and month does not appear in the record—PIETER CORNELISE BREYANDT (BRYANT) and Hendriktie Arents (Aerts), had a dau. Lysbeth bap. in the church at Hackensack, N. J. It is probable he is the same Pieter Cornelise, who had by wife Hendrikje Aerts (Arents), the following named children bap. in the Dutch Church at New York, and in Bergen, N. J. 1. Annetje, bap. N. Y., Sept. 10, 1671 ; 2. Geertruyd, bap. N. Y. Nov. 8, 1673 ; 3. Cornelis, born in B., April 18, 1676 (*see* Winfield's Land Titles, Hudson Co., N. J., p. 363), bap. N. Y., May 3, 1676 ; 4. Arent, bap. B., Oct. 7, 1678 : 5. Andries, bap. B., Aug. 21, 1681, d. young ; 6. Andries, bap. B., June 30, 1684. Presuming that Pieter Cornelise and Hendrikje Aerts, of New York, 1671-6, and Bergen, 1676-84, are identical with Pieter Cornelise Breyandt (Bryant) and his wife, of Hackensack, in 1687, we trace their children as follows : Annetje (Antie) Bryant, m. 1st about 1692, Nicasius Kip ; m. 2d at Hackensack, Oct. 10, 1713, Isaac Van Gysse, widower of Hillegond Claes Kuyper. Geertruyd Bryant, m. at H., Oct. 26, 1695, Roelof Bougart, who was born at Flatbush, L. I. He m. 2d at H., Aug. 23, 1718, Elisabet Bertholf, widow of Jan Albertse Terhmyne. Cornelis Bryant, m. at H., Dec. 7, 1700, Margrita Simonse Van Winkle, widow of Martin Winne. Arent and Andries Bryant probably died without issue. Lysbeth Bryant, m. at H., April 12, 1707, Egbert, son of Laurens Ackerman and Geertie Egberts, he was bap. in N. Y., Feb. 23, 1685.

[**] Romeyn's Hist. Discourse, Hackensack, May, 1869.

H., Sept. 2, 1726, Lucas Van Voorhees, son of Albert Stevense Van Voor-
hees and Helena Van der Schure ; he was bap. at H., Feb. 26, 1699 ; 7.
Catarina,[4] bap. Sept 12, 1708, m. at H., Oct. 15, 1727, Dirk Terhuyne ; 8.
Elisabeth,[4] bap. March 11, 1711, m. at H., Nov. 19, 1731, Hendrick Blink-
erhof (Brinckerhoff), son of Jacobus Hendrickse Blinkerhof and Angenitie
Banta ; he was bap. at H., Nov. 9, 1710.*

Petrus Kip,[3] prob. a son of Hendrick,[2] and Anna (De Sille) Kip, m. in
N. Y., April 24, 1702, Immetie Van Dyck, dau. of Dirck Franszen Van
Dyck and Urseltie Jans Schepmoes ; she was bap. Jan. 11, 1675. They
had ten children bap. in the Dutch Church at New York.

28. ISAAC KIP[3] (12), son of Isaac Hendrickszen[x] (8), bap. Jan. 15, 1662 ;
m. Oct. 20, 1686, Sara De Mill, dau. of Anthony De Mill, Sheriff of New
York, 1673–4, and Elisabeth Vander Liphorst ; she was bap. Dec. 30,
1663, and died about 1726. He was a Cooper, and lived and died in New
York. His will is dated Nov. 19, 1746 ; proved June 6, 1750. To his
grandson, Abraham Kip, eldest son of his eldest son, Anthony Kip, deceased, he gives ten shillings current money, etc., to be paid him at the age
of twenty-one years, and if he should die before that time without issue,
then to his brother Isaac Kip, " or whoever else of my sons or grand sons
that may legally be deemed my heir at law, which ten shillings shall be a full
bar of all claim or pretence of being my heir at law." The rest of his estate
he divides as follows : one-sixth part to the children of his son Anthony,
deceased ; one-sixth part to his dau. Catlyntie, wife of Peter Marschalk ;
one-sixth part to the children of his son Isaac Kip, deceased ; one-sixth
part to his son Jacob Kip ; one-sixth part to his son Petrus Kip ; and one-
sixth part to his son Abraham Kip. Appoints as executors his loving
friends Francois Marschalk and Evert Byvank of the city of New York,
Bakers, and John Kip, of said city, Merchant. He had *issue :*

29. i. CATALINA,[4] bap. Oct. 19, 1687 ; died young.
30. ii. ANTHONY,[4] bap. Jan. 8, 1690 ; m. 1st Jan. 3, 1713, Maria Byvank,
prob. a dau. of Johannes Byvank and Belitje Evertse Duyckinck, of Albany ;
she was bap. there Feb. 12, 1688. He m. 2d, 1719 (?), Catlyntje Kip, his
cousin, dau. of Abraham Kip, of Albany. He had the following named
children bap. in the Dutch Church at New York. 1. Belitje,[6] bap. Nov. 1,
1713 ; 2. Sara,[6] bap. March 27, 1720 ; 3. Abraham,[6] bap. June 3, 1722 ;
4. Isaac,[6] bap. Sept. 30, 1724 ; and Sara,[6] bap. Jan. 30, 1728.
31. iii. CATALINA,[4] bap. Oct. 21, 1691 ; m. June 3, 1722, PETRUS MARS-
CHALK of New York, son of Andries Marschalk and Elizabeth Van Gelder ;
he was bap. Feb. 19, 1696. They had *issue :* Andries, bap. March 24,
1723 ; Isaac, bap. July 18, 1725 ; Sara, bap. Aug. 17, 1729 ; and Elizabeth,
bap. Aug. 23, 1730.
32. iv. ISAAC, JR.,[4] bap. Oct. 1, 1693 ; m. May 13, 1716, Anna Van
Noortstrant of New York, prob. a dau. of Jacob Van Noortstrant and
Annetje Croesvelt, who was bap. Feb. 12, 1696. They had *issue :*
1. Isaac,[6] bap. June 19, 1717 ; 2. Anna,[5] bap. Sept. 23, 1719 ; and Sara,[5]
bap. April 25, 1722.
33. v. JACOB,[4] bap. July 14, 1695 ; m. Dec. 7, 1717, Engeltje (Angelina)
Pels, of New York, dau. of Evert Pels and Grietje (Margaret) Melcherts

* For Marriages and Baptisms in the Church at Hackensack, I am indebted to the courtesy of James W.
Quackenbush, Esq., of that place.

Van Deurse (Van Deusen) ; she was bap. July 25, 1697. He was a Cordwainer and Tanner in New York, and died in October, 1754, leaving his wife, son Evert, and dau. Elizabeth surviving him. He had *issue :* 1. Margrietje,[b] bap. Feb. 24, 1721 ; m. July 20, 1740, Hans (Johannes) Hansen, Jr. ; 2. Isaac,[b] bap. July 25, 1725, d. young ; 3. Sara,[c] bap. July 23, 1727, d. young ; 4. Betje[c] (Elizabeth), bap. March 18, 1733 ; and 5. Evert,[b] bap. Jan. 11, 1738.

34. vi. JOHANNES,[4] bap. April 11, 1697 ; died unmarried.

35. vii. ELIZABETH,[4] bap. July 16, 1699 ; died young.

36. viii. PETRUS,[4] bap. June 19, 1700 ; m. Dec. 6, 1724, Margrietje Blom, dau. of Jacob Blom and Mayke Janse Bosch (Bos), of New York. She was bap. Nov. 4, 1702. They had *issue* bap. in the Dutch Church in New York : 1. Maria,[5] bap. Sept. 1, 1725 ; 2. Isaac,[5] bap. Sept. 4, 1726 ; 3. Jacob,[5] bap. June 23, 1728 ; 4. Abraham,[5] bap. Feb. 23, 1733 ; 5. Maria,[5] bap. Jan. 22, 1735 ; and 6. Sara,[5] bap. Sept. 24, 1738.

37. ix. ELIZABETH,[4] bap. Aug. 12, 1702 ; died unmarried.

38. x. ABRAHAM[4] (39), bap. Aug. 19, 1705.

39. ABRAHAM KIP[4] (38), bap. Aug. 19, 1705 ; m. Feb. 13, 1729, Maria (Mary) Van den Berg, of New York, dau. of Huybert Gerritzen Van den Berg* and Maria Lansing ; she was bap. Feb. 27, 1709. He was a Cooper, and died in New York about 1750, leaving his wife surviving. Her will is dated July 19, 1765, and proved Jan. 5, 1785. In it she is described as Mary Kip, of the City of New York, widow of Abraham Kip, late of the City of New York, Cooper, deceased, and one of the daughters of Huybert Van den Berg, late of the said city, Cartman, deceased. She bequeaths her estate to her daughter Mary, and after her death directs it to be divided equally among her three other children, to wit : Sarah, wife of Gerrit Harsen ; Abraham Kip, and Gerrit Kip. Appoints her son-in-law, Gerrit Harsen, of said city, Baker, her son, Abraham Kip, of said city, Painter, and her friend, Mr. Nathaniel McKinley, of said city, executors. Abraham Kip and his wife Maria Van den Berg had *issue :*

40. i. ISAAC,[5] bap. June 29, 1729; died young.

41. ii. ISAAC,[5] bap. Feb. 14, 1731 ; died young.

42. iii. HUBERT,[5] bap. Sept. 30, 1733 ; died unmarried.

43. iv. ISAAC,[5] bap. March 23, 1735 ; died young.

44. v. SARA,[5] bap. Feb. 27, 1736 ; m. Nov. 28, 1757, GERRIT HARSEN, Baker of New York.

45. vi. MARVTJE,[5] bap. Jan. 1, 1738 ; died unmarried.

* HUYBERT GERRITSZEN (VAN DEN BERG) and his wife Maria Lansing came from Albany, and joined the Dutch Church in New York, Dec. 2, 1696. He was probably a brother of Barent Gerritse Van den Berg of the Manor of Rensselaerswyck, in 1687, and perhaps the son of Gerrit Van den Bergh, of Albany, 1663. His wife was a dau. of Hendrick Lansing and Elizabeth Caspers, of Albany. They were married at Albany, Dec. 20, 1693, and had dau. Lysbeth bap. there July 29, 1694. (*See Pearson's First Settlers of Albany, pp. 53 and 70.*) She is probably the Elizabeth Van den Berg who married in New York, Feb. 22, 1713, Johannes Ostrander. Their children bap. in New York were :
1. Theuntie Van den Berg, bap. Nov. 17, 1695.
2. Gerretje Van den Berg, bap. June 16, 1697 : died young.
3. Gerretje Van den Berg, bap. Jan. 11, 1699 ; m. Aug. 8, 1718, Pieter Van der Lyn, and had Elizabeth bap. Sept 2, 1719.
4. Gerrit Van den Berg, bap. Aug. 31, 1701 : died young.
5. Gerardus Van den Berg, bap. April 9, 1704.
6. Hendrikus Van den Berg, bap. Nov. 13, 1706.
7. Marytje (Maria) Van den Berg, bap. Feb. 27, 1709 ; m. Abraham Kip as noticed in the text.
8. Ariaantje Van den Berg, bap. Dec. 26, 1710 ; died young.
9. Ariaantje Van den Berg, bap. July 27, 1712.
10. Gerrit Van den Berg, bap. Nov. 14, 1714.

46. vii. ISAAC,[5] bap. May 4, 1740 ; died unmarried.

47. viii. ELIZABETH,[5] bap. Feb. 7, 1742 ; died unmarried.

48. ix. ABRAHAM,[5] bap. May 27, 1744.

49. x. GERRIT[5] (50), born May 11, bap. May 18, 1746.

50. GERRIT KIP[5] (49), born May 11, bap. May 18, 1746 ; m. Feb. 12, 1768, Ellenor or Nelletje Brouwer. She was a daughter of Johannes Brouwer* and Susanna Druljet (Droljitt, Droljet, Driljet, Draljet, Deroill-het), and born in New York, June 9, bap. June 12, 1745. They had *issue.*

51. i. ABRAHAM[6] (56), bap. June 2, 1768.

52. ii. ELIZABET DRULJET,[6] bap. Aug. 12, 1770 ; m. RICHARD WILKIN-SON, and had 1. Ellenor, d. s. p. ; 2. Eliza, m. William Gallaer ; 3. Maria, m. John Brown ; 4. Rachel ; 5. Susan, d. s. p. ; and 6. Sarah d. s. p.

53. iii. GERRIT,[6] bap. July 19, 1772 ; m. Ann Leech, and had 1. Jane ;[7] 2. John ;[7] 3. Ellenor,[7] m. Asa Wells ; and Mary Ann,[7] m. David Fulkerson.

54. iv. JOHN[6], bap. Sept. 18, 1774 ; died unmarried.

55. v. HUBERT[6], born 1777 (?) ; died unmarried.

56. ABRAHAM KIP[6] (51), bap. June 2, 1768 ; m. 1789, Rachel Blank. He was a mason and bricklayer in the city of New York, where he died early in 1797. His wife was a descendant in the sixth generation, of Jeuriaen (George) Blank, Goldsmith, of New Amsterdam, who came to New Netherland with his wife Tryntje Claes, prior to 1643. She married second in 1798, PETER NAYLOR†, bricklayer, of New York, the son of Richard Naylor of England. He died June 13, 1818 ; she died March 5, 1836. Abraham Kip and Rachel Blank had *issue.*

57. i. RACHEL[7], born May 11, 1790 ; m. Feb. 8, 1806, JAMES LYNCH, Hairdresser. He was born Dec. 5, 1781, in Monmouth Co., N. J., but re-

---

* JOHANNES BROUWER (Brower), was a great-grandson of Adam Brouwer, from Ceulen, who married in New Amsterdam, March 19, 1645, Magdalena Verdon. Adam Brouwer was an early settler in Brooklyn, Long Island, and in 1661, was the owner, with Isaac De Forrest, of the old Gowanus Mill, on the Gowanus Creek, later known as Freeke's Mill, supposed to be the first erected on Long Island. (*Brooklyn Manual*, 1863, p. 375.) In his will, dated Jan. 22, 1692½, proved March 21, 1692, he is styled Adam Brouwer, Berkhoven, inhabitant of the town of Brookland. He left surviving him his wife, Magdalena, and the following named children : Pieter ; Matthew ; William ; Maria ; Aeltje ; Fytje ; Jacob[2] ; Helena ; Adam ; Abraham ; Anna ; Sarah ; Nicholas, and Rachel. Jacob,[2] son of Adam Brouwer,[1] born at Gowanus, married at Flatbush, Jan. 7, 1682, Anetje, dau. of William Bogardus, and Wyntie Sybrants. Their marriage also appears in the Dutch Church records of New York, under date Feb. 4, 1682. They had bap. in Brooklyn, Sybrant (?) ; Jacob,[3] Nov. 30, 1684 ; Willem, May 8, 1687 ; Everardus, Dec. 8, 1689 ; Elisabet, Nov. 15, 1694 ; Adam, March 29, 1696, and baptized in the Dutch Church in New York, Wyntje, Oct. 1, 1701, and Magdalena, March 8, 1704. Jacob,[3] bap. Nov. 30, 1684, son of Jacob Brouwer,[2] married Oct. 28, 1709, Pieternella De La Montagne, of New York, dau. of Jan de La Montagne and Annetie Josephs Waldron. They had *issue* ; Jacob, bap. in Brooklyn, Sept. 24. 1710, and the following bap. in New York : Johannes,[4] March 19, 1712 ; Abraham, Feb. 6, 1717 : Antje, March 13, 1720 ; Adam, Feb. 14, 1722, and Antje, March 30, 1726.

JOHANNES BROUWER,[4] bap. March 19, 1712, son of Jacob,[3] married Oct. 9, 1734. Susanna Deroillhet (Druljet), probably the dau. of Paulus and Susanna Druljet. (The latter was a widow Sept. 5, 1735.) The tradition in the Kip family is, that Susanna, wife of Johannes Brouwer,[4] was a French woman. They had bap. in New York the following named children : Susanna, bap. Sep. 5, 1735 ; Annetje, bap. Feb. 8, 1738 : Jacob, bap. March 26, 1740 ; Antje, bap. Nov. 7, 1742 ; Nelletje or Ellenor, born June 9, bap. June 12. 1745 ; m. Gerrit Kip, as noticed in the text ; and Johannes, bap. Dec. 2, 1747.

† PETER NAYLOR and Rachel Blank had *issue :*
1. Richard Naylor, born Feb. 8, 1799 ; died May 11, 1829, unmarried.
2. Peter Naylor, born Feb. 9, 1801 ; m. Dec. 23, 1823, Margaret N. Cormer, of New York.
3. Eliza Ann Naylor, born Nov. 4, 1803 ; died Feb. 2, 1807.
4. John Naylor, born Dec. 19, 1806 ; m. Jan. 6, 1829, Eliza Higbee.
5. Matilda Naylor, born June 17, 1809 ; died Dec. 24, 1812.
6. Alexander Naylor, born July 2, 1812 ; died March 10, 1813.
7. Elmira Naylor, born Nov. 28, 1814 ; m. Nov. 28, 1831, Jonathan Freeman Morgan, of New York.
8. Joseph Naylor, born Feb. 6, 1816 ; m. Aug. 10, 1836, Eliza Osborn.

sided nearly all his life in New York; he died in Brooklyn, March 20, 1857; she died in Brooklyn, Jan. 8, 1852. They had *issue:*

1. ELLEN LYNCH, born May 23, 1808; died Sept. 17, 1809.
2. RACHEL LYNCH, born April 17, 1810; died Aug. 27, 1811.
3. SARAH LYNCH, born March 8, 1812; m. June 25, 1831, William Simmons, of Mexico; she m. 2^d —— Palmer, and died Aug. 5, 1854.
4. JAMES LYNCH, born Dec. 23, 1813; m. Nov. 23, 1835, Olevia Ann Marsac, dau. of Michael and Rachael (Jennings) Marsac; she was born on Staten Island, Nov. 23, 1810; he died in 1864, at Governor's Island, while in the U. S. service. *Issue:* 1. Sarah Olevia, born Aug. 23, 1836; died Feb. 20, 1849; 2. Mary Frances, born Oct. 24, 1839; m. July 29, 1868, William H. son of Charles H. Close; 3. Eliza Cornelia, born Jan. 5, 1849; died May 30, 1849.
5. WASHINGTON LYNCH, born March 3, 1816; m. 1st June 4, 1838, Maria Davenport, of New York; m. 2^d ——, at St. Louis; he was killed by falling from the roof of a building at St. Louis, Mo., Jan. 19, 1861.
6. ANN ELIZA LYNCH, born March 23, 1818; m. June 12, 1839, Burdett E. P. Randolph, of Brooklyn, L. I.
7. MATILDA LYNCH, born Jan. 12, 1820; m. Feb. 28, 1839, Franklin Laughlin, of New York.
8. MARY VAN ANTWERP LYNCH, born Dec. 13, 1821; m. Sept. 3, 1839, Charles Hawley Close, son of Henry and Arney (Reynolds) Close; he was born August 5, 1819, at Stamford, Ct., but resided from his boyhood in New York City. He was prominently connected for thirty-five years with the drug trade in New York, and was for many years a member of the firm of M. Ward, Close & Co. He died in Brooklyn, Dec. 7, 1873. She resides, 1877, in New York. *Issue:* 1. Emma Louisa, born Aug. 2, 1840; m. Jan. 19, 1860, Charles Peter Schuyler, Broker, of New York, son of Philip M. Schuyler, of Boonville, Oneida Co., N. Y. He died in New York City, Oct. 10, 1874. They had *issue:* 1. Mary V. Schuyler, born in Harlem, N. Y., Dec. 23, 1861. 2. Arney Amelia, born July 21, 1842; m. May 13, 1863, Louis Franklin Georger, Furrier, of New York, son of Louis F. and Emily (Gunther) Georger. He was born in New York, April 26, 1841. They had *issue* (all born in New York): Francis Frederick Georger, born April 6, 1865; Arney Amelia Georger, born May 17, 1870; died March 14, 1871; and Julia Helene Georger, born July 25, 1872. 3. William Henry, born March 29, 1844; m. July 29, 1868, Mary Frances, dau. of James and Olevia Ann (Marsac) Lynch. They had *issue:* Harry Albert Close, born on Staten Island, July 12, 1869; died same place, Aug. 13, 1870; Louis Franklin Close, born in Brooklyn, June 8, 1871; and Emma Olevia Close, born in Brooklyn, Aug. 23, 1873. 4. Charles Augustus, born Feb. 4, 1846; m. Nov. 15, 1874, Lottie Marshall. They had *issue:* Edith Lottie Close, born on Staten Island, Oct. 2, 1876. 5. Mary Frances, born Dec.

26, 1847; m. Feb. 13, 1868, Edwin Ruthven Purple.*
Lawyer, of California, Arizona, Utah, Montana, and New
York, son of Lyman Smith and Minerva (Sheffield) Purple.
He was born in Sherburne, Chenango Co., N.Y., June 30,1831.
They had *issue* (all born in New York City) : Mary V. Pur-
ple, born April 9, 1869; died April 11, 1869; Mary Close
Purple, born May 30, 1870; Frances Minerva and Amelia
Georger Purple, twins, born Sept. 29, 1872 ; and Sarah Shef-
field Purple, born May 30, 1875; died July 5, 1876. 6.
James Wood, born Sept. 30, 1850; died Feb. 22, 1859. 7.
Walter McDougall, born July 19, 1852; m. March 17, 1874,
Matilda Marsac. They had *issue:* Mary V. Close, born in
New York, Feb. 10, 1875.

9. ELIZABETH LYNCH, born March 6, 1823 ; m. Nov. 12, 1843,
John Bishop, of Brooklyn ; she died Oct. 4, 1854.

10. ELIAS LYNCH, born May 26, 1827 ; he has been thrice married ; no further particulars.

11. MARGARET LYNCH, born Dec. 26, 1833; died Sept. 13, 1837.

58. ii. THOMAS HENDERSON,[7] born June 13, 1792 ; m. Jan. 12, 1817,
Ann Ross, and had *issue:* Abraham ;[8] Jane ;[8] Thomas ;[8] Mary ;[8] and
Sarah Ann.[8]

59. iii. SARAH,[7] born June 23, 1794; m. June 3, 1809, JOHN GALLA-
HER, and had *issue:* Margaret ; Abraham ; George ; Alexander ; William W. ; Rachel ; Sarah ; John ; Eliza ; Ruth ; Jane ; Peter ; and Al-
mira.

60. iv. JAMES,[7] born Nov. 23, 1796 ; died in 1819, unmarried.

---

* EDWARD PURPLE[1], the common ancestor of the family bearing his name in this country, was admitted
an inhabitant of the town of Haddam, Ct., in May, 1674. It is probable that he was a descendant of
Christopher Purple, who purchased land in Essex County, England, in 1580, and died there about 1605,
leaving a son Christopher, but the connection has not yet been clearly traced. It is supposed that the first
Christopher Purple was a native of France, from which country he fled to England at the time of the massacre of St. Bartholomew.

Edward Purple[1] was a Farmer, or as described in an old deed still extant, a Husbandman, and married,
1675, at Haddam, Hannah, daughter of Nicholas Ackley, one of the original proprietors of that town, and a
resident. 1638-39, of Hartford. He died at Haddam, Jan. 4, 1719-20, leaving his wife surviving and
three sons, Edward[2], John and Richard.

EDWARD PURPLE[2], born about 1676, died about 1727, married Mary ——, and had Edward[3] and
Mary, twins, born March 28, 1713 ; Elias, born March 27, 1716 ; and John, born June 14, 1718.

EDWARD PURPLE[3], born March 28, 1713. In early life he removed from Haddam to Middletown, Ct.,
where he married, 1740, Ruth Hollister, of Glastenbury. He was an active business man, and though com-
paratively young at the time of his decease, had accumulated a large amount of property, and was regarded
wealthy. He died in August, 1752, and his widow married, September 29, 1757, Nathaniel Spencer, of
Middletown. His children were Ruth, born August 1, 1741 ; Mary, born July 19, 1743 ; Edward[4], born
March 18, 1745 ; Dorothy, born May 9, 1747 ; Ezra, born January 18, 1749 ; Josiah, born Dec. 4, 1750.

EDWARD PURPLE[4], born March 18, 1745, a Farmer, married in 1768, Mary Hodge. He died August.
1794. His widow married, December 31, 1795, Stephen Knowlton. The children of Edward Purple and
Mary Hodge were Edward, born August 14, 1769 ; Polly, born May 25, 1771 ; Ansel[5], born 1773 ; Samuel,
born May 28, 1784 ; Ruth, baptized July 9, 1784 ; Deborah, born April 25, 1788 ; Statira, born 1790 ; Ann,
born March 30, 1793.

ANSEL PURPLE[5], born in Middle Haddam, Ct., 1773. He was a Farmer, and removed in 1797 to Whites-
town, N. Y., and subsequently to Otsego County, where he married, Feb. 19, 1798, Dolly, daughter of Dr.
Ephriam Smith and his wife Abigail Higgins. He died while on a visit to Middle Haddam, November
16, 1808. His widow married, October 5, 1809, Elisha Harris, and removed to Chenango Co., N. Y., and
afterwards to Cuyahoga Co., Ohio, where she died March 25, 1857. Their children were Lyman Smith[6],
born in Burlington, Otsego Co., N. Y., Jan. 19, 1799 ; Ansel, Lavina, and Elisha.

LYMAN SMITH PURPLE[6], born in Burlington, Jan. 19, 1799. Removed when young with his mother to
Chenango Co., N. Y., where he married, January 27, 1820, Minerva, daughter of Dr. James [Fones] Sheffield and his wife Sarah Calkins. She was born in Northumberland, Washington Co., N. Y., July 4, 1801,
and died in the City of New York March 27, 1868. He was a Tanner, Currier, and Shoemaker, and located
after his marriage in the town of Lebanon, Madison Co., N. Y., and a few years after removed to the town
of Sherburne, Chenango Co., N. Y. He was for many years Deacon of the Baptist Church in Earlville, N. Y.,
was a man of exemplary piety and singularly pure and upright in all the relations of life. He died at
Earlville, May 7, 1839. Their children were : 1, Samuel Smith, born in Lebanon, June 24, 1822, a Physician
for the past thirty-three years in the City of New York, and unmarried. 2, Ansel Sheffield, born in Lebanon,
Nov. 15, 1825, a Farmer, and after 1846 a resident of Troy, Bradford Co., Penn., where he married Sept.
3, 1846, Mary E., daughter of Aaron Baldwin and Harriet (Lawson) his wife. He died in the U. S. Volunteer Service at Bardstown, Ky., March 4, 1862. 3, Edwin Ruthven[7], born and married as noticed in
the text.

☞ On page 47, it is stated that the last mention found of HENDRICK KIP[1], SENIOR, is April 19, 1665. It is not improbable that he is the Hendrick Kip, Sen[r], whose name appears in a Tax List made in New York, on the 10th of November, 1676, for the purpose of defraying the charges in building the New Dock, and paying the city debts, etc. This List will be found on page 36, Vol. ii. of the N. Y. Genealogical and Biographical Record, to which the reader is referred.

On the same page the statement is made, that perhaps *Kippenburg* was identical with *Incleuburg*, or Fire Beacon Hill, near 36th Street and Fourth Avenue, at the period referred to. This part of the Island was called *Kipsborough* in 1746, which gives additional warrant for the belief that the *ancient Kippenburg* was in the vicinity of the old Kip farm, from which the name was probably derived. See extract from the N. Y. Weekly Post Boy, in Valentine's Manual for 1865, p. 795.

HENDRICK KIP, JR[2], noticed on page 56, made an affidavit, August 1, 1662, while on the Delaware, in which he says he was then "about 29 years old." This gives the date of his birth in Amsterdam about the year 1633. *See* Doc. Rel. to Colonial History of New York, Vol. 12, p. 401.

MEYER—MYER—MYERS—MEIR.

THE name of Meyers (or Myer) is a very ancient and common one both in Germany and Holland, and is supposed to take its derivation from *Meÿer*, a country Mayor, or Sheriff, sometimes, though rarely, translated Farmer ; *Meÿery*, a Manor, Mayoralty, or Lordship ; or, perhaps, from *Meir*, a lake. Its exact designation among the individuals here given, we have not more definitely attempted to trace. The orthography varies in the same family, but the most common form of the name as it appears in the records is MEYER and MVER. There were four persons,* early residents of New Amsterdam, who do not appear to have been related to each other, but from whom sprung four distinct lines of this family in New York. These were JILLIS (or GILLIS) PIETERSZEN [MEYER], JAN DIRCKSZEN MEYER, MARTEN JANSZEN MEYER, and ADOLF MEYER, whom we propose to notice briefly in the order of their names, as mentioned.

1. JILLIS (or GILLIS) PIETERSZEN [MEYER[1]], commonly called Jillis Pieterszen Van der Gouw, or Van der Gouda—the ancient town of Gouda, or Tergouw, in Holland, having been the place of his nativity— was a house-carpenter, and came to New Amsterdam prior to 1638, and probably as early as 1633, in company with Director General Van Twiller. On the 16th of April, 1639, then aged 27 years, in company with Jacob Stoffelsen and Tymen Janszen, he makes declaration as to the condition of the Fort, Church, Mills, and other public property, at the time of Governor Kieft's arrival in New Amsterdam.† On the 3[d] of June, 1638, he was appointed Master Carpenter at Fort Orange ‡ (Albany), but probably did not long reside there. He married at New Amsterdam, July 6, 1642, ELSJE HENDRICKS, born in Amsterdam, dau. of Hendrick Janszen Snyder —otherwise, Hendrick Janszen, the tailor—and his wife, Geertje Scheerburch. On the 25th of October, 1653, he obtained a patent for a house

---

* NICHOLAS MEYER, who m. in 1655, Lydia Van Dyck, was the ancestor of the DE MEYER family, of whom hereafter.
† Coll. New York Hist. Society, vol. 1 (New Series), p. 279.
‡ Cal. N. Y. Hist. MSS. Dutch, p. 62.

and lot in Beverwyck * (Albany), and perhaps lived there during the last years of his life. It does not appear that he was himself known by the name of Meyer, his children having adopted that as *their* family name, for reasons at present unascertained. His children were baptized in New Amsterdam, but probably all of them who reached years of maturity were married at Beverwyck. His residence in New Amsterdam, according to Mr. Valentine, was on the site of the present Wall Street, his house fronting the public road running along the East River, now Pearl Street. He deceased prior to 1656, and the following year his heirs sold the property above mentioned to the city, the lot then becoming a part of the public street, now Wall Street.† He owned another house and lot in Pearl Street, near the Fort, a two-thirds interest in which, owned by his heirs, Captain Hans Hendrickse and Johannes Wendel, of Albany, was conveyed by them, July 25, 1676, to his son, Hendrick Jillise Meyer; the other third part belonging to said Hendrick Jillise, " as his inheritance of the third part of all the effects of Gillis Pieterse, deceased, according to the will."‡ The division of this property, as above set forth, indicates that only three of his children survived him. *Issue :*

2. i. Eva Jillise Meyer[2], bap. April 26, 1643; m. Capt. Hans Hendrickse, an early resident and trader at Beverwyck. His descendants assumed the surname of Hansen. He made his will Feb. 12, 169¾, and was deceased in 1697, leaving the following named children : Hendrick; Margareta, m. Jan. 13, 1692, Frederick Harmense Visscher, of Albany, and died Aug. 30, 1701 ; Johannes, and Elsje.§

3. ii. Pieter Jillise Meyer[2], bap. Nov. 20, 1644 ; probably died young.

4. iii. Tryntje Jillise Meyer,[2] bap. April 22, 1647 ; died young.

5. iv. Tryntje Jillise Meyer,[2] bap. July 4, 1648 ; probably died young.

6. v. Hendrick Jillise Meyer,[2] bap. March 6, 1650. He joined the Dutch Church, in New York, Feb. 28, 1672 ; m., 1671, probably at Albany, Elsje Claes Roosevelt, dau. of Claes Martenszen Van Rosenvelt [Roosevelt] and his wife, Jannetje Samuels, or Thomas. (Both names are given in the baptismal record of their children.) She was bap. Feb. 11, 1652. In 1686 they resided in Pearl, near the present Whitehall Street, in New York. He was a cordwainer, and, in 1699–1700–1, an Assistant Alderman from the South Ward. In 1703 his family consisted of 1 male, 1 female, and 3 children. *Issue :*

    1. Elsje,[3] bap. Sept. 15, 1672 ; died young.

    2. Jannetie,[3] bap. Sept. 19, 1674 ; m. May 27, 1701, Abraham Provoost, from Albany. For a further account of this family, see vol. vi., page 20, of the N. Y. G. and B. Record.

    3. Elsje,[3] bap. March 12, 1677 ; m. Oct. 30, 1698, Bernardus Smith, from Bushwick, L. I., for many years a resident of New York. She was his first wife, and died in 1704 ; he m., second, June 30, 1705, Anna Colevelt, widow of Laurence Hedding.

* O'Callaghan's Hist. of New Netherland, vol. 2, p. 588.
† Valentine's History of New York, p. 119.
‡ Pearson's Early Records of Albany, p. 130.
§ Pearson's First Settlers of Albany, pp. 59–144.

4. MARRITIE,³ bap. June 25, 1679 ; m. April 21, 1700, HENDRICK
   VAN DER HEUL. See page 49.
5. RACHEL,³ bap. March 1, 1684.
6. CATHARINA,³ bap. June 13, 1686; m. Dec. 25, 1706, HAR-
   MANUS RUTGERS,* from Albany. He was a prominent
   brewer in New York city, and died there Aug. 9, 1753.
   His wife, Catharina Meyer, died Feb. 28, 1737. He m.,
   second, at Hackensack, N. J., Sept. 17, 1739, Margaret De
   Foreest, whom he survived, and by whom had no issue.
7. HENDRICK,³ bap. Nov. 4, 1688. (Perhaps the Hendrick
   Meyer who m. at Hackensack, N. J., June 24, 1716, Elsie
   de Vouw.) (?)
8. JOHANNES,³ bap. May 15, 1692. (No further account.)
   7. vi. MARIA JILLISE MEYER,² bap. Jan. 21, 1652 ; m. Capt. JOHANNES
WENDELL, of Albany. (See Pearson's First Settlers of Albany, p. 148, and
Genealogy of the Brattle Family, p. 39.)

---

1. JAN DIRCKSZEN MEYER and his wife, TRYNTJE ANDRIESSE GREVEN-
RAET, were residing in New Amsterdam prior to 1652, but the time of their
arrival here is unknown. Their names are recorded in the list of Old
Members of the Dutch Church, many of whom, it is certain, were settled
here before 1649. There is reason to believe that he was by trade a *Painter*, and that he is the Jan Dirckszen who was admitted to the rights of a
small burgher April 14, 1657. Mr. Valentine estimates his wealth, at the
final cession of New York to the English in 1674, at $2,000. He then
resided in the present Bridge Street, but in 1686 was living in Stone Street,
between Whitehall and Broad. Tryntje or Catharine Grevenraet, his first
wife, was, as her name indicates, the daughter of Andries, and probably a
sister of Isaac, Metje † and Lysbeth Grevenraet, the latter of whom was the

* He was a grandson of Ruth Jacobszen, *alias* Rut Van Woert, of Rensselaerswyck, and his wife, Tryntje Janse Van Breestede, and the son of Harmen Rutgers, of Albany, and his wife, Catharina, dau. of Anthony de Hooges. His father and mother removed from Albany to New York, and joined the Dutch Church in the latter place, Sept. 3, 1696. Pearson says Harmen, the elder, was still living in 1720. HARMANUS RUT-GERS and CATHARINA MEYER³ had *issue:*
1. HARMANUS RUTGERS, bap. May 2, 1708; m. June 7, 1729, ELIZABETH, dau. of Robert and Cornelia (ROOS) BENSON. She was bap. Nov. 24, 1708. They had the following named children baptized in the Dutch Church, in New York: 1. Harmanus, bap. April 5, 1730; 2. Robert, bap. July 4, 1731; 3. Harmanus bap. Oct. 8, 1732; 4. Antony, bap. Jan. 20, 1734; 5. Cornelia, bap. Oct. 31, 1736; 6. Catharina, bap. June 2, 1738; 7. Margarita, bap. Feb. 13, 1740; 8. Maria, bap. Sept. 13, 1741; and 9. Hendrick, bap. May, 23, 1743.
2. ELSJE RUTGERS, bap. Feb. 1, 1710; m. Jan. 27, 1731, JOHN MARSHALL, and had baptized in the Dutch Church, in New York: 1. Anna Maria, bap. Oct. 6, 1731; 2. Harmanus, bap. March 14, 1739; 3. Edward, bap. April 29, 1741; and 4. John, bap. June 22, 1743.
3. HENDRIK RUTGERS, bap. Feb. 24, 1712; m. Jan. 29, 1732, CATHARINA, dau. of Capt. Johannes and Anna (Bancker) DE PEYSTER. She was bap. July 22, 1711. They had the following named children bap-tized in the Dutch Church, in New York: 1. Catharina, hap. Oct. 8, 1732; 2. Johannes, bap. Jan. 1, 1735; 3. Anna, bap. Jan. 9, 1737; 4. Harmanus, bap. Oct. 22, 1738; 5. Elizabeth, bap. Jan. 17, 1742; 6. Har-manus, bap. Nov. 27, 1743; 7. Hendrik, bap. Oct. 20, 1745; 8. Maria, bap. Nov. 1, 1747; and 9. Har-manus, bap. Oct. 4, 1749.
4. CATHARINA RUTGERS, bap. Feb. 21, 1714; m. Dec. 27, 1729, ABRAHAM, son of John and Catharina (Meyer) VAN HORNE. He was bap. Oct. 31, 1708. They had the following named children baptized in the Dutch Church, in New York: 1. Catharina, bap. May 14, 1732; 2. Abraham, bap. Jan. 9, 1737; 4. Margareta, bap. Oct. 3, 1739; 4. Elizabeth, bap. April 28, 1742; 5. Jacobus, bap. April 21, 1745; 6. Her-man, bap. Sept. 27, 1747; and 7. Eva, bap. March 4, 1750.
5. MARIA RUTGERS, bap. April 11, 1716; died young.
6. ANTHONY RUTGERS, bap. June 8, 1718; died young.
7. EVA RUTGERS, bap. Aug. 30, 1719; m. about 1741, JOHN, son of Samuel and Maria (Spratt) PROVOOST. See N. Y. G. AND B. RECORD, vol. VI., p. 17.
8. JOHANNES RUTGERS, bap. Feb. 11, 1722; died young.

† METJE GREVENRAET, a widow as early as 1664, and who then occupied a small house on the east side of Whitehall, north of Stone Street, is said by Mr. Valentine to have been the mother of Isaac Grevenraet, named in the text, to whom she bequeathed considerable real estate in this city. There is reason to doubt this rela-tionship. In the list of Old Members of the Dutch Church her name is entered Metje Andries, which seems

ancestress of the De Riemer family of New York, but perhaps better known in her day as "Mother Drisius." *Gestorven* is written opposite Tryntje Grevenraet's name in the Church Members' book, but no clue is given to the time of her decease. The last notice found of her is on Dec. 31, 1664, at which date she was sponsor at the baptism of Dirckje, dau. of Jan Dircks-zen (Van Aernam). He married second, Dec. 12, 1677, Baertje, dau. of Hendrick Kip, Sen., and widow of Jan Wanshaer, by whom he had no issue. He was living Feb. 24, 1689, but had deceased before June 12, 1700. He had 3 sons and 3 daughters; the eldest son and daughter were born in Amsterdam, of which city both parents were probably natives. *Issue:*

2. i. ANDRIES,[2] born in Amsterdam; joined the Dutch Church in New York Aug. 4, 1669. His name appears sometimes in the records Andries Janszen. In 1674 he resided near his father in Bridge Street, and followed the trade of house-carpenter. He married, Nov. 5, 1671, VROUWTJE IDEN VAN DER VORST or VAN VORST, dau. of Ide Corneliszen Van Vorst and Hilletje Jans. She was bap. Aug. 24, 1653, and joined the Dutch Church in New York July 28, 1670. Her father resided at Ahasimus, now within the corporate limits of Jersey City, and is said to have been the first white male child *born and married* in New Netherland.* They had *issue* bap. in the Dutch Church in New York: 1. Catryntie,[3] bap. Sept. 8, 1672; m. March 20, 1693, JOHANNES, son of Cornelis Janszen and Anna Maria (Jans), VAN HORNE. 2. Annetie,[3] bap. Feb. 21, 1677; m. July 29, 1702, JAMES SEBREN [CEBRA?]. 3. Aefje,[3] bap. June 4, 1679. 4. Johannes,[3] bap. May 14, 1681; m. Sept. 22, 1704, SARA, dau. of Isaac and Lysbeth (Van der Spiegel, DE FOREEST; she was bap. March 10, 1686. They had 12 children bap. in the Dutch Church in New York. 5. Andries,[3] bap. Nov. 24, 1686; m. Feb. 23, 1708, GEERTIE WESSELS, dau. of Laurens Wessels and Aeltje Jans Hendrickse Van Bommel, *alias* Aeltje Splinters. ANDRIES MEYER[3] was a Cordwainer in New York, and died early in the spring of 1767, leaving his wife Geertie surviving, and naming in his will only beside her his eldest son Andries. They had 10 children bap. in the Dutch Church in New York. 6. Cornelis,[3] bap. April 12, 1689, of whom we have no further account. It is probable that ANDRIES MEYER[2] and his wife Vroutje Van Vorst had beside the children above named the follow-ing, viz.: 1. Hillegond,[3] who m. July 12, 1696, JOHANNES HARDENBURG, who settled in New York from Albany; 2. Elsje,[3] who m. Feb. 3, 1704, EVERT DUYCKINCK; and 3. Ide,[3] born about 1674; m. Oct. 25, 1704, ANNATJE, dau. of Claes Gerritszen RAVESTEYN or RAVENSTEIN and Maria Jans Van Rollegom; she was bap. June 3, 1687. They had 10 children bap. in the Dutch Church in New York.

---

to have been one of the family names of the Grevenraets. In Dominie Selyn's list of the Members of the Church in 1686 her name appears as Metje Grevenraet, the widow of Anthony Jansen. Their children, if any they had, would, according to the Dutch rule, have borne the family name of Antonissen. A Dutch woman usually retained after marriage, and even in her widowhood, her maiden name, which, of course, dif-fered from that of her children. Hence, in the absence of proof, we deem it more likely that Metje Greven-raet was the sister rather than that she was the mother of Isaac Grevenraet.

* Valentine's *Manual*, 1862, p. 768. A correction of this statement, as well as the one that Sara Rapalje was the first child of European parents born in the Colony of New Netherland, will be found in Dankers and Sluyter's Journal in the *Memoirs of the Long Island Historical Society*, Vol. I., p. 114. From the state-ment there made it appears that to Jean Vigne (also written Vinge) belongs the honor, so long accorded to Sara Rapalje, of being the *first white child* born in New Netherland, and claimed by Mr. Valentine for Ide Corneliszen Van Vorst as the *first white male child* born and married in the Colony. The marriage of Jean Vigne to his first wife, Emmerentia Van Nieuwerzluys, antedates the earliest records of the Dutch Church of New Amsterdam. He married his second wife, Weiske Huytes (Niesje Huytes), widow of Andries Andries-zen, in Brooklyn, in the spring of 1682 (date of betrothal in New York Feb. 15, 1682), and died, it is supposed, without issue, in 1691, aged 77 years. Gosen Vinge joined the Dutch Church in New York Sept. 4, 1673. What relation, if any, he was to Jean Vinge is unknown.

3. ii. DIRCKJE,[2] born in Amsterdam; sometimes called DIRCKJE JANS; joined the Dutch Church in New York January, 1660; m. June 3, 1670 (the Bergen Church record says June 20, 1670), ENOCH MICHIELSZEN [VREELAND], son of Michiel Janszen * and Fytie Hermans. His name appears indifferently in the records as Enoch Michielszen and Enoch Vreeland. He was probably that child of Michiel Janszen whose name at the baptism, Oct. 24, 1649, has been omitted from the record. They lived in Bergen, N. J. She died Oct. 5, 1688; he m. second, Sept. 16, 1691, GRIETIE WESSELS,† widow of Jan Janszen Langedyck, by whom he had no issue; she died Nov. 20, 1697; he m. third, Jan. 13, 1704, AEFJE, dau. of Joris Janszen and Maria (Rutgers) VAN HORNE; she was bap. March 16, 1680. He died Aug. 17, 1714.‡ He had issue by his first wife five sons and three daughters, bap. in New York, as follows:

1. ELSJE VREELAND, bap. Nov. 12, 1671; m. Feb. 13, 1688, EDWARD EARLE, young man from Maryland, who settled at Secaucus, N. J., in 1676. Will dated May 16, 1709, proved May 8, 1717.§ They had bap. in the First Ref. (Dutch) Church in Hackensack, N. J.: 1. Marmeduke, bap. —— —, 1696; m. —— De Maree; 2. Willem, bap. Oct. 13, 1700; m. at Hackensack, June 14, 1723, Maria Frans (French); 3. Elsje, bap. Dec. 7, 1701; m. at Hackensack, May 24, 1728, George Simmons, from Philadelphia; 4. Philippus, bap. June 10, 1703; 5. Jammesyn (?), bap. March 18, 1705; 6. Silvester, bap. Aug. 10, 1707; m. Magtel Zabriskie; 7. Tiodora, bap. April 10, 1709; 8. Nataniel, bap. Nov. 26, 1710; m. at Hackensack, Aug. 19, 1737, Fransintje Banta. The record of the Ref. Church in Bergen, N. J., gives the name and date of birth of some of Edward and Elsje (Vreeland) Earle's children as follows: 1. Edward, bap. April 22, 1690; m. Elizabeth Frans, and had bap. at Hackensack Edward, April 11, 1720, and Jan, June 15, 1723; 2. (Son), born May 28, 1692. (This was probably Enoch Earle, who m. a De Maree, by whom he had Anna and Mary, bap. at Hackensack, June 15, 1723); 3. Hannah, born March 26, 1695; 4. Maanedirck (Marmaduke), born Oct. 6, 1696; 5. Johannis, born Sept. 8, 1698; 6. (Son), born May 1, 1703 (prob. Philip); 7. (Daughter), born Oct. —, 1704.‖

2. CATHARINA VREELAND, bap. May 15, 1673; m. May 27, 1692, AERT ELBERTSZEN. (In the Bergen Church record this name is *Aert Albertse*, and the date of marriage June 26, 1692.) They had bap. in the Dutch Church in New York: 1. Dirckje, bap. Nov. 5, 1692; 2. Elbert, bap. Dec. 17, 1693; 3. Enoch, bap. July 14, 1695; 4. Johannes, bap. March 27, 1698; 5. Abraham, bap. April 28, 1700; 6. Wessel, bap. Jan. 28, 1702; 7. Benjamin, bap. Sept. 12, 1703; and 8. Benjamin, bap. June 2, 1705.

---

* MICHIEL JANSZEN, the common ancestor of the VREELAND family in this country, came from Broeckhuysen, and left Holland Oct. 1, 1636, in the ship Reosselaerwyck, with his wife and two children. He was a *boereknecht*, or farm servant, and settled at first at Greenbush, opposite Albany. He became a resident of New Amsterdam about 1644. His own and wife's name appear in the list of Old Members of the Dutch Church there. In 1646 they removed to Communipaw (N. J.). He died in 1663. His wife died Sept. 21, 1697. For a further account of them and their children *see* Winfield's History of Hudson County, N. J., p. 439.

† GRIETIE WESSELS was probably the dau. of Wessel Evertszen and Geertie Boute, bap. March 28, 1644, her father's name being entered at the baptism *Wessel Kever* (?). She married first, Aug. 15, 1666, Elbert Aertsen, and joined with him the Dutch Church in New York Nov. 4, 1670. They had two sons, Arent, bap. June 19, 1667, and Wessel, bap. April 7, 1669. She m. second, April 28, 1672, Jan Janszen [Langedyck], from St. Martin, in Holland, by whom she had no issue bap. in the Dutch Church in New York.

‡ For a fuller account of him and his descendants, particularly of his son Joris Vreeland, born Sept. 25, 1710, and bap. in the Church at Bergen, *see* Winfield's History of Hudson Co., N. J., pp. 443-45.

§ Winfield's Land Titles in Hudson Co.. N. J., pp. 130-31.

‖ Winfield's Land Titles in Hudson Co'., N. J., p. 366.

3. MICHIEL VREELAND, bap. Jan. 27, 1675 ; died unmarried.   He was *non compos mentis.**

4. JOHANNES VREELAND, bap. April 7, 1677 ; m. June 8, 1701, *Maria Beger*, so says the marriage record.   The right name, however, is MARIA CREGIER ; she was the dau. of Ma tin Cregier, Jr., of Albany, and his wife Jannetje Hendrickse Van Doesburgh.† They had bap. in the Dutch Church in New York.   1. Maria, bap. Nov. 29, 1702 ; 2. Catharina, bap. Nov. 19, 1704 ; 3. Enoch, bap. Jan. 22, 1707 ; and 4. Martinus, bap. April 3, 1709.

5. ABRAHAM VREELAND, bap. June 22, 1678 ; m. at Bergen, Oct. 28, 1699, MARGRIETJE JACOBSE VAN WINCKEL.

6. FYTIE VREELAND, bap. Feb. 28, 1680 ; m. PERIGRINE SANDFORD, son of Capt. William and Sarah (Whartman) Sandford, of New Barbadoes, N. J.

7. ISAAC VREELAND, bap. Jan. 14, 1683 ; m. at Hackensack, March 23, 1706, TRINTIE SIMESE VAN WINCKEL.   Mr. Winfield gives this name *Tryntje Newkirk*, with date of marriage as above.   Isaac and Trintie Simese (Van Winckel) Vreeland had two children bap. in the Church at Hackensack, viz., Simon, bap. June 5, 1709, and Annetie, bap. March 18, 1712.

8. ENOCH VREELAND, bap. Aug. 4, 1687 ; m. Oct. 22, 1709, MARIA ST. LEGER, widow, nee Van Horne.   She was probably the dau. of Cornelis Janszen and Anna Maria (Jans) VAN HORNE ; she was bap. July 23, 1681. Enoch and Maria (Van Horne) Vreeland had *issue* bap. in the Dutch Church in New York :   1. Enoch, bap. Oct. 4, 1710 ; 2. Cornelus, bap. Jan. 28, 1713 ; and 3. Efje, bap. Aug. 12, 1722.

ENOCH MICHIELSE VREELAND and AEFJE JORIS VAN HORNE, his third wife, had four children bap. in the Dutch Church in New York, as given below, his name appearing in the baptismal record as *Enoch Michielse*, *Enoch Michielse Vrelant*, and *Enoch Vrelant, Sen.*   The youngest son, Benjamin, must have been over three years old at the time of his baptism, as that event took place long after the death of his father.

9. JACOB VREELAND, bap. March 28, 1705.

10. HELENA VREELAND, bap. Jan. 14, 1713.

11. ELIAS VREELAND, bap. March 4, 1715.

12. BENJAMIN VREELAND, bap. December 11, 1717.

4. iii. JOHANNES², bap. Feb. 25, 1652 ; frequently called Jan Janszen Meyer, and by trade a carpenter ; joined the Church in New York, August 4, 1669 ; m. June 13, 1677, ANNETJE VAN VORST, sister of his brother Andrie's wife.   In 1686, they were living in Smit Straat, now William, below Wall Street.   About 1694, he removed to Tappan, where his two youngest children were born and baptized.‡ They had *issue* bap. in New York.   1. Jan,³ bap. March 27, 1678 ; 2. Catharina,³ bap. Feb. 4, 1680 ; 3. Iden,³ bap. Jan. 27, 1682 ; 4 and 5, Johannes³ and Judith,³ twins, bap. May 11, 1684 ; 6. Ide,³ bap. Jan. 16, 1687 ; 7 and 8. Hillegond³ and Dirckje,³ twins, bap. Aug. 30, 1689 ; 9 and 10. Cornelis³ and Annetje,³ twins, bap. June 12, 1692 ; 11. Elizabeth,³ bap. at Tappan, June 1, 1695 ; 12. Andries,³ bap. at T., Oct. 14, 1697.§   For a further account of this

---

* Winfield's History of Hudson Co., p. 445.
† Pearson's First Settlers of Albany, p. 35.
‡ Cole, *Genealogy*, pp. 32–33.
§ Idem.

family, *see* Cole, *Genealogy*, or "Isaac Kool (Cool or Cole) and Catharine Serven, &c., their descendants, &c., by Rev. David Cole, D.D.," New York, 1876, pp. 32–33.

5. iv. LYSBETH,[2] bap. Jan. 31, 1655 ; m. Dec. 29, 1678, ELIAS CORNE-LISZEN, from New Castle on the Delaware, then living in New York. They had two sons baptized in New York, viz., Cornelis, bap. Sep. 3, 1679, and Johannes, bap. Jan. 14, 1682, of whom and their parents we have no further account.

6. v. PIETER,[2] bap. March 25, 1657; m. Jan. 16, 1678, BATJE [*Betty, or Elizabeth*] JANS, *Van Haert in Gelderland.* She joined the Dutch Church in New York, Feb. 26, 1673, while it appears he was never a member. In 1686 they were living in Marketfield Street. In 1703, his family consisted of one male, one female, and five children.* He had *issue* bap. in the Dutch Church in New York : 1. Catharina,[3] bap. Nov. 8, 1678 ; m. August 9, 1696, ZACHARIAS WEEKS, from New England. 2. Marritie,[3] bap. Jan. 20, 1680 ; died young. 3. Cornelia,[3] bap. Oct. 6, 1681 ; died young. 4. Cornelia,[3] bap. Dec. 10, 1682 ; she is probably the Cornelia Meyer who m. April 23, 1704, CORNELUS TIMMER or TIMBER, who was prob. son of Wydt Cornelis Timmer and Jannetje Joris Van Alst. She became a widow, and married second, Jan. 17, 1718, MICHIEL BASSETT, and was again a widow the same year. She had no children by either husband bap. in the Dutch Church in New York. 5. Maryken,[3] [Maria] bap. Feb. 13, 1687 ; m. June 15, 1707, DR. JOHANNES VAN BUREN,† from Amsterdam. 6. Lysbeth,[3] bap. Sept. 28, 1690 ; m. 1711,

* Valentine's History of New York, p. 356.

† DR. JAN or JOHANNES VAN BEUREN, said to have been born about 1678 (N. Y. G. & B. RECORD, vol. vii., p. 46), was a native of Amsterdam, a graduate of the University of Leyden, and came to New York in 1700. About 1724, he removed with his family from New York to Flatbush, L. I. In 1728-9, he returned to New York, where he probably continued to reside until his death. He was living July 31, 1751, but deceased prior to Oct. 16, 1757, leaving his wife and at least five of his children surviving him. His name appears in the records of the Ref. Dutch Church in New York, indifferently as Van Buren, Van Beuren, Van Bueren, and Van Büüren. His descendants, we believe, now spell the name VAN BEUREN, in contradistinction to the VAN BUREN family of the Upper Hudson, of whom Cornelis Maas Van Buren was the ancestor. It is to be questioned, however, whether this orthography obtains among all his descendants. He had *issue* bap. in the Dutch Church in New York as follows :

1. PIETER VAN BEUREN, bap. Sept. 18, 1709 ; died young.
2. CHRISTINA VAN BEUREN, bap. March 2, 1711 ; died young.
3. PIETER VAN BEUREN, }
4. MARIA VAN BEUREN,   } twins, bap. Jan. 21, 1713.
5. MICHIEL VAN BEUREN, bap. Jan. 26, 1715 ; died young.
6. CORNELIA VAN BEUREN, }
7. ELIZABETH VAN BEUREN, } twins, bap. Jan. 30, 1717.
8. CATHARINA VAN BEUREN, bap. Aug. 31, 1718 ; m. at Flatbush, Aug. 3, 1743, GERRIT DE GRAUW, and had bap. in the Dutch Church in New York. 1. Johannes, bap. June 21, 1747 . 2. Walter, bap. June 22, 1749, and 3. Maria, bap. July 31, 1751.
9. ELIZABETH VAN BEUREN, bap. Feb. 1, 1721 ; m. August 6, 1746, DR. ENGELBERT KEMMENA, sometimes written *Kammega* and *Cammena.* There were several of this name at Hackensack, N. J., in the early part of the last century, probably descendants of Hendrick Janszen Cammega, of Flatbush, 1686 8, but I have been unable to trace any connection between them and the Doctor, and probably there was none. These were Henry Kammega, who m. at H. Feb. 9, 1717, Margariet Mattyse ; Johannes Kammega, of New Utrecht, L. I., who m. at H., Jan. 19, 1723, Vroutie Jonkbloet, widow ; Daniel Cammena, from Long Island, who m. at H., Aug. 29, 1735, Geesje Loots ; and Abraham Cammega and wife, Lija Maris, who had dau. Maria bap. at H., April 10, 1726. DR. ENGELBERT KEMMENA, was naturalized in 1750, and admitted a Freeman of the city of New York in 1765, being then engaged and for some years previously in practice there as a Surgeon. On the 3d of July, 1775, he endorsed the application of John Hammell for appointment as Surgeon in the Provincial Army, certifying that said Hammell had studied Physic and Surgery with him "full seven years," and recommending him as a proper person capable of practising the healing art. (Val. Manuel, 1856, Hist. MSS. Rev. Papers 1-109.) He sold a lot of ground in "Market Street, formerly called Maiden Lane," on the 9th Sept. 1794, to Wm. Wilmerding, merchant, and was then a "Practitioner of Physic" in the city. This is the last notice found of him, and he probably died soon after, having survived his wife some years. He had no children bap. in the Dutch Church in New York.
10. MICHIEL VAN BEUREN, bap. Jan. 1, 1723. He was a Cordwainer in the city of New York, and admitted a Freeman of the city in 1765. His wife's name was JANNETJE HENDRICKS. They had bap. in the Dutch Church in New York : 1. Johannes, bap. May 19. 1757 ; 2. Elizabeth, bap. Jan. 31, 1759 ; 3. Johannes, bap. Dec. 17, 1760 ; 4. Daniel, bap. Nov. 10, 1762 ; 5. Elizabeth, bap. Sept. 16, 1764 ; 6. Beekman, bap. Aug. 31, 1766 ; 7. Michiel, bap. Sept. 15, 1770 ; and 8. Elizabeth, bap. Sept. 22, 1772.

ANTHONY HAM, of New York. They had 10 children bap. in the Dutch Church in New York. 7. Barentje,[3] bap. Oct. 26, 1692. 8. Johannes,[3] bap. Feb 4, 1694; m. May 27, 1719, ELIZABETH, dau. of William and Elizabeth (Van Thuyl) PELL; she was bap. Sept. 1, 1700. They had 11 children bap. in the Dutch Church in New York.

7. vi. ELSJE, bap. Feb. 25, 1663; no further account.

---

1. MARTIN JANSZEN MEYER,[1] Van Elsvliet, married in New Amsterdam. Oct. 28, 1662, HENDRICKJE HERMANS from Amsterdam. Their marriage is also recorded in the Brooklyn Church Records under date of Nov. 19, 1662. It is not improbable that he is identical with the Martin Janszen, also called Martin Janszen Van Breuckelen, who was a resident of Amersfort, L. I., as early as 1653, and a magistrate there in 1656-7, and 1658. He followed the occupation of Blacksmith, and his name frequently appears in the records as Martin Janszen Smit, and sometimes Martin Meyer Smith; at the baptism of his youngest dau., Helena, it is recorded Martin Smidt. It appears that neither he nor his wife were members of the Dutch Church of New Amsterdam.* On the 17th July, 1664, he obtained a patent for a lot, garden, and orchard in Smith's valley, then without the city limits, and in the vicinity of the present Pearl, north of Wall Street. This was in exchange for his former premises, situated under the city fortifications, which, with a number of others was—in order to strengthen the city defenses—ordered to be demolished, by an ordinance passed Oct. 16, 1673. On the 22d November, 1683, he and his wife conveyed a portion of this property to George Heathcote,† and December 17, 1685, a city commission of four persons was ordered to examine the grounds and report "what incon-

---

11. JACOBUS VAN BEUREN,
12. CHRISTINA VAN BEUREN, } twins, bap. August 3, 1729.

13. BEEKMAN VAN BEUREN, bap. Nov. 5, 1732. Adopting the profession of his father, he settled in New York, where he was engaged in the practice of Physic until the beginning of the Revolutionary War. Dr. Francis says that "strong opposition was met in those days to the adoption of inoculation for the small-pox, as pursued by Dr. Van Beuren in the Old Alms House, prior to 1770." He m. First, April 12, 1754, HYLTJE DE PEYSTER, dau. of William and Margaret (Roosevelt) de Peyster, by whom he had one dau., Margaret, bap. Sept. 12, 1755. He m. Second, Dec. 25, 1756, ELIZABET GILBERT, dau. of William and Maria (Van Zandt) Gilbert. They had bap. in the Dutch Church in New York: 2. Johannes, bap. Oct. 16, 1757; 3. William, bap. Nov. 22, 1758; died young; 4. Maria, bap. Jan. 27, 1760; died young; 5. Maria, bap. April 29, 1764; 6. Beekman, bap. Feb. 9, 1766, 7. William, bap. Nov. 15, 1767; 8. Hendrikus, bap. July 30, 1769; 9. Catharina, bap. Aug. 4, 1771; died young; and 10. Catharina, bap. Feb. 14, 1773.

DR. JOHANNES VAN BEUREN, and his wife, Maria Meyer,[2] had besides the thirteen children above named, two sons, viz., JAN VAN BEUREN, JR., who m. Femetie ———. and had bap. at New Utrecht, L. I., Maria, bap. May 18, 1729, and Jan, bap. Nov. 7, 1730, and probably others; and DR. HENDRICK VAN BEUREN, born at Flatbush, Nov. 12, 1725; who m. First, at Flatbush, Nov. 28, 1747, Johanna Albertsen, dau. of Johannes Albertse, of Bushwick, L. I. He m. Second, Catryntie Van Voorhees, by whom he had son Johannes, bap. at Flatbush, July 21, 1754, and probably others. He was engaged in the practice of Physic and Surgery at Flatbush as early as 1754, and was a noted Loyalist in Kings County during the Revolutionary War.

* The number of persons who were not church members, was always large in proportion to the number of the residents of the city. In 1686, the population of New York was about 3,800, the majority of whom were of course Dutch, or of Dutch descent, while there were only 354 men and women, and 702 children belonging to the Dutch Church at that time. (*Olden Time in New York, &c, New York,* 1833, *p.* 45.) The whole number of communicants received in the church from 1649, to Feb. 1701 inclusive, was 1812.

† GEORGE HEATHCOTE came from the parish of Stepney, County of Middlesex, England. He was a Merchant and Shipmaster, in which latter capacity he was engaged in the English and West India trade from New York, as early as 1674-5. In August, 1676, he purchased a lot in Albany, which Professor Pearson says was probably held by him for the purpose of occasional trade, till 1684, when he sold it to Robert Sanders. In Oct., 1676, he was fined and his liberty to trade restricted, for alleged seditious words, and declaring he had not the privileges of an Englishman, &c. This fine was afterwards returned, and he was allowed to trade freely, though he had much trouble with the authorities, who charged him with frequent violation of the revenue laws. After 1692, he removed to Fall's Township, Bucks County, Pennsylvania, where he died in Nov., 1710. In this will he speaks of his two grandchildren, "the children of John Barber, in London, which he had by my daughter, Deceased;" also of his two sisters, Hannah Browne and Anna Lupton. Bequeaths a portion of his estate to his cousin, Caleb Heathcote, of the province of New York, who is appointed executor of the will.

veniency or convenience the laying out of a street through the same "
would cause to said Heathcote and Meyer.*

MARTIN JANSE MEYER and his wife Hendrickje, made a joint will dated
in New York, March 16, 169¾, at the probate of which, Aug. 17, 1714,
the fact is recited, "that Martin Meyer dying first some years ago, the said
Hendrickje is also lately dec^d." The children named in their will are, Johannes Meyer, eldest son and heir ; Hartman [Hermanus] ; Martin ; Elsie
Meyer married with Burger Myndertz ; Belitje Meyer married with Claas
Gysbertsz ; Helena married with Eduard Cock ; Catharina and Anna
Meyer "*ongetrout.*" It is probable that they resided during a portion of
their married life out of New York, as there is no record here of the bap-
tism of three of their children. *Issue :*

2. i. ELSJE², bap. June 10, 1663 ; m. BURGER MYNDERTSZEN, who in
1702, was a Blacksmith in New York. He was probably the son of Myndert Frederickse, one of the early settlers of Beverwyck, who came from
Iveren, and married in New Amsterdam, Aug. 5, 1656, Catharyn Burcharts
[Burger] of the latter place. "The unsettled condition," says Prof. Pearson, "of the early Dutch family names, is well shown by the descendants
of Myndert Frederickse ; some took the surname of *Myndertse,* his Christian name ; whilst others took that of *Van Iveren,* the place from whence
he came in Holland." Burger Myndertszen was born in 1660,† but the
place and date of his marriage are unknown. He probably had, besides
other children not traced, one son, *Martin Van Iveren,* who m. Feb. 1,
1718, Judith Holmes, and had son Burger, bap. Nov. 13, 1718, in the
Dutch Church in New York.

3. ii. BELITJE², bap. Feb. 22, 1665, m. CLAAS GYSBERTSZEN, of whom
we have no notice except that in his father-in-law's will.

4. iii. JAN,² bap. June 12, 1657. This is probably the JAN or JOHANNES
MEYER, of New York, who m. at Hackensack, N. J., Aug. 22, 1696, JAN-
NETIE CORNELISE BANTA, of the latter place. They had a son Martin,³
bap. at H. Feb. 25, 1700, and probably others.

5. iv. ANNETIE,² bap. Aug. 29, 1668 ; unmarried in March, 1693, the
date of her father's will. There was an Anna Meyer—perhaps the same—
wife of Samuel Lee, who had son Samuel, bap. Feb. 3, 1714, in the Dutch
Church in New York.

6. v. HELENA,² bap. Dec. 23, 1674, m. Oct. 12, 1692, EDWARD KOCX
(Cock), of whom we have no further account.

7. vi. HARTMAN² (HERMANUS), named in his father's will, was admitted
a Freeman‡ of the city of New York in 1698. He m. March 6, 1702,
HELENA, dau. of Elias and Marritie (Cornelis) POST. She was bap. Sept.
29, 1680. They had bap. in the Dutch Church in New York : 1. Maria,³
bap. Oct. 4, 1702 ; 2. Martinus,³ bap. March 8, 1704 ; 3. Martinus,³ bap.

* Cal. N. V. Hist. MSS. English, pp. 30–143.
† Pearson's First Settlers of Albany, p. 82.
‡ The Mayor, Aldermen, and Commonalty of the City of New York, in their petition Nov. 9, 1683, to
Gov. Dongan for a charter, enumerated among other ancient municipal customs, privileges, &c., that
"None were to be esteemed Freemen of the Citty but who were admitted by ye Magistrates afores'd [May-
or and Aldermen], and none before such admission to sell by retayle, or exercise any handycraft, trade or
occupation, and every merch't or shop-keeper was to pay ffor ye publick use of ye Citty £3-12s, every
handycraft £1-4s, on being made ffree."
"No freeman of ye Citty was to be arrested, or have their goods attached, unless it was made to appear
that they were departing or conveying away their estates to defraud their credit'rs."
"No person was admitted to trade up hudson's River except he was a Freeman, and had been an arrivall
inhabitant in the Citty ffor ye space of 3 years, and if any ffreeman should be absent out of ye Citty ye space
of 12 months, and not keep ffire and candle, and pay scott and lott should loose his ffreedom."—Valentine's
Manual for 1844-5, p. 312.

Feb. 18, 1711 ; and 4. Hermanus,[3] bap. Feb. 17, 1714. He died in 1714, and his widow, Helena Post, m. second, July 1, 1715, GERRIT BRAS, of New York, by whom she had 3 sons and 4 daus., bap. in the Dutch Church in New York.

8. vii. MARTIN[2] (MARTINUS), mentioned in his father's will ; m. May 28, 1705, EMMETJE, dau. of Jacobus Franszen and Magdaleen (Cornelis) VAN DYCK. She was bap. Oct. 17, 1686. They had bap. in the Dutch Church in New York, one dau. Catlyntje,[3] bap. April 24, 1706. She m. Nov. 19, 1726, PETER BOND, JR., sometimes written *Bant, Band* and *Bondt.* They had 8 children bap. in the Dutch Church in New York. She died in 1743, and her husband m. second, Aug. 7, 1744, Elizabeth Becker, widow of Jonathan Friend.

9. viii. CATHARINA[2], unmarried at the date of her father's will.

----

1. ADOLF MEYER[1] was from Ulfen in Westphalia, at least it is so stated in the record of his marriage, which took place in New York, April 29, 1671, to MARRITJE VER VEELEN, of Amsterdam. His wife was a near relative, perhaps a dau. of Johannes and Anna (Tjersvelt) Ver Veelen, who were among the first settlers of New Harlem. She joined the Dutch Church in New York Dec. 7, 1673 ; he joined March 1, 1674, and soon after removed to New Harlem. He was Corporal of the First Night Watch there, Dec. 6, 1675.* He was a farmer by occupation—a prominent man in public affairs—one of the patentees in Gov. Dongan's patent of March 7, 1686, confirming the New Harlem patent of Oct. 11, 1666, granted by Gov. Nicolls—and an Assistant Alderman from the Out Ward, as Harlem was then designated, in 1693-4. On the 11th of Dec., 1691, he was chosen by the freeholders of Harlem, in company with Jan Hendricks Brevoort, Samuel Waldren, and Peter Van Oblinus, to lay out the undivided land belonging to the town. These persons, as trustees of the town, confirmed to John Loweson Bogert certain of these lands on the 14th of Sept., 1706,† which is the last notice found of him. His wife was a widow, March 7, 1711. His will is dated Feb. 13, 1710, but not proven until Sept. 2, 1748. In it he mentions his wife Maria, and the following named children, 6 sons and 3 daughters :

2. i. JOHANNES[2], bap. Aug. 13, 1671. He was a farmer, and settled in Harlem ; m. Jan. 30, 1702, TRYNTJE VAN DALSEN (also written *Dalden* and *Dalsing*). They had bap. in the Dutch Church in New York, 1. Jacob[3], bap. May 8, 1709, and, 2. Maria[3], bap. May 6, 1711.

3. ii. HENDRICK[2], bap. Sept. 3, 1673 ; m. Dec. 10, 1697, WYNTJE RHEE, probably the dau. of Jan Rhee (Ree) and Claesje Dircks, who was bap. Feb. 18, 1682. They had bap. in the Dutch Church in New York : 1. Maria[3], bap. May 14, 1699 ; died young. 2. Adolph[3], bap. Oct. 29, 1701. 3. Johannes[3], bap. Jan. 27, 1703 ; died young. 4. Johannes[3], bap. July 9, 1704 ; died young. 5. Abraham[3], bap. July 8, 1705. 6. Maria[3], bap. Sept. 14, 1707. 7. Hendrick[3], bap. Aug. 10, 1712 ; died young. 8. Hendrick[3], bap. July 26, 1713 ; m. Sept. 23, 1735, Maria, dau. of Abraham and Mary (Leisler) Gouverneur. 9. Johannes[3], bap. April 15, 1716 ; died young. 10. Johannes[3], bap. July 5, 1719 ; m. Oct. 1, 1747, Anna Crommelyn.

* Valentine's *Manual for* 1848, p. 387.
† *Deduction of Title of* Benj. L. Benson *to* 80 *acres of Land at Harlem, etc., New York,* 1836, 8°.

4. iii. ANNA CATHARINA[2], bap. March 12, 1677; m. Dec. 24, 1698, ABRAHAM RYCKE, of the Poor Farm, or Bouwery.* Though married as Rycke, his proper name, or the one he afterward assumed, was ABRAHAM LENT. He was the son of Ryck Abrahamsen [Lent] and Tryntje Hercks, born March 10, 1674, and bap. May 12, 1675. His father was the eldest, and his uncle Hendrick the youngest, son of Abraham Rycken, "who for some reason not clearly ascertained, renounced their own cognomen and assumed that of Lent." Abraham Lent lived for some years in Westchester County, but in 1729 returned to Newtown, L. I. He died Feb. 5, 1746, and his widow July 21, 1762. For a very full account of their family see Riker's Annals of Newtown, p. 317, to which we are indebted for some of the particulars here given.

5. iv. MARIA[2], bap. April 26, 1679; m. July 29, 1699, SAMSON BENSON, JR., from Albany. His name is sometimes written *Samuel* in the Dutch Church records. They had bap. in the Dutch Church in New York, 1. Johannes, bap. Feb. 4, 1700; and, 2. Catharina, bap. Jan. 10, 1705. There was a Samson Benson, Jr., perhaps the same person, who m., Dec. 10, 1710, Maria Bocke (Bocquet), dau. of Abraham and Tanneke (Andries) Bocke, and had 7 children, bap. in the Dutch Church in New York. This statement, however, must be regarded as entirely problematical.

6. v. ABRAHAM[2], bap. March 3, 1682. He was a farmer in Harlem, and owned a farm of 85 acres there in 1713. He m. May 10, 1706, ENGELTJE BUSSING, and had bap. in the Dutch Church in New York, Abraham[3], bap. Feb. 8, 1716.

7. vi. ISAAC[2], bap. April 13, 1684; was living at date of his father's will.

8. vii. JACOB[2], bap. May 16, 1686. He m. (1710?) ANNATJE HENDRICKSE KAMMEGA, and had bap. in the Dutch Church in New York, 1. Adolph[3], bap. March 7, 1711. They also had bap. in the Dutch Church in Hackensack, N. J., 2. Adolph[3], bap. May 10, 1712; and, 3. Annatie[3], bap. May 20, 1722, and probably others, the record of whose baptism is lost.

9. viii. ADOLF[2], bap. July 24, 1692; m., first, Oct. 25, 1716, MARGRITJE WALDRON, by whom he had no *issue* bap. in the Dutch Church in New York. He m., second, CATHARINA, dau. of PETER HARING (Herring.) By his second wife he had bap. in the Dutch Church in New York, 1. Maria[3], bap. Aug. 9, 1724; 2. Petrus[3], bap. Oct. 22, 1729.

10. ix. ANNETJE[2], bap. Aug. 3, 1698; m. May 2, 1718, JOHANNES SICKELS, of Harlem. Of them and their descendants we have no account.

DE MEYER—DE MEYERT.

Perhaps no class among the early residents of New Amsterdam was more distinguished for the rapid strides they made to wealth and social distinction, in their adopted home, than those who came from the old commercial cities of Germany. The most prominent representative of this class—which included, among others, the heads of the Vander Beeck, Santford, Ebbing, Leisler, and Schrick families—was Nicholas De Meyer, a native of Hamburg, who settled here as early as 1655, engaged exten-

---

* This was a large farm " in the occupation and tenure (as early as 1654) of the deacons and officers of the Dutch Church at New Amsterdam "—situated at Newtown, L. I.—which was kept under cultivation by them for the benefit of the poor. It was called the Armen Bouwery, or the Poor's Farm, from whence the name of Poor Bowery, still applied to that section of the town.—(*Riker's Annals of Newtown*, pp. 35-36.)

sively in trade, and in less than twenty years became next to Fredrick Philipse, the wealthiest inhabitant of the city, his fortune being equalled only by that of one other person—Cornelius Steenwyck, from Haerlem.   He was admitted to the rights of a small burgher April 14, 1657 ; Schepen, 1664 ; Alderman, 1669–1670 and 1675, and appointed Mayor of the city in 1676.*   He was also an Assistant Alderman for the South Ward in 1686. He belonged to the anti-Leislerian party, and appears to have been more moderate and conservative in his politics than the majority of his political associates.   In 1689–90 he was appointed a member of Gov. Sloughter's Council,† but had deceased before Sloughter's arrival, in March, 1691.

1. NICHOLAS DE MEYER[1], the ancestor of the DE MEYER family, of New York, m. first, June 6, 1655, LYDIA, dau. of Hendrick VAN DVCK. His name appears in the record of his marriage, and also in the list of members of the Dutch Church, without the prefix De, but it is always attached in the record of the baptism of his children.   He joined the Church in New Amsterdam, in April, 1660 ; his wife was a member for some time prior to her marriage.   She died about 1687.   He m. second, SARA KELLENAER, of Kingston, who was, says Mr. Valentine, the widow of John Wicksteen. She joined the Dutch Church, in New York, Sept. 1, 1689, and was then the wife of De Meyer.   He died in 1690, and had bap. in the Dutch Church in New York, 3 sons, and 3 daus., all by his first wife, viz. :

2. i. JOHANNES[2], bap. Jan. 26, 1656.   On the 13th August, 1680, John and William De Meyer and Mathias Mathisen, obtained a grant of about 60 acres of land at the fall of the Platte Kill, in Ulster County.‡   He is not mentioned in his brother Henry's will, dated Nov., 1692, but is probably the JAN DE MEYER, who by wife EVA MATHYSE, had son Mathys[3], bap. March 10, 1697, in New York.

3. ii. WILHELMUS[2], bap. Nov. 21, 1657 ; m. Oct. 23, 1678, CATHARINA BAYARD, from Bergen op Zoom, an old and strongly fortified town near the sea coast, in Holland.   She was a near relative of Balthazar and Anna (Stuyvesant) Bayard, probably a dau. of the latter and sister of the former. Soon after his marriage he removed to Ulster County, N. Y., having purchased, April 11, 1679, a parcel of land, with house and lot at Kingston. He was a witness at Kingston, Jan. 19, 1681, at a renewal of the treaty of peace with the Esopus Indians.§   In 1684, he returned to New York, rejoining with his wife the Dutch Church here, on the 5th Sept. of that year.   He again removed a few years after to Kingston, where he was engaged in trade, as a merchant, and represented the county of Ulster in the Colonial General Assembly during the years 1691–1693 and 1695–98. In 1692, he bore the title of Captain, and some years later that of Colonel. He was Clerk of Ulster County, 1704, and living at Kingston as late as May, 1709, and probably died there.   He and his wife Catharina Bayard had bap. in the Dutch Church in New York, one dau. Anna[3], bap. Nov. 1, 1685.   They probably had son Nicholas[3], a freeholder and inhabitant of the County of Ulster, in 1701–2 ; also a dau. Lydia[3], who became the second wife of Andries Douw, of Manor Rensselaerswick, and had dau. Catharina, bap. at Albany, Nov. 26, 1704.‖

---

* Valentine's Manuals.
† Doc. Rel. to Col. Hist. of N. Y., Vol. 3, pp. 685–756.
‡ Calendar of Land Papers, p. 20.
§ Coll. Ulster Hist. Society, 1–64.
‖ Pearson's First Settlers of Albany, p. 43.

4. iii. ANNA CATHARINA[2], bap. June 19, 1661 ; joined the Dutch Church in New York, Feb. 28, 1678 ; m. Oct. 13, 1680, JAN WILLEMSZEN NEE-RING, a young man from Bordeaux. In July, 1690, he is described in a deed made by William De Meyer, to him and others, as a resident of New Castle, in the Province of Pennsylvania, and in August, 1692, as a resident of New Castle, in Delaware, where, probably, he lived and died. They had bap. in the Dutch Church in New York :

    1. SARA NEERING, bap. July 23, 1681.

    2. LYDIA NEERING, bap. May 20, 1685.

    3. JOHANNES NEERING, bap. May 22, 1687.

    4. ELIZABETH NEERING, bap. May 17, 1691.

5. iv. DEBORA[2], bap. June 25, 1664 ; joined the Dutch Church, March 5, 1681. Married first, Sept. 17, 1684, THOMAS CRUNDALL, a young man from London. He was a merchant in New York, and Alderman of the Dock Ward, in 1686 and 1687. They lived "Along the Strand," then the most aristocratic quarters of the city. He was living in July, 1689, and was active in his opposition to Leisler and his adherents. She m. second, Oct. 2, 1691, THOMAS LYNDON (LYNDALL), a young man from old England. He was Sheriff of the city of New York, from March to October, 1691. His will is dated Aug. 27, 1694 ; proven, March 3, 1696–7 ; names only his wife Deborah, and dau. Frances, to whom he gives his estate ; speaks of loving brother and four sisters in England, without naming them. She m. third, Oct. 10, 1697, WILLIAM ANDERSON. He was engaged in mercantile pursuits, in New York, was Treasurer of the city from 1703 to 1706, and Sheriff from Oct., 1708 to July, 1710,[*] and a vestryman of Trinity Church, from 1698 to 1717. His family, in 1703, consisted of 1 male, 1 female, 2 children, 2 negroes, and 1 negro child. His wife was living March 14, 1710, but died prior to June 18, 1712, at which date a bill was introduced into the Legislative Council, to enable William Anderson to sell ground in Queen Street, the estate of said William in right of Deborah his wife, deceased, for the payment of debts contracted by her before their intermarriage. She had no children bap. in the Dutch Church, except by her first husband. These were :

    1. THOMAS CRUNDALL, bap. July 29, 1685.

    2. SARA CRUNDALL, }

    3. LYDIA CRUNDALL, } twins, bap. May 25, 1687.

    4. LYDIA CRUNDALL, bap. Feb. 6, 1689.

Of her dau. FRANCES LYNDALL, no mention is found, except in her father's will.

6. v. LYSBETH,[2] bap. Aug. 29, 1666 ; joined the Dutch Church in New York, Feb. 25, 1685 ; m. Aug. 24, 1687, PHILIP SCHUYLER, of Albany, son of Col. Philip Pieterse Schuyler and his wife Margareta Van Slichtenhorst ; born Feb. 8, 1666.[†] Soon after their marriage they removed to Esopus (Kingston), where he was engaged in trade. On the 1st of March, 1693, they both joined the Dutch Church in New York, by certificate or letter from the Church at Esopus. They had bap. in New York, one son,

    1. NICHOLAS SCHUYLER, bap. Sept. 21, 1692 ; was a Surveyor and Indian trader in the Mohawk Country. He was a member of the Provin-

---

    [*] Valentine's Manual for 1864.
    [†] Pearson's First Settlers of Albany, p. 98.

cial Assembly from Schenectady, in 1727-8; m. at Albany, Dec. 2, 1714, Elsie Wendel, and was buried July 8, 1748. He had bap. at Albany, 1. Elisabeth, Sept. 18, 1715; 2. Philip, Oct. 27, 1717, and at Schenectady, 3. Ariaantje, March 6, 1720, m. Col. Kiliaen Van Rensselaer, and died Oct. 17, 1763; 4. Harmanus, Jan. 28, 1722; 5. Catharina, Aug. 11, 1723, m. John Jacobse Lansing, gentleman, of Albany, Dec. 12, 1747; 6. Harmanus, b. April 2, bap. April 3, 1727; and 7. Johannes, Feb. 4, 1733. (See Pearson's First Settlers of Schenectady, p. 166, and Pearson's First Settlers of Albany, pp. 98, 130.)

7. vi. HENRICUS,[2] bap. Nov. 7, 1668. He was a prominent and successful merchant in New York, and m., May 14, 1689, AGNIETJE DE KEY, dau. of Jacob Theuniszen and Hillegond (Theunis) De Key ;* she was bap. July 6, 1670, and joined the Dutch Church in New York, Sept. 2, 1688. His will is dated Nov. 9, and proven Nov. 22, 1692; names wife *Angenieta*, dau. Lydia, and the child his wife " is now bigg withal ; " his brother William De Meyer ; his sisters, Anna Katharina Willems, wife of John Willems [Neering] of the town of New Castle ; Deborah, wife of Thomas Lyndall, of New York, gentleman ; and Elisabeth Schuyler, wife of Philip Schuyler, of New York, merchant. Appoints his wife and brothers-in-law, Theunis and Jacobus De Key, executors of his estate. He had *issue* bap. in New York : 1. Lydia,[3] bap. Feb. 4, 1691 ; and 2. Henricus,[3] bap. Nov. 13, 1692 ; he is probably the H. De Meyer who was a witness at Harlem, March 28, 1721, to a conveyance (unrecorded) of lands made by Elizabeth Benson, widow and executrix of Johannes Benson, late of the Island of New York, and others, to Sampson Benson.†

Agnietje De Key, the widow of Henricus De Meyer,[2] m. second, in August, 1696 (m. l. dated Aug. 11), WILLIAM JANEWAY, gentleman. He was an Englishman, and came to New York in 1693, as purser of H. M. Ship Richmond, commanded by Capt. John Evans. He was admitted a freeman of the city in 1695. In 1700 he was acting as Capt. Evans' agent, to whom an extensive grant of land had been made lying on the west side of Hudson River, about 40 miles in length, and 20 in breadth ; but which was afterwards " cancelled for its magnitude, uncertainty, and want of consideration."‡ William Janeway was a vestryman of Trinity Church in 1697, and from 1702 to 1704.

---

* This name furnishes another illustration of the changes in early Dutch family names, which render the tracing of their pedigree so difficult and perplexing. The ancestor of the DE KEY family of New York was, JACCE TOENISZEN [Theuniszen] VAN TUYL, in Guilderland, who married in New Amsterdam, March 29, 1658, HILLETJE [Hillegond] TOENIS [Theunis], born in the latter place. At the baptism of their first child Theunis, April 4, 1659, their names are recorded JACOB VAN THUYL and HILLEGONO THEUNIS. At the baptism of their next child, Jannekin, Dec. 15, 1660, the fathers name is recorded simply JACOB THEUNISZEN ; at the baptism of their third child Johannes, Jan. 28, 1662, the fathers name appears JACOB THEUNISZEN KEY, while at the baptism of their fourth child Johannes, June 8, 1664, he comes out full fledged as JACOBUS DE KEY, which surname he ever after retained. There is reason for his being called VAN THUYL, after his native place, but why he adopted the surname of DE KEY remains a mystery. He was a man of some note in his day, and an active oppouent of Lieut. Gov. Leisler, who caused his arrest and imprisonment.

His son CAPT. THEUNIS DE KEY, bap. April 4, 1659, married May 26, 1680, Helena Van Brugh. He was a merchant of good repute, an Assistant Alderman from the North Ward in 1685, 6, 7, 1691, and 1692, and one of the Church Wardens of the Dutch Church in New York, in 1698.

† *Deduction of Title of* Benj. L. Benson *to* 80 *acres of Land at Harlem, etc. New York*, 1836. 8°.

‡ Doc. Rel. to Col. Hist. N. Y., Vol. 3, 55 ; Vol. 4, 391–784, Valentine's Hist. of New York.

VAN DYCK.

HENDRICK VAN DYCK,[1] came from Utrecht to New Amsterdam about 1639-40—accompanied probably by his wife, DIVERTJE [DEBORA] COR-NELISE, *alias* BOTJAGERS—as ensign in the service of the West India Company. In March, 1642, he was sent by Gov. Kieft in command of an expedition against the Weckquaesgeeks Indians in West Chester; and early in 1644, with Capt. John Underhill, against the Long Island and Connecticut Indians. He soon after returned to Holland; was commissioned *Schout-fiscal*, June 28, 1645, and again embarked for New Netherland, in company with Governor Stuyvesant, in December, 1646, the bickerings of the "Churlish Director" with Van Dyck furnishing the staple themes of scandal on the voyage. "At Saint Christophers," says Brodhead, "the Fiscal Van Dyck, claiming a seat at the council board, to dispose of a captured prize, was rudely repelled—'When I want you I will call you,' was Stuyvesant's haughty reply. Renewing his attempt at Curaçoa, the insulted fiscal met a still sterner rebuff, and was not allowed even a 'stroll ashore' during the three weeks the ship lay at anchor there." It would be difficult to form an excuse for this outrageous treatment, on the part of the Director, of his chief officer. Upon their arrival he was admitted to a seat in the Council, and held office until March 28, 1652, when he was dismissed by Stuyvesant, from which action he appealed to the States General for redress. In September, 1655, he unfortunately killed an Indian squaw, whom he detected in stealing peaches from his orchard, situated a short distance below the present Rector Street. To avenge this murder the Indians invaded the town, wounded Van Dyck, cut down his next door neighbor Paulus Leendertszen Van der Grist with an axe, and in three days massacred one hundred inhabitants of the surrounding settlements, and carried one hundred and fifty more into captivity.* Divertje Cornelise, the first wife of Hendrick Van Dyck, became a communicant of the Dutch Church, in New York, May 30, 1672, shortly prior to her death. It appears somewhat remarkable that her husband's name is not recorded in the list of Church members. He m., second, in Midwout, June 20, 1675, Magdalena [Jacobs] Ryssens, widow of Jacob [Van] Couwenhoven, both living in New York, by whom he had no issue. He and his first wife made a joint will, August 13, 1655, before the notary, Dirck Van Schelluyne, which was proved March 22, 168⅜, and in which they mention their dau., Lidia Van Dyck, married with Nicholas [De] Meyer; their dau. Rycke Van Dyck, married with John Durett; also their "two underaged children, by name, Cornelis Van Dyck, old thirteen years, and Janneke Van Dyck, old nine years."

CORNELIUS VAN DYCK,[2] son of Hendrick; bap. in New Amsterdam, March 10, 1642; settled in Albany; became a Chirurgeon, and practised his profession there until his death in 1686. His first wife was Elisabeth Lakens; the second, Elisabeth Beck, the widow of Captain Sylvester Salisbury. For an account of his children *see* Pearson's First Settlers of Schenectady, p. 219, and First Settlers of Albany, pp. 125-6. The other children of Hendrick Van Dyck[1] named in his will were:

LYDIA VAN DYCK,[2] born in Utrecht; m. NICHOLAS DE MEYER.

RYCKE [ULRICA] VAN DYCK,[2] born in Utrecht; m. NOV. 1, 1654, JAN

---

* Brodhead's History of the State of New York, vol. 1.

DARETH (Durett, Dret, Droit, De Ret), also from Utrecht, who soon after removed to Beverwyck, where he died in May, 1669 (Pearson.) They had no children baptized in the Dutch Church, in New York.

JANNETJE VAN DYCK,[2] born in 1644, in Enckhuysen, on the Zuider Zee, probably came to New Amsterdam with her parents on their return to New Netherland in 1647 ; joined the Church in New Amsterdam Oct. 12, 1664 ; m. March 22, 1665, JOHANNES COLY (Coely, Coelie, Cooly, Cooley), a young man from London. The most frequent form of this name in the records is COELY. He was a blacksmith, and furnished the iron work to repair Fort James in 1672–3, and also to repair it during the time of Gov. Sloughter in 1691.* Though his wife was a communicant of the Dutch Church, he was reputed to be, in 1696, one of the few Roman Catholics in New York. His will is dated in New York, Jan. 22, 168⅔ ; proven March 22, 1709. In it he mentions his wife, Jane, and 8 children, viz. : *William Cooley*, his "eldest and only son ; " his daughters, Elizabeth, Deborah, Lydia, Hannah, Mary, *Rickey*, and Cornelia. Appoints his wife Jane sole executrix. They had baptized in the Dutch Church : .

1. WILHELMUS COELY, bap. Dec. 20, 1665 ; died young.

2. LYSBETH COELY, bap. Aug. 28, 1667 ; joined the Dutch Church Feb. 25, 1685 ; m. Sept. 6, 1688, BERNARDUS, son of Abel and Annetje (Meynderts) HARDENBROOK. He was baptized August, 1662. They had baptized in the Dutch Church : 1. Anna, June 30, 1689 ; 2. Janneken, Oct. 25, 1691 ; 3. Anneken, Dec. 31, 1693 ; 4. Elizabeth, Dec. 15, 1695 ; 5. Maria, Jan. 9, 1698 ; 6. Abel, Nov. 19, 1699 ; and 7. Margareta, Dec. 17, 1701.

3. DEBORA COELY, bap. June 18, 1671 ; m. Aug. 26, 1694, NICHOLAS FIELDING. She joined the Dutch Church in New York, June 1, 1698. He was the first Sexton of Trinity Church, appointed Oct. 25, 1697, and described as "a person reputed of honest behaviour and conversation, who offered his service gratis, till the Corporation of the Church should be formally established." He held the office but a short time—about a year. (Berrian.)

4. WILLIAM COELY, bap. March 16, 1673 ; m. by Do. Dubois, June 7, 1700, to DINA, dau. of Cornelis Janszen and Heyltie (Pieters) CLOPPER. She was bap. March 15, 1675. They had bap. in the Dutch Church one dau., Heyltie, April 13, 1701, who married Jan. 10, 1725, Gerardus, son of Johannes and Sara (Van Laer) Hardenbrook. WILLEM COELY died about 1703, and his widow Dina m. second, Jan. 29, 1706, STEPHEN VAN BRAKEL (Ver Brakel, á Brakele, Brakele), probably son of Gysbert Gerritse Van Brakel, and his wife Reintje Stephens. They had bap. in the Dutch Church : 1. Margrietje Van Brakel, Nov. 19, 1706 ; died young ; 2. Reintje Van Brackel, Jan. 9, 1709 ; m. Sept. 1, 1727, John Stephens, Jr., and had son John, born Jan. 13, bap. Jan. 20, 1744, in the Presbyterian Church, in New York ; 3. Margritje Van Brakel, April 11, 1711.

5. LYDIA COELY, bap. Nov. 24, 1674 ; m. April 7, 1695, PIETER MASKELT (Masjet, Machet, Makkett), and removed to New Rochelle, Westchester County, N. Y., where they resided until 1697, when they returned to New York. They had one dau. bap. in the Dutch Church, Lydia, Nov. 17, 1697, who m. Dec. 31, 1720, Abraham Santvoort (Santford), widower of Vroutje Van Horne, by whom she had no issue. For a further account of Abraham Santford, see RECORD, vol. vi., p. 23, and vol. vii., p. 118.

* Cal. N. Y. Hist. MSS. English, pp. 104-222.

6. RYCKIE COELY, bap. April 26, 1679 ; died young.

7. HENDRICK COELY, bap. Oct. 27, 1680 ; died young.

8. RYCKIE COELY, bap. Aug. 5, 1682.

9. CORNELIA COELY, bap. May 27, 1687. Cornelia Coely, probably the same, who m. Jan. 24, 1729, JOHN FREDERICKS KUNTER.

10. MARY (MARIA) COELY (mentioned in her father's will) ; m. Nov. 22, 1699, GABRIEL THIBOÚ, from England.

11. HANNAH COELY (mentioned in her father's will).

VARLETH—VARLET—VARLEET—VERLET—VERLETH.

THE name of Varleth, in its various orthographic forms in the early records, has an unmistakable French structure, a corruption perhaps of *Valet*, and it is not improbable it was borne by some French exile who took refuge in Holland, in order to escape the religious persecutions of his native land, which prevailed during the latter part of the sixteenth century. The first members of the family in New Netherland were natives of Utrecht and Amsterdam, and though not to be deemed unprolific, their name, for nearly two centuries, has disappeared from the annals of our colonial and State history. It appears to have died out in the male line, in the third generation from the emigrant ancestor CASPER VARLETH,[1] but, as if to make amends for the swift decay of its male stem, we find the mater-lineal branches of the family blooming and fruitful with the historic names of Bayard, Schrick, Philipse, Brockholst, Schuyler, Livingston, Jay, Clarkson, French, Morris, Robinson, Van Horne and others, who, if perchance of equal worth, are of lesser note among the ancient families of New York.

The first notice of the name found in the records, is on the 21st of Sept., 1642—the substitution of Hendrick Van Dyck, as attorney of Peter Verlet & Co., and July 17, 1647, in the report of the referees on a difference between Augustine Hermans, agent of Catharina Verlet of Amsterdam, and David Provoost, respecting a legacy. In September and October, 1652, Anna Verlet, described as the wife of George Hack (Hawks?), was a party plaintiff and defendant in various suits in the court at New Amsterdam, in one of which she claims, as her private property, a certain lot of tobacco sent to her from Virginia by her husband.* It is probable she was a sister of Casper Varleth,[1] and assisted her husband in his business affairs, as well as engaging occasionally in trade on her own account, a not uncommon practice for merchants' wives at that time. Her husband was probably the *George Hacke*, who was one of the signers with other inhabitants of the county, of the "*Engagement of Northampton*," in Virginia, March 25, 1651, relating to the surrender of Virginia to the British Parliament, or rather to Cromwell, who had sent out a naval force to reduce the colony to his sway.† George Hack was in New Amsterdam in Sept., 1652, and his wife's name is frequently found in the records here as late as January, 1661, but Virginia was probably their permanent place of residence. There was an Abraham Varleth here in 1651, perhaps a brother or son of Casper,[1] if the latter, he had deceased before the death of his father in 1662. He was a sponsor, Jan. 1, 1651, at the baptism of Abraham, son of Nicholas Varleth,[2] which is the only notice found of him.

---

* Cal. N. Y. Hist. MSS. Dutch, pp. 20, 38, 129.

† Virginia Hist. Register, vol. i. p, 163.

1. CASPER OR JASPER VARLETH,[1] the ancestor of the family bearing his name in New Amsterdam, was an early resident of the Dutch settlement of Fort Good Hope, at Hartford, Conn., and was there, according to Mr. Savage, perhaps as early as the completion of the Fort in 1633. He may have been domiciled for a short time at New Amsterdam, as we find reference made to an inventory of articles taken at his house in July, 1651, and that his son-in-law, Paulus Schrick, on the 17th of October, 1661, petitioned for a deed of a house and lot on the Fresh Water,* Manhattan Island, sold to him by his said father-in-law. He is mentioned by Savage as a Dutchman of some consequence at Hartford in 1656, "who may have lived there near thirty years," and died there in September, 1662, who had wife Judith who died before him, and children, Nicholas, Mary, Judith, and Jane.† Beside these he probably had Catharina, born in Amsterdam, who married Francois De Bruyn in New Amsterdam, in August, 1657.

A judgment against him and his son Nicholas,[2] dated Dec. 9, 1652, in New Amsterdam, for the payment of freight by the ship Fortune, indicates the fact that they were engaged in trade together, but their partnership seems to have been of a limited character. He was an active business man at Hartford, enjoying 'the respect of the English settlers there, and designated sometimes in the proceedings of the General Court of the colony as *Mr. Varleet*, an honorable distinction in those days—" the prefix *Master* or Mr., corresponding very nearly in meaning to the English word, gentleman,"‡ or the title " Honorable " as at present used. From the respectful terms in which the following request is couched, it may be inferred that he possessed also, in a high degree, the friendship and esteem of the authorities at New Amsterdam.

" TO CASPER N[V]ERLEITH :

" At the request of the Burgomasters and Schepens of the city of New Amsterdam you will please to repair to the Stadt house of this city aforesaid, on the morning of to-morrow, the 21st inst., and there show the pass which you received from Jan Jongh [John Young], in so doing will confer on us a friendship with which we remain yours affectionately.

" Signed by order of Burgomasters and Schepens,

JACOB KIP, Secretary."

" New Amsterdam,
20 March, 1654."§

About this time he was engaged in aiding Johannes Van Beeck in his attempt to marry his daughter Maria, the peculiar circumstances of whose marriage we shall have occasion to notice hereafter. Judith Varleth, his wife, was associated with Anna, the wife of George Hack, before mentioned, in some business enterprises that gave rise, in September, 1652, to a suit in New Amsterdam, respecting a number of negroes and other property which Mrs. Varleth had purchased, and which were taken away in the night time by one Capt. Geurt Tyssen.‖ Casper Varleth,[1] and his wife Judith, appear to have been enterprising, industrious, and thrifty persons—qualities of character for which their descendants have also been noted. They

---

* PAULUS SCHRICK obtained a patent, Jan. 31, 1662, for two morgens (about four acres), of land at the Kolck, or Fresh Water, in New Amsterdam (O'Callaghan's Hist. of New Netherland, vol. ii. p. 591), perhaps the property above alluded to.
† Savage's Genealogical Dictionary, vol. iv. p. 365.
‡ Col. Records of Conn., 1636-1665, pp. 322, 372, 387. Hollister's Hist. of Conn., vol. ii. p. 424.
§ Valentine's Manual, 1853, p. 444.
‖ Cal. N. Y. Hist. MSS. Dutch, pp. 127, 128.

had *issue*, one son and four daughters, which we give in the order of their marriage, as follows:

2. i. NICHOLAS VARLETH,[2] probably came to New Netherland with his father, and resided for some time with the family at Hartford. His daughter Susanna[3] was born in Amsterdam, of which city he too was probably a native. His name first appears in the records at New Amsterdam on the 1st January, 1651, at the baptism of his son Abraham.[3] His first wife was Susanna Jillis, supposed to have been a sister of Margaret Jillis, the wife of David Provoost. On the 14th of October, 1656, he married his second wife, Anna Stuyvesant,[*] widow of Samuel Bayard, and sister of Governor Stuyvesant, by whom he had no issue. This alliance, as well doubtless as his own personal merit, secured for him at once honorable position in the public service at New Amsterdam, and, subsequently, in the adjoining province of New Jersey. He was appointed April 7, 1657, Commissary of Imports and Exports, *vice* Adriaen Van Tienhoven, and the following year Searcher, Inspector, and Guager, *vice* Warnaer Wessels dismissed. April 17, 1657, he was admitted to the rights of a small burgher, and April 23, 1658, took the oath of office as Collector of Duties on Exports and Imports to and from New England and Virginia. On the 27th Feb., 1660, he was commissioned, with Brian Newton, Ambassador to Virginia, and soon after concluded, with the General Assembly of that colony, a treaty of Amitie and Commerce, highly satisfactory to both New Netherland and Virginia. He was one of the Commissioners that signed the articles of capitulation, on the surrender of New Netherland, Sept. 6, 1664, his name appearing in that document, NICH. VARLETH, which, among the diverse methods of spelling in the records, we have adopted as the correct orthography.†

He was, for some years, one of the chief merchants of New Amsterdam, and in June, 1660, a partner of his brother-in-law, Jacob Backer,‡ engaged

---

* ANNA STUYVESANT was the dau. of Balthazar Stuyvesant and his first wife MARGARET HARDENSTEIN. "The name is derived from *Stuiven*, to stir or raise a dust, and *sand*, being the same in both the Dutch and English." Her father was a clergyman, who settled, July 19, 1622, at Berlicum, a small town in Friesland, having come from Scherpenzeel in the same province, "where he was the minister previous to 1619." He left Berlicum in 1634, for Delfzyl in Guelderland, where he died in 1637. His first wife died at Berlicum, May 2, 1625, aged fifty years. Gov. Peter Stuyvesant and Anna, and perhaps others, were the issue of this marriage. He married second, July 22, 1627, Styntie Pieters, of Harlem, by whom he had Margaret (two of that name) Tryncke (Tryntje?) and Balthazar. *See* Anthology of New Netherland, pp. 181, 182.

ANNA STUYVESANT married her first husband, SAMUEL BAYARD, in Holland, and by him had four children (Winfield's Land Titles), who came with her to New Netherland in 1647, in company with Governor Stuyvesant. These were—1. BALTHAZAR BAYARD, born in Amsterdam, m. in New Amsterdam, Nov. 12, 1664 (Family Bible), Marritje Loockermans. 2. NICHOLAS BAYARD, born in Alphen, a small town near Utrecht, m. in New Amsterdam, May 23, 1666, Judith Verlet. 3. PETRUS BAYARD, born in Alphen, m. in New Orange, as New York was then called, Nov. 28, 1674, Blandina Kierstede. 4. CATHARINE BAYARD, born in Bergen Op. Zoom, m. in New York, Oct. 23, 1678, William De Meyer.

† O'Callaghan's Register of New Netherland. O'Callaghan's Hist. of New Netherland. vol. ii. p. 535. Cal. N. Y. Hist. MSS. Dutch, pp. 183, 195, 207, 214, 217, 259. Valentine's Hist. of New York, p. 147.

‡ JACOB OR JACOBUS BACKER, a prominent merchant in New Amsterdam, came from Old Amsterdam, and married Oct. 30, 1655, Margariet Stuyvesant, from Delfzyl in Guelderland, born there about 1635. She was the dau. of Rev. Balthazar Stuyvesant and Styntie Pieters, and half sister of Governor Stuyvesant, and of Anna, the wife of Nicholas Varleth. Mr. Backer's trading operations were extensive and his wife actively aided him in his business enterprises. He was admitted to the rights of a small burgher April 11, 1657; Schepen in 1660, and President of the Board in 1664. Besides these and other official positions, he was one of the Provincial Agents to Holland in 1663, and a representative, from New Amsterdam, in the General Assembly held at that place, at the City Hall, April 10, 1664, also one of the signers, Sept. 8, 1664, of the ratification of the Articles of Capitulation on the surrender of New Netherland to the English. He returned to Holland in 1666, leaving his wife Margariet in charge of his business affairs, but his property having been heavily mortgaged before his departure to Jean Cossean, was foreclosed by him in 1670. It was reported that Mr. Backer died in the East Indies. He resided on the east side of Broad near Beaver Street, where he also had his warehouse. These premises were purchased in October, 1670, at public sale, by Mr. Balthazar De Hart a wealthy merchant, who died in 1672, unmarried, leaving most of his estate to his brothers Daniel, Matthias and Jacob. Among other bequests he makes one to his natural son Matthias and another to his "Naturall son Daniel De Hart, procreated by Margarett Stuyvesant." This son Daniel was bap. in the Dutch Church in New York, Sept. 1, 1671, and is perhaps the same who had by wife

in the Curaçao trade and importing tobacco from Virginia. He resided on
the west side of the present Whitehall, between Pearl and State Streets, on
property purchased in Feb., 1658, of Paulus Schrick, and which he subsequently sold to Jacob Leisler. Some time prior to October, 1665, he left
New York, and settled permanently in Bergen, N. J., where he had acquired
extensive landed possessions.

In March, 1656, Nicholas Varleth[2] was a resident of Hoboken, N. J.,
and his request for six or eight soldiers, for his defense, having been
denied, "for fear of a collision with the Indians," he, at the same time,
"asks permission to transport to New Amsterdam from Hoboken, a frame
house which he had sold Michael Jansen [Vreeland] for 230 guilders." *
How long he had resided there does not appear. On the 5th Feb., 1663, he
obtained a patent for a tract of land at Hoboken, supposed to be the same
that was in his possession previous to March, 1656. From Winfield's History of the Land Titles in Hudson County, N. J.—a work replete with
valuable information concerning the early settlers of New Netherland, no-
where else to be found—we learn that "he was appointed Captain of the
militia in Bergen, Gamoenepan [Communipaw], Ahasimus and Hooboocken,
October 6, 1665; on the same day a member of the court at Bergen, and on
the first of November following a member of Carteret's Council. These
positions he continued to hold for several years. He died in the summer of
1675," leaving his wife, Anna Stuyvesant, and two children surviving him.
His widow was living January 19, 1683, but the date of her decease is
unknown. His children, both by his first wife, were :

1. SUSANNA,[3] born in Amsterdam ; m. June 8, 1673, JAN DE FOREEST,
son of Isaac and Sarah (de Trieux) De Foreest ; he was bap. March 27,
1650. In 1686, they resided in the present Beaver street, between Broad
and William. They had issue bap. in the Dutch Church in New York : 1.
Nicholas, bap. Feb. 4, 1674 ; 2. Susanna, bap. Jan. 4, 1676 ; 3. Sara,
bap. April 10, 1678, and 4. Sara, bap. March 12, 1670. These children
all died in childhood, except Susanna, who married Robert Hickman, of
New Jersey.†

2. ABRAHAM,[3] bap. Jan. 1, 1651. He was a clerk in the Provincial Secretary's Office in 1673, and one of the Commissioners the same year to
administer the oath of allegiance to the inhabitants of the towns in Achter
Çol, and also to the inhabitants of the towns on Long Island, east of
Oyster Bay.‡ From Winfield's Land Titles, we learn that "he left the
Province in 1675, entered the Dutch East India Company's service, and
afterwards died in the city jail at Ceylon."

3 ii. JANNETJE OR JANE VARLETH,[2] born in Utrecht. Married in New
Amsterdam, Dec. 10, 1651 (1650) AUGUSTYN HERMANS (HARMAN HEER-
MANS) a native of Prague in Bohemia, whose life and history fills no
inconsiderable space in the early annals of New Netherland. He was a

Catharine Van Pelt, son Balthus [Balthazar], bap. in New York April 6, 1709, and who was living in 1695
in Elizabeth Town, N. J.

In April, 1676, Margaret Stuyvesant (named Margaret Baker in the patent) having obtained a patent for
224 acres of land there, became a resident of Elizabeth Town, N. J. On the 11th of March, 1677-8, was recorded
a covenant of marriage "between Hendrick Droogestradt and Mrs. Margarita Stuyvesant, both of Elizabeth Town, in which Hendricus, Nicholas and Abraham Backer are mentioned as her children." (New
Netherland Register. Valentine's Hist. of New York, p. 110. Hatfield's Hist. of Elizabeth, N. J., p. 250.)

JACOB BACKER and Margariet Stuyvesant had issue bap. in New York: 1. [Nicholas] bap. March 25,
1657; 2. Balthazar, bap. Sept. 18, 1658; 3. Hillegond, bap. Sept. 7, 1659; 4. Henricus, bap. Sept. 26,
1660, and 5. Abraham, bap. Nov. 23, 1664.

* Whitehead's East Jersey under the Proprietors, p. 28 ; Cal. N. Y. Hist. MSS. Dutch, p. 164.
† Winfield's Land Titles in Hudson Co:, N. J., p. 39.
‡ O'Callaghan's Register of New Netherland, pp. 29-164.

man of good education, a surveyor by profession, skilled in sketching and drawing,* an adventurous an enterprising merchant—"the first beginner of the Virginia tobacco trade"—and possessed of little or none of that phlegmatic disposition which has often been ascribed as a characteristic of the Dutch settlers of New Amsterdam. A friendly notice of his speculative genius is given by Van der Donck, who speaks of him as a "curious man and a lover of the country," who made an experiment in planting indigo seed near New Amsterdam, "which grew well and yielded much," samples of which sent to the Netherlands, "were found to be better than common."† His wife was a member of the church here prior to her marriage, and though his name does not appear as a communicant, the evidence is not lacking that he was a man of deep religious feeling, and one who reverently recognized the Divine Power which controls in wisdom the destinies alike of men and nations.

At what time Augustyn Hermans came to New Netherland is not precisely known. He was in the employ of the West India Company, and was in company with Arent Corssen in 1633, at the time of the Dutch purchase from the Indians of the lands, which included the site of Philadelphia, on the Schuylkill, near the mouth of which Fort Beversrede was subsequently erected.‡ He probably went back to Holland and returned again to this country under different auspices than those of his first adventure here. In June, 1644, he was with Laurens Cornelisson, an Agent of Peter Gabry & Sons,§ and Mr. Brodhead says he "came out under the patronage of the Chamber of Enckhuysen, as agent of the mercantile house of Gabry of Amsterdam."‖ The same year he was established in trade of that general character common at the time, and afterward made several voyages to Holland in the prosecution of his commercial enterprises. Some years later we find him interested in privateering, and one of the owners, in 1649, of the frigate *La Garce*, engaged in depredations on the Spanish commerce. On the 6th of Dec., 1651, he purchased of the Indians, for Cornelius Van Werckhoven, an influential member of the provincial government of Utrecht, the "Raritan Great Meadows," and other large tracts of land in New Jersey, which acquisitions being objected to by the Amsterdam Chamber, Van Werckhoven was compelled the following year to abandon.¶

For reasons not apparent he was unfortunate in his business operations, and in September, 1652, "a fugitive" from his creditors, his affairs in the hands of assignees Paulus Leendertsen (Van der Griest) and Allert Anthony, who were finally discharged as such March 18, 1653. In May, 1653, he was granted "liberty and freedom" by the Council, and excused for having broken the Company's Seal, "having settled with his creditors;"

---

*A view of New Amsterdam, sketched by Augustyn Hermans, was engraved on Nicolas Jan Vischer's map *Novi Belgii Novæque Angliæ nec non partis Virginiæ*, published in 1650-6, and also on a reduced scale from Visscher's map on the map prefixed to the second edition of *Vanderdonk's Description of New Netherland*. (Memoirs of the L. I. Hist. Soc., Vol. I., p. 230, foot note.) It will be found at the bottom of the latter map in the Coll. of N. Y. Hist. Society, Vol. I. (second series) facing the title; also in O'Callaghan's Hist. of New Netherland, Vol. II., p. 312. and in Valentine's Hist. of New York.

"In the Grenville Library is the only map ever made by Faithorne, an artist distinguished for crayon portraits and delicate copper-plate engraving. On it is this statement: "Virginia and Maryland; as it is planted and inhabited this present year, 1670: surveyed and drawn by Augustus Hermann Bohemiensis;" also a beautiful portrait of the original settler of Bohemia Manor. (O'Neil's Terra Mariæ, page 164.)

† Coll. N. Y. Hist. Society, Vol. I., Second Series, p. 156.
‡ O'Callaghan's Hist. of New Netherland, Vol. I., p. 156. O'Neill's Terra Mariæ, p. 158.
§ The firm name in April, 1652, was John and Charles Gabry. They were prominent merchants in Old Amsterdam.
‖ Brodhead's Hist. of N. V., I., 476. In Van Tienhoven's answer to the Remonstrance of New Netherland (Nov. 29, 1650), he says that "AUGUSTYN HEERMANS went out in the [ship?] *Maecht Van Enchuysen*, being as he now is clerk to Gabri in the trading business."
¶ Brodhead's Hist. of New York, Vol. I., p. 537.

the same month he was bearer of dispatches from Gov. Stuyvesant to the New England authorities at Boston respecting an alleged conspiracy of the Dutch and Indians against the English. In December, 1658, he obtained permission to make a voyage, doubtless for trade, to the Dutch and French Islands in the West Indies, and arrived at the island of Curaçao, April 18, 1659. He left there the 16th of May following for New Netherland, and the next year made arrangements for settling permanently in Maryland.*

In his public positions he rendered useful and important service to the colony. He was one of the board of Nine Men, organized Sept. 25, 1647, and held that office in 1649 and 1650 ; one of the Ambassadors to Rhode Island in April, 1652, and in the same capacity, in company with Resolved Waldron, was sent to Maryland in September, 1659. On this latter embassy they were instructed "to request the surrender of fugitives or threaten retaliation, and to demand reparation for the seditious proceedings and 'frivolous demands, and bloody threatenings' of Col. Utie on the South River." Hermans kept a journal of their travels and proceedings while on this service, and with his associate urged, with great ability, before the Maryland governor and his council, the rights of the New Netherland Government, in opposition to Lord Baltimore's claim to the South River. "Indeed, it may be safely claimed that the independent existence of the present State of Delaware is mainly owing to the very reasons which they maintained so ably" at that time. The authorities at New Amsterdam were not unmindful of his influence, when, upon despatching Capt. Newton and Varleth on their mission to Virginia, in Feb., 1660, they instructed them "to inquire in Maryland if danger threatened the South river, and to avail themselves of the 'aid and tongue of Augustine Heermans,'" who was then in Virginia. Nor was the proprietary of Maryland—to which colony he returned in 1660—slow to recognize his talents and accomplishments, for, in that year, "as a compensation for his services in preparing for Lord Baltimore a map of the country," he obtained a patent for a large tract of land, embracing upwards of twenty thousand acres, "situated at the junction of the Elk River and Bohemia River at the head of Chesapeake Bay, and lying mostly in the present State of Maryland, but partly in the State of Delaware," to which he gave the name of Bohemia Manor.† To this place,‡ described by the Labadist travellers as "a noble piece of land," the best they had seen in all their journey south, he removed with his family about the year 1664, and there spent the remainder of his days.

In the Journal of a Voyage to New York, &c., in 1679-80, by Jaspar Dankers and Peter Sluyter, translated by Henry C. Murphy, Esq., and published in the Memoirs of the Long Island Historical Society, vol. i., will be found many interesting particulars relating to Augustyn Hermans and his family. Dankers and Sluyter belonged to the community of Labadists—a religious sect founded by Jean de Labadie, born near Bordeaux, in 1610—who, having made an unsuccessful attempt to colonize at Suri-

---

* Cal. N. Y. Hist. MSS. Dutch, pp. 28, 30-5-6-7, 43-7, 92, 127-8, 131-2, 204, 331. O'Callaghan's Register of New Netherland, pp. 56-57, 137-8.

† Doc. Rel. to Col. Hist. of N. Y. vol. ii. p. 88. Brodhead's History of New York, vol. i. pp. 666-9, 673. O'Callaghan's Hist. of New Netherland, vol. ii, pp. 381-388. Memoirs of the Long Island Hist. Society, pp. xxxi, 230.

‡ HERMAN, or HARMAN, as the name was afterwards changed to, was the first proprietor of the celebrated Bohemia Manor, consisting of eighteen thousand acres of land, which lays partly in St. George's and Pencader hundreds, in Newcastle county, and partly in Cecil county, Maryland. This land is supposed to be the best in Delaware. (Extract from Vincent's History of Delaware, vol. i. p. 319.)

nam, came to New York and the adjoining colonies, as detailed in their journal, on a tour of observation, having for its ultimate object the establishment here of a colony of their co-religionists. Ephraim Hermans, the oldest son of Augustyn Hermans, became tinctured with their doctrines, and persuaded his father into an agreement to convey a portion of his manor to Dankers, Sluyter, and others, with the view of drawing a large community near his domain, and thus enhancing its value. Afterwards, believing that some deceit had been practised upon him in the matter, he refused to make the conveyance, but was finally compelled to do so by the court. On the 11th of August, 1684, he conveyed 3,750 acres of his manor lands "to Peter Sluyter, *alias* Vorsman, Jasper Danckaerts, *alias* Schilders, of Friesland ; Petrus Bayard, of New York ; and John Moll and Arnoldus de la Grange, of Delaware, in company." Upon this tract, the Labadists settled, but " nothing of them remained as a religious community" five years after the death of Peter Sluyter, which occurred in 1722.

When the Labadist travellers first visited Augustyn Hermans at his Manor, Dec. 3, 1679, they brought a letter from his son Ephraim, and were treated with "every kindness," although he was sick "and very miserable, both in body and soul ;" he had none but negroes to serve him, and his misery was increased " by a miserable, doubly miserable wife," so miserable that they " will not relate it here." In the entry of their journal, Dec. 26, 1679, they speak of the family as follows :—"Ephraim Hermans is the oldest child of Augustine Hermans, there being two brothers and three sisters, one of whom lives now at Amsterdam. They are all of a Dutch mother, after whose death their father married an English woman, who is the most artful and despicable creature that can be found. He is a very godless person, and his wife, by her wickedness, has compelled all these children to leave their father's house and live elsewhere." Full of self-righteousness, these men regarded every one outside of their own persuasion as special objects of God's wrath, and doomed to endless perdition. A part at least of this tirade was doubtless due to the fact that Hermans had as poor an opinion of their religious tenets as they had of his godliness, and, in his will, " speaks in emphatic terms of condemnation of the connection of his son Ephraim with the Labadists."

JANNETJE VARLETH, his first wife, died some time after their removal to Bohemia manor, and probably prior to 1666. In that year, " Augustine Harman, of Prague, in the kingdom of Bohemia, petitioned the Maryland Assembly for the naturalization of himself, his sons Ephraim Georgius, Casparus, and his daughters Anna Margaritta, Judith, and Francina." * The custom then obtained of naturalizing the wife, as well as the other members of a family, and as her name is not mentioned in this petition, there is little doubt she was not living at that date. His second wife was a MISS WARD, of Cecil County, Maryland,† by whom he probably had no issue ; the statement made by Mr. Hanson that his daughter, Anna Margaret, was the fruit of this second marriage, is shown to be an error by the Labadists' account of the family, and the baptismal records of the Dutch Church in New York.

AUGUSTYN HERMANS died in 1686,‡ and had *issue* by his wife JANNETJE

* O'Neil's Terra Mariæ, p. 164, foot note.
† Hanson's Old Kent, Maryland, p. 80.
‡ Memoirs of the Long Island Hist. Society, vol. i. p. xxxiv. foot note. The date of his death, as here given by Mr. Murphy, is undoubtedly correct. In Vincent's History of Delaware, vol. i. p. 468, the statement is made that " his death must have occurred about the last of December, 1669, as on the 14th of De-

VARLETH, two sons and three daughters, baptized in the Dutch Church in New Amsterdam, viz. :

1. EPHRAIM GEORGIUS HERMANS, bap. Sept. 1, 1652. His second name, Georgius, is usually dropped in the records. He accompanied his father's family on their removal to Maryland, but, in 1673, was a resident of New York city. He was a man of note, and held several offices under the English government in New York and Delaware, to which latter place he removed about 1676, and settled at Newcastle. He subsequently became a Labadist, and his father, it is said, pronounced a curse upon him " that he might not live two years " after joining that sect. He married in New York, September 3, 1679, Elizabeth Rodenburg, who appears to have been a favorite with the Labadists. They speak of her as having " the quietest disposition we have observed in America," and as being " politely educated." For a further account of them and their children, *see* page 32, foot note.

2. CASPARUS HERMANS, bap. Jan. 2, 1656. On the 16th Feb., 1674, he and his brother, Ephraim, obtained a patent for a tract of land near Newcastle on the Delaware. In 1679, he was residing about twenty-two miles from his father's manor, on a place named Augustine, which the Labadists found well situated, and of which they remark, it " *would not badly suit us.*" He was a member of the Pennsylvania General Assembly from Newcastle, in 1683, 1684, and 1685. There was a Casper Augustine Herman, perhaps the same with his name slightly " *dutchified,*" a member of the Legislature of Maryland, from Cecil county in 1694.* His first wife was SUSANNA HUYBERTS, whom he probably married on the Delaware. He married second, in New York, August 23, 1682, ANNA REVNIERS. He had one son (and perhaps other children), named Ephraim Augustine Herman, who was a member of the Legislature of Maryland, from Cecil county, in 1715, 1716, 1728, and 1731.

3. ANNA MARGARETA HERMANS, bap. March 10, 1658. She was keeping house for her brother Ephraim, at Newcastle, when the latter was visited by the Labadists in December, 1679. They speak of her as "a little volatile, but of a sweet and good disposition." She complained to them " that she was like a wild and desolate vine, trained up in a wild and desolate country ; " that she wanted to know more of God and to serve him, and hoped the Lord would be merciful to her. She treated them " with great affection, and received thankfully " what they said to her. She became the wife of MATTHIAS VANDERHEYDEN or VANDERLEYDEN, who was a member of the Maryland Legislature, from Cecil county, in 1709, 1713, 1715, and 1716. They had *Issue* :†

    1. JANE VANDERHEYDEN, m. MR. COUTS, of Scotland.
    2. ANNA FRANCINA VANDERHEYDEN, m. EDWARD SHIPPEN, son of Edward Shippen and Elizabeth Lybrand. He was born at Boston, Dec. 10, 1677–8, and died at Philadelphia, Dec.

---

cember," after the Labadists left him, " they were informed that he was very sick and at the point of death." An account is then given of his " *tombstone,*" which was taken by the Bayards (who, after his death, came into possession of that portion of the manor in which his grave was situated), for a door for their family vault. The inscription on it is as follows :—" AUGUSTINE HERMAN, Bohemian, the first founder and seater of Bohemian Manor, Anno 1669."

The Labadists visited him in December, 1679, and the error in the date on the tombstone (?) described by Mr. Vincent is so palpable, that it hardly seems necessary to point it out. May it not have been a stone inscribed with the actual date of the settlement of the Manor?

* Proud's Hist. of Pennsylvania, vol. i. pp. 236, 286, 292. Hanson's Old Kent, p. 380.
† Hanson's Old Kent. Letters and Papers Relating, &c., to Provincial History of Penn. Privately Printed, 1856. (Shippen Genealogy.) Gibson's Biog. Sketches of Bordley family.

26, 1714. They had one dau. Margaret, who m. John Jekyll, Esq., then collector of the Port of Boston. After Mr. Jekyll's death, she lived in Philadelphia, and died there about 1750. Their dau. Fanny Jekyll m. July 19, 1758, William, son of Edward Hicks, Esq. Another dau. Margaret Jekyll, m. Mr. Chalmers.

After the death of Edward Shippen, his widow,

ANNA FRANCINA, m. Col. Hynson of Chestertown, Md., where she died before 1768, aged ninety years.

3. AUGUSTINA VANDERHEYDEN, born in 1685, m. JAMES HARRIS, of Kent county, Maryland, and had son Matthias Harris. She died in 1775, aged 90 years.

4. ARIANA VANDERHEYDEN m. Feb. 9, 1713, JAMES FRISBY, son of James and Sarah Frisby, of Cecil county, Maryland, and had Sarah Frisby, born Dec. 7, 1714; Ariana Margaret Frisby, born Sept. 18, 1717, and Francina Augustina, born Aug. 16, 1719. JAMES FRISBY, died Dec. 18, 1719, aged 35 years, and his widow, ARIANA VANDERHEYDEN, married Sept. 1, 1723, THOMAS BORDLEY, born 1682 in Yorkshire, England; he came to Kent Co., Md., in 1694, and finally settled at Annapolis; they had *Issue*: three sons, Thomas, Matthias, and John Beale Bordley. Thomas Bordley died Oct. 11, 1726, O. S., and his widow ARIANA married for her third husband, in Nov., 1728, EDMUND JENINGS, ESQ., of Annapolis, where they resided until 1737, when they went to England. She was inoculated for small-pox there, of which she died in April, 1741. He died in 1756, while on a visit to England. They had *Issue:* one son, Edmund Jenings, born in 1731, and one dau. Ariana Jenings.

4. JUDITH HERMANS, bap. May 9, 1660. Her name appears in the petition of her father to the Maryland Assembly, in 1666, for the naturalization of himself and children, and is the last notice found of her.

5. FRANCINA HERMANS, bap. March 12, 1662. She went from Maryland to Holland before 1679, but soon returned to this country. She joined the Dutch Church, in New York, by letter, or certificate, from the church in Old Amsterdam, Dec. 5, 1684, and was then single. She subsequently married JOSEPH WOODT (WOOD), and had bap. in the Dutch Church, in New York, Jenneken Wood, bap. Oct. 18, 1693.

4 iii. MARIA VARLETH[2] was probably the second daughter of Casper Varleth[1] and his wife Judith. She was thrice married: 1st to JOHANNES VAN BEECK, 2d to PAULUS SCHRICK, and 3d to WILLIAM TELLER, whose widow she was at her death, in 1702. Her first marriage, in the spring of 1654, was the source of much trouble to the authorities of New Amsterdam. On the 10th of Feb., 1654, Johannes Van Beeck petitioned the Court of Burgomasters and Schepens that the banns of matrimony between him and Maria Varleth might be registered and proclaimed. This had previously been done through the court at Gravesend (L. I.), a proceeding which the New Amsterdam court objected to as contrary to the "practice and custom of our Fatherland," because the parties were not domiciled there. Upon the earnest prayer and remonstrance of Casper Varleth and Johannes Van Beeck, the Court, on the 19th of Feb., 1654, enquired more fully into the matter, and, in an elaborate opinion, preserved in their minutes, finally ad-

judged "that the aforesaid young persons having made their proper Ecclesiastical proclamation with the earliest opportunity, that they follow it up with the bonds of matrimony immediately thereafter." *   On the 2d of March following, Governor Stuyvesant requested a copy of this opinion or resolution of the Board of Burgomasters and Schepens, with "the written reasons why such resolution was not submitted to the Director-General and Councillors for their approbation," and alleging that Johannes Van Buckly's [Van Beeck's] marriage was "not only without the knowledge of his Father but expressly against his prohibition against marrying abroad." †   In the meantime Van Beeck had resolved to consummate his matrimonial purpose elsewhere, and, on the 27th Feb., 1654, posted notices in various places in New Amsterdam, setting forth the difficulties opposed by Director Stuyvesant to his marriage at Gravesend, and protesting against the same, also giving his reasons for leaving the neighborhood.   On the same day an order for his arrest was made, and a letter of the Director and Council was addressed to all Governors, Deputy Governors, Magistrates, and Christian Neighbors, stating that he and Maria Varleth, assisted by Caspar Varleth and Augustine Hermans, had run off to New England to get married, and requesting them not to solemnize such marriage, but send back the runaways.   It appears, however, that they were married at Greenwich by Richard Crabb, a noted character and Acting Magistrate of that place.   On the 14th of Sept, 1654, by a decree of the Council in the case of Johannes Van Beeck, "who was married to Maria Varleth at Greenwich, Conn., by an unauthorized farmer named Goodman Crab," the marriage was declared unlawful, and the parties ordered to live separate.‡   It is probable that this decree was finally annulled, for, after the death of Van Beeck, Maria was recognized by the court as his lawful widow.

JOHANNES VAN BEECK was probably a younger son of Isaac Van Beeck of Amsterdam, one of the Directors of the West India Company, and perhaps came here with his brothers, Nicholas and Joost Van Beeck, about 1650.§   On the 9th of Sept., 1653, he obtained a deed from Ariaen Keyser of a house and lot in Pearl Street.   From the following it appears that he was killed by the Indians in the terrible massacre of September, 1655 : "9th Nov^r., 1655, Orphans' Court.—Whereas John Van Beck came to his death by the late misfortune [irruption of the Indians] leaving a widow and minor child, &c." . . . "16 Nov^r., 1655, The Court appointed Joost Van Beck, brother of the deceased, and Nicholas Verleth, brother of the widow, guardians, &c., of the child." . . . "20 Jany., 1656. Joost Van Beck refuses to serve as guardian, as he doubts the legality of the marriage and has a claim against the estate, so both he and Verleth are dismissed, and Paulus L. Van der Grist and Govert Loockermans appointed." ‖   In May, 1656, Joost Van Beeck having obtained a judgment against Maria Varleth, widow of Johannes Van Beeck, she petitioned for its annulment.   In the mean time he sued her for slander, to which she paid no attention ; but the Council, on the 3d May, 1656, ordered her ar-

---

* Register of the Burgomasters and Schepens, etc., Valentine's Manual, 1844-5, pp. 306-8.
† Valentine's Manual, 1853, pp. 443-444.
‡ Cal. N. V Hist. MSS. Dutch, pp. 135, 136, 141, 162, 165, 167, 378.
§ In a letter from the Directors at Amsterdam, dated April 18, 1651, Gov. Stuyvesant was instructed that permission had been given the agents of Gerard Smith, Nicolas and Joost Van Beeck to select lands for their colonies in New Netherland and one or two lots in the Manhattans (Cal. N. Y. Hist. MSS. Dutch, p. 276). Joost Van Beeck Isaacksen and his wife, Maria Anna Saffe, had a son, Petrus, bap. in New Amsterdam, August 22, 1655.   He probably returned to Holland with his family before the English conquest.
‖ Minutes of the Orphans' Court, pp. 5, 7, and 12.   I am indebted to William Clarkson, Esq., of New York, for the above memorandum, and also for valuable data relating to the Brockholst family.

rest for contempt in not answering his complaint. No further reference to
the matter appears, and probably here her legal troubles ended. Johannes Van Beeck and Maria Varleth[2] had *issue*, one daughter:

1. JUDITH VAN BEECK, bap. May 9, 1655. She m. in Willemstadt (Albany) August 29, 1674, GABRIEL MINVIELLE, a native of Bordeaux in
France. They both joined the Dutch Church in New York, Dec. 13, 1674.
He afterwards became a communicant of the French Church, but returned
to the Dutch Church again June 1, 1676. His wife's name not appearing
with his at the latter date, and there being no further account of her, it is
supposed that she died the year after her marriage, without issue. He was
a merchant, one of the prominent men of his time, and Mayor of New
York in 1684. He married, second, m. l. dated Jan. 25, 1676-7, Susanna,
dau. of John Lawrence, and died in Sept., 1702, leaving no children. His
widow married William Smith, m. l. dated Dec. 22, 1702.

MARIA VARLETH[2] m. second, Nov. 29, 1658, PAULUS SCHRICK, a native
of Neurenberg (Nuremburg). He is noticed by Mr. Savage as of "Hartford,
one of the little colony of Dutch from New York, that had planted before
the English went thither," and his wife's name mistakenly given as "Mary,
widow of Josephus Ambeck." On the 29th of Oct., 1652, he obtained a
deed from Claes Janszen Van Naerden of a lot in Pearl Street in New
Amsterdam, and was, perhaps, a resident here for a short time, his name
first appearing in the records Dec. 24, 1651, as a sponsor at the baptism of
Warnar, son of Hendrick Van Diepenbroeck. He was a merchant—a Free
Trader—and resided chiefly at Hartford, Conn., until his death in 1663.
His son Paulus was born there, and probably his daughter Susanna Maria,
though both were baptized in New Amsterdam. He is frequently styled
de Heer, or the *Honorable*, in the records, and was an important personage
among the burghers of New Amsterdam and Beverwyck (Albany), to which
places, and to Holland, his trading enterprises extended. Paulus Schrick
and Maria Varleth[2] had *issue*, one daughter and son, both baptized in the
Dutch Church in New Amsterdam the same day, viz.:

I. SUSANNA MARIA SCHRICK, bap. Sep. 2, 1663. Her second name,
Maria, is dropped in the record of her marriage and baptism of her children. She joined the Dutch Church in New York, Nov. 30, 1676, and married at Albany, May 2, 1681, CAPT. ANTHONY BROCKHOLST.* This name
was usually spelled *Brockholes*, but the Captain's autographs in the Secretary of State's office at Albany are written *Brockholls*, in the records of the
New York Dutch Church it is *Brockholst, Broeckholt, Brockholt, Brochols,
Brochold*, and *Brokholes*, while in the Surrogate's office it is written Brocholst and BROCKHOLST, which latter seems to have been the name pre-
ferred by his descendants.

When the Duke of York commissioned Major Edmund Andros in 1674
as his Lieutenant and Governor, Lieut. Anthony Brockholst, in case of his
death, was to succeed him in the government of New York and its depen-
dencies. Of a Roman Catholic family in Lancashire, England, seated at
Claughton for many centuries, he was "a profest Papist." He was a
member of Andros' first Council, and in his temporary absence from
New York in 1677-8, administered the government. He succeeded Sylvester Salisbury, who died in the winter of 1680, as Commandant at Albany,
and on the departure of Andros for England, in January, 1681, was appointed
by special commission Commander-in-Chief, etc., of the New York Govern-

* Pearson's First Settlers of Albany, p. 27.

ment, in which capacity he acted until the arrival of Gov. Dongan, in
August, 1683. He was also a member of Dongan's Council, and in 1684
bore the title of Major. In October, 1688, he accompanied Gov. Andros
on his journey to New England, and was left in command of Fort Charles
(Pemaquid), Maine, in March, 1689, from whence he was sent to Boston the
following month. In January, 1690, Lieut.-Gov. Leisler ordered his arrest,
but it does not appear that he suffered much on this account.* On the 11th
of Nov., 1695, Major Anthony Brockholst and Capt. Arent Schuyler, in behalf of themselves and their associates, Samuel Bayard, George Ryerson,
John Mead, Samuel Berrie, David and Hendrick Mandeville, obtained a
Patent (having purchased, June 6, 1695, the Indian title to the same)
for 5,500 acres of land from the East Jersey proprietors at *Pacquanac*,
now known as Pompton Plains, Morris County, N. J.† He was afterwards reported in June, 1696, as one of the ten Roman Catholics residing
in the city of New York, but in that or the following year he and Arent
Schuyler settled permanently on their Jersey lands in the Pompton valley,
on the east side of the river, and were, in all probability, the pioneers in
that region of country. He was living at Pompton in June, 1710, and is supposed to have died in 1723. An allusion is made to the exemplification
of Major Brockholt's will in a letter of Michael Kearney to Isaac Bobin,
dated at Perth Amboy, Sept. 5, 1723,‡ but where the original was entered
of record we have been unable to ascertain. His wife was living April 8,
1722, and was at that date a sponsor at the baptism in the Dutch Church,
in New York, of Anna dau. of Philip French. Anthony Brockholst and
his wife Susanna Schrick had seven children baptized in the Dutch Church,
at New York, and one in Albany. Beside these, they had a son Henry,
whose baptism is unrecorded. Only Mary, Henry, Judith, Susanna and
Jannetie or Johanna, of their children, were living in November, 1701, the
date of Maria (Varleth) Teller's will. *Issue :*

1. MARIA BROCKHOLST, born July 5, bap. July 29, 1682. She never
married. Her will is dated Sept. 12, 1761, proven July 25, 1766. She d.
June 10, 1766. In her will she styles herself Mary Brockholst, of the city
of New York, Spinster ; names her three nieces, viz. : Anna wife of David
Van Horne ; Susanna the wife of William Livingston ; and Elizabeth the
wife of David Clarkson, the children of her deceased sister Susanna formerly the wife of Philip French ; also refers to the children, without naming
them, of her late niece Mary Browne, late wife of the Hon. William
Browne of Beverly, in New England, who was also a dau. of her said
deceased sister Susanna ; names her nephews, Frederick and Philip
Philipse, and her two nieces, Susanna wife of Beverly Robinson, and Mary
wife of Roger Morris, the children of her sister Johanna wife of the late
Col. Frederick Philipse. Appoints David Van Horne, Beverly Robinson,
William Livingston and David Clarkson, Executors.

2. HENRY BROCKHOLST, born Dec. 28, 1684 ; m. MARIA VERPLANCK,
probably the daughter of Samuel (and Ariaentie) Verplanck, who was bap.
Sept. 2, 1692. But little of his personal history has been gleaned, and the
Clarksons of New York, a model of family history, is the only work, save
Schenk's Historical Discourse at Pompton, N. J., in which we have found
his name even alluded to. He was a sponsor at the bap. in the Dutch

* Brodhead's History of New York, vol. 2, Index. Burke's Landed Gentry.
† Schenk's Hist. Discourse at Pompton Plains, 1871.
‡ Cal. N. Y. Hist. MSS. English, p. 480.

Church in New York, Feb. 3, 1723, of Susanna, dau. of Frederick Philipse ; also at the bap. Jan. 1, 1725, of Elizabeth, dau. of Philip French, and Sept. 6, 1741, at bap. of Charles, son of Gulian Verplanck. Henry Brockholst Livingston, the fifth son of Gov. William Livingston, of New Jersey, was named after him, he being his maternal uncle. He resided probably all his life in New Jersey. In 1755, a division of a part of the land acquired by his father in 1695 at Pompton was made between him and Philip, son of Arent Schuyler, and the sons of Samuel Bayard. His will is recorded at Trenton. His property was bequeathed to his nephews and nieces, the same as his sister Mary's. He died March 4, 1766.

MARIA VERPLANCK, wife of Henry Brockholst, was a sponsor with David Clarkson at the bap. July 13, 1735, of Anthony, son of Frederick Philipse. At the bap. of Adriana, dau. of Gulian and Maria (Crommelin) Verplanck, July 13, 1748, Charles Crommelin and *his wife, Maria Brockholst*, were sponsors. It is not improbable that this Maria Brockholst, of whom we have no other mention, was the dau. of Henry and Maria (Verplanck) Brockholst, and the *first wife* of Charles Crommelin, his second being Sarah Roosevelt, whom he married Sept. 29, 1750.

Mary Brocholst, of the city of New York, widow (prob. the widow of Henry Brockholst), made will dated March 9, 1775 ; proven Dec. 17, 1784 ; names her friend, Mrs. Margaret Stuyvesant, wife of Peter Stuyvesant, and their two daughters, Judith and Cornelia, to each of whom she makes a small bequest, devising the residue of her estate to her nephews, Samuel and Gulian Verplanck, and her nieces, Ann Ludlow, wife of Gabriel Ludlow, and Mary McEvers, wife of Charles McEvers. Appoints her nephews, Samuel and Gulian Verplanck, Executors.

3. ANTHONY BROCKHOLST, bap. at Albany, Aug. 14, 1687 ; died in infancy.

4. ANTHONY BROCKHOLST, born July 25, 1688 ; bap. same day ; died in infancy.

5. JUDITH BROCKHOLST, born June 30, bap. July 2, 1690. At the bap. in the Dutch Church, in New York, March 30, 1726, of Maria, dau. of Frederick and Johanna (Brockholst) Philipse, DIRK VAN VEGTEN *and his wife, Judith Brocholst*, were sponsors. He was probably the son of Michael Dirkse Van Veghten and Maria Parker, of Albany, where he was bap. Jan. 26, 1690. From an old deed, dated April 20, 1742 (for a synopsis of which I am indebted to Mr. G. H. Van Wagenen, of Rye, N. Y.), it appears that Michael Van Veghten removed from Albany to New Jersey as early as 1724. In this deed, Dirck Van Veghten, of Somerset Co., N. J., Gentleman, described as the son and heir of Michael Van Veghten, late of said county, deceased, conveys jointly with his wife Judith, to John Watson, merchant, of Perth Amboy, N. J., a lot of land in PERTH AMBOY, which was purchased by his father, Sept. 30, 1724, of William Loveridge, of Perth Amboy. It is probable that Judith was his first wife, and his second Elizabeth Ten Broeck, who became a communicant of the First Ref. Dutch Church in New Brunswick, in March, 1744, of which it appears he was a member as early as 1732–5.*

6. JENNEKEN BROCKHOLST, born Sept. 16, bap. Sept. 18, 1692 ; died in infancy.

7. ANTHONY BROCKHOLST, born Oct. 6, bap. Oct. 7, 1694 ; died in infancy.

* Steele's Hist. Discourse.

8. SUSANNA BROCKHOLST, born Feb. 19, bap. Feb. 23, 1696; m. in 1720, PHILIP FRENCH, son of Philip French, Jr., and Anna (Philipse) French; he was bap. Nov. 17, 1697. His father, who is described in the record of his marriage (July 6, 1694) in the Dutch Church in New York as *Mr.* Philip French, " Van London," was a native of Kelshall, Suffolk County, England, born in 1667, and came to New York in June, 1689. He was a prosperous merchant, and an active anti-Leislerian. He was Speaker of the Assembly in 1698, and Mayor of the city in 1702. In his will, dated May 29, 1706, proven June 3, 1707, he mentions his wife, Anna, son Philip, and daughters Elizabeth, Anna and Margaret, and refers, not by name, to the children of his brother John.*

PHILIP FRENCH probably lived in New York city until about 1727, when he became a resident of New Brunswick, N. J., where he owned a large estate in land, comprising it is said the greater portion of the present site of that town. In 1732–5 he was a member of the First Ref. Dutch Church there, of which he or his son, Philip, was a liberal benefactor in 1765. His wife, Susanna, died in Holland, whither he accompanied her for the benefit of her health in 1729–30. He married second about 1732, ANNA FARMER. He had four daughters by his first wife and one son by his second, all baptized in the Dutch Church in New York, viz. :

1. ANNA FRENCH bap. April 8, 1722. At her baptism her mother's name is recorded *Susanna Brokholls, Jr.;* the sponsors were *Adolph Philips* and *Susanna Brokholls*, who was without doubt the wife of Major Anthony Brockholst. She m., Sept. 25, 1744, DAVID VAN HORNE, son of Abraham and Maria (Provoost) Van Horne; he was bap. July 20, 1715. They had issue one son and six daughters, viz. : 1. Capt. David Van Horne, of the Revolutionary Army, subsequently known as Gen. David Van Horne, m. Sarah Miller; 2. Mary, m. Levinus Clarkson; 3. Cornelia, m. Philip P. Livingston; 4. Catharine, m. Gen. Jacob Reed; 5. Elizabeth, m. Charles Ludlow; 6. Susan, m. George Trumbull; 7. Anne, m. William Edgar.

2. SUSANNA FRENCH, bap. June 19, 1723; the sponsors were *Cornelus Van Hoorn* and *Maria Brockholst.* She m., about 1745, WILLIAM LIVINGSTON, son of Philip and Catharine (Van Brugh) Livingston; he was bap. at Albany, Dec. 8, 1723. Governor of the State of New Jersey from 1776 to 1790. He died July 25, 1790. His wife died July 17, 1789. They had thirteen children, six of whom died during the Governor's life-time,† viz. : 1. a son, born 1746, died in infancy; 2, a son, born 1747, died in infancy; 3. Susannah, born 1748, m. John Cleve Symmes; 4. Catharine, born Sept. 16, 1751, m., first Matthew Ridley and second John Livingston; 5. Mary, born Feb. 16, bap. Feb. 25, 1753, m. James Linn; 6. William, born March 21, bap. March 31, 1754; 7. Philip Van Brugh, bap. July 28, 1755; 8. Sarah Van Brugh, born Aug. 2, 1756, m., April 28, 1774, John Jay;

---

* The Marriage License of a John French and Mary White, dated Oct. 21, 1694, appears in vol. iii., p. 92, of the N. Y. G. & B. RECORD; also one of John French and Katherine Benson, dated June 8, 1704, is published in vol. ii., p. 26, of the same work.
† Sedgwick's Life of William Livingston, p. 446.

9. Harry Brockholst, born Nov. 26, bap. Dec. 4, 1757; 10. Judith, born Dec. 30, 1758, bap. Jan. 7, 1759, m. John W. Watkins; 11. Philip French, born Sept. 1, bap. Sept. 4, 1760; 12, John Lawrence, born July 15, bap. July 25, 1762; 13. Elizabeth Clarkson, born April 5, bap. April 25, 1764.

3. ELIZABETH FRENCH, born Dec. 27, 1724; bap. Jan. 1', 1725; the sponsors were *Henry Brokholst* and *Elizabeth Van Hoorn.* She m., May 3, 1749, DAVID CLARKSON, JR., second son of David and Anna Margareta (Freeman) Clarkson, and grandson of Matthew Clarkson, Secretary of New York from 1689 to 1702; he was born June 3, bap. June 8, 1726. He was an opulent and prosperous merchant in New York for many years before the war of the revolution, but as he was an uncompromising whig during the war, nearly the whole of his fortune was lost by his devotion to the popular cause. His death occurred Nov. 14, 1782. His wife died June 14, 1808, and was buried by his side in the cemetry of the Dutch Church, at Flatbush, L. I. They had issue seven sons and one daughter, viz.: 1. David, b. July 30, 1750; d. young. 2. David, b. Nov. 15, 1751, a captain in the Rev. Army, m. Jane Mettick, and d. s. p. June 27, 1825; 3. Philip, b. April 4, 1754, d. young. 4. Freeman, b. Feb. 23, 1756, m. Henrietta, his cousin, dau. of Levinus Clarkson, and d. Nov. 14, 1810; she d. Sept. 18, 1850. 5. Matthew, b. Oct. 17, 1758; a distinguished colonel in the Rev. Army, aid-decamp to Arnold and Gates, and subsequently known as General Matthew Clarkson; m., 1st, May 24, 1785, Mary Rutherfurd; she d. July 2, 1786; m., 2d, Feb. 14, 1792, Sarah Cornell; she d. Jan. 2, 1803; he d. April 25, 1825. 6. Ann Margaret, b. Feb. 3, 1761; m. Nov. 16, 1784, Gerrit Van Horne, and d. Nov. 2, 1824; he d. Feb. 22, 1825. 7. Thomas Streatfeild, b. April 5, 1763; m. Oct. 30, 1790, Elizabeth Van Horne, and d. June 8, 1844; she d. Aug. 9, 1852, in her 82d year. 8. Levinus, b. March 31, 1765; m., Feb. 25, 1797, Ann Mary Van Horne, and d. Sept. 28, 1845; she d. June 23, 1856, in her 79th year.

4. MARIA FRENCH, bap. June 19, 1726; the sponsors were *Fredrik Philips* and *Johanna Brocholst, his wife.* She became the second wife of HON. WILLIAM BROWNE, of Beverly, Mass., son of Samuel Browne, of Salem, Mass., and had issue: 1. Anne, b. Aug. 25, 1754, and d. unmarried in New York. 2. Sarah, b. Feb. 13, 1758; m. in 1780 (m. l. dated Nov. 1 of that year) Edward Hall of Maryland. She d. in 1761. He d. April 27, 1763. His first wife was Mary, dau. of Gov. William Burnet, by whom he had an only son, William Burnet Browne.*

5. PHILIPPUS FRENCH, bap. April 1, 1733; the sponsors were *Col. Thomas Farmer* and *Anna Billop, his wife;* d. s. p. 1803.

9. JOHANNA BROCKHOLST, born Feb. 15, 1700, bap. Nov. 6, 1700; m., about 1719, FREDERICK PHILIPSE, only son of Philip and Maria (Sparks)

---

* N. E. Hist. Geneal. Register, Vol. 5, p. 49. Clarksons of New York, 1–180.

Philipse, and grandson of Frederick* and Margaret (Hardenbroeck) Philipse, of New York.   He was born at Spring Head, so-called, on the estate of his father, in Barbadoes, in 1695.   Left an orphan in 1700, he was sent to New York the next year by desire of his grandfather, who immediately sold the Spring Head estate, so that his grandson might not afterwards be induced to settle in Barbadoes, an arrangement that gave great displeasure to his mother's relatives.   His grandfather died Nov. 6, 1702, leaving him a large estate, including the "Yonkers plantation," and by the death of his uncle, Adolph Philipse, the whole manor of Philipsburg, in Westchester County, with the upper Highland patent of Philipstown, in Putnam County, became vested in him as the nearest male heir of his grandfather, Frederick.†   He died in New York, July 26, 1751, of consumption, and was buried in the family vault in the Dutch Church, at Sleepy Hollow, near Tarrytown.   The following notice of his death is from the *New York Gazette*, etc., for July 29, 1751:‡ "New York, July 29, 1751: Last Friday Evening departed this Life, in the 56th year of his Age, the Honorable FREDERICK PHILIPSE, Esq., one of his Majesty's Justices of the Supreme Court of this Province, and a Representative in our General Assembly for the County of Westchester.   He was a Gentleman conspicuous for an abundant Fortune; but it was not his Wealth that constituted his Merit; his Indulgence and Tenderness to his Tenants, his more than Parental Affection for his Children, and his increased Liberality to the Indigent, surpassed the Splendor of his Estate, and procured him a more unfeigned Regard than can be purchased with Opulence, or gained by Interest. There were perhaps few Men that ever equalled him in those obliging and benevolent Manners, which, at the same Time that they attracted the Love of his Inferiors, created him all the Respect and Veneration due to his Rank and Station.   That he was a Lover of his Country, is gloriously attested by his being repeatedly elected into the Assembly for the last 27 Years of his Life.   He had a Disposition extremely social, and was what few ever attain to be, a *good Companion*.   But what I have said of his Character is far from being a finished Portrait; it is only a sketch of some few of his Excellent Qualities, many features I am sure, have escaped me; but I dare say, that those I have attempted, are not set off with false colours, but drawn faithfully from the Life."

He left surviving him his wife Johanna, two sons, Frederick his heir, and Philip, to whom was devised (in equal portions with his sisters) the upper highland patent of Philipstown, and three daughters, Susannah, wife of Mr. Beverley Robinson, Mary, whom he calls in his will his *second* daughter, and Margaret, called his *youngest*.   They had nine children baptized in the Dutch Church in New York, but their dau. Mary's baptism (who married Col. Roger Morris) does not appear here, if the published date of her birth, July 5, 1730, is correct.§
His wife was killed by a fall from her carriage, on the Highland estate, in 1765.   Frederick and Johanna (Brockholst) Philipse, had *issue*;

> 1. FREDERICK PHILIPSE, born Sept. 12, bap. Sept. 14, 1720.
> The sponsors at his baptism were *Adolphe Philipse* and *Susanna Brokholls*.   From Sabine's Loyalists, we learn that

---

* The best account of this ancestor of the Philipse family will be found in the Memoirs of the Long Island Hist. Society, vol. 1, p. 362.
† Bolton's Hist. of Westchester County.   Burke's Dictionary of the Landed Gentry.
‡ Valentine's Manual, 1856, p. 681.
§ They had a dau. Maria (Mary) bap. March 30, 1726, but she probably died young.

though holding an elevated position in Colonial society, he was not a prominent actor in public affairs. He was, however, a member of the Assembly and Colonel in the militia. On account of his loyalty to the British crown during the war of the Revolution, his estate, one of the largest in the province, was confiscated by the New York Legislature, and upon the withdrawal of the British troops from New York in 1783, he went to England, where he died at the city of Chester, April, 30, 1785.* He married ELIZABETH RUTGERS, a widow, the dau. of CHARLES WILLIAMS, ESQ., and had with other issue, Frederick, Jr., for an account of whom see Burke's Dictionary of the Landed Gentry, etc., and Bolton's History of Westchester, vol. 1, p. 322.

2. SUSANNA PHILIPSE, bap. Feb. 3, 1723. The sponsors were *Henry Brockholls* and *Catharina Philips.* She died young.

3. PHILIPPUS PHILIPSE, bap. Aug. 28, 1724. The sponsors were *Philip French* and *Maria Brokholst.* He was a merchant for some years in New York,† and died there, May 9, 1768. He married MARGARET, dau. of Nathaniel MARSTON, and had with other issue, Frederick, for an account of whom see Burke's Landed Gentry and Bolton's History of Westchester. His widow married Rev. John Ogilvie, m. l., dated April 15, 1769, afterwards the Rev. John Ogilvie, D.D., who was at the time of his death (Nov. 26, 1774), Assistant Minister of Trinity Church in New York, and whose first wife was Catharine, dau. of Lancaster Symes.

4. MARIA (MARY) PHILIPSE bap. March 30, 1726. The sponsors were *Dirk Van Vegten* and *Judith Brocholst, his wife.* She probably died young.

5. SUSANNA PHILPSE, bap. Sept. 20, 1727. The sponsors were *Henry Brokholst* and *Susanna Brokholst, the wife of Philip French.* She married, about 1750, CAPT. BEVERLEY ROBINSON, son of Hon. John Robinson, of King and Queen County, Virginia, and where he was prob. born in 1722. His father, on the retirement of Sir William Gooch as Governor of Virginia, in August, 1749, became President of the Council of that Colony, but died a few days thereafter. His mother, Catharine Beverley, was a dau. of Robert and Catharine (Hone) Beverley, of Virginia, and a sister (not the dau., as Bishop Meade has it) of Robert Beverley, author of the history of that colony, first published in 1705.‡ He came to New York as early as 1746, and was Captain of a "Company of Foot lying in Fort George," in November of that year. His marriage made him wealthy, giving him as it did, the possession of his wife's large estate on the Hudson River, near West Point. He was living here at the commencement of the Revolution, and opposing the separation of the colonies from the mother country, he raised the Loyal American Regiment, and sought to prevent that glorious re-

* Bolton's Hist. of the Church in Westchester, pp. 491-2.
† N. V. Hist. MSS. English, pp. 582, 617.
‡ Beverley's History of Virginia. Meade's Old Churches and Families of Virginia, vol. 1, p. 378, and Campbell's History of Virginia, p. 448-9.

sult.   Of this Regiment he was commissioned Colonel.   In
the treason of Arnold, Col. Beverley Robinson's name is
conspicuous, and it is supposed he was aware of that officer's
defection, before any other person.   It is said he was much
opposed to Major André's trusting himself to the honor
"of a man who was seeking to betray his country."   After
the capture of that unfortunate gentleman, he was conveyed, Sept. 26, 1780, to Col. Robinson's own house, which
Arnold had occupied as headquarters, and then used by
Washington temporarily as such.   He and his wife and his
son Beverley, Jr., were included in the "Act for the Forfeit-
ure and Sale of the Estates of Persons who have adhered
to the Enemies of this State, etc," passed by the New York
Legislature, 22d October, 1779, and the whole of their im-
mense estate passed from the family.   The British Government granted him the sum of £17,000, which was con-
sidered only a partial compensation for his loss.   At the
conclusion of peace in 1783, Col. Robinson left for England, where he lived in retirement at Thornbury, near Bath,
and died there in 1792, aged 70 years.   Susanna his wife
died at the same place, in November, 1822, aged 94.*
For an account of their children, see Burke's Landed Gentry,
Burke's Peerage and Baronetage, and Sabine's Loyalists of
the American Revolution, vol. 2, p. 221 to 229.

6. MARY PHILIPSE, born July 5, 1730.   The association of this
lady's name with that of Washington, lends attractiveness to
her personal history, and is so interesting, that more than a
brief allusion to it is deemed necessary.   In February, 1756,
Col. Washington left Winchester, Virginia, to have a personal interview concerning his rank in the Virginia forces,
with General Shirley, Commander-in-chief of the British Army
in America, at Boston.   Upon this journey, performed on
horseback, in the depth of winter, he was absent seven weeks.
"While in New York," says Mr. Sparks, "he was lodged
and kindly entertained at the house of Mr. Beverley Robinson, between whom and himself an intimacy of friendship
subsisted, which indeed continued without change till severed
by their opposite fortunes twenty years afterwards in the
Revolution.   It happened that Miss Mary Philipse, a sister
of Mrs. Robinson, and a young lady of rare accomplishments, was an inmate in the family.   The charms of this lady
made a deep impression upon the heart of the Virginia colonel.   He went to Boston, returned, and was again welcomed to
the hospitality of Mr. Robinson.   He lingered there, till duty
called him away ; but he was careful to intrust his secret to
a confidential friend, whose letters kept him informed of
every important event.   In a few months intelligence came
that a rival was in the field, and that the consequences could
not be answered for, if he delayed to renew his visits to New
York.   Whether time, the bustle of a camp, or the scenes

* Sabine's Loyalists.

of war, had moderated his admiration, or whether he despaired of success, is not known. He never saw the lady again, till she was married to that same rival, Captain Morris, his former associate in arms, and one of Braddock's aids-de-camp." * Burke declares positively that she "refused the hand" of Washington, while Mr. Sabine regards this statement as very doubtful, and says, "the passage just cited seems to utterly disprove the assertion." Mary Philipse was married, Jan. 19, 1758, to COL. ROGER MORRIS, of an ancient English family, who was born in England, Jan. 28, 1727. He was a Captain in the 17th Foot, at the age of 17, one of General Braddock's aid-de-camps, and wounded at the defeat of that officer, July 8, 1755, on the Monongahela. He accompanied Wolfe in 1759 to Quebec, and participated in the battle on the plains of Abraham. On the 19th of May, 1760, he was made Lieutenant-Colonel of the 47th Foot, and in June, 1764, retired from the army. He settled in New York, and was a Member of the Council, from 1765 to the commencement of the war. Col. Morris' country-seat was situated on the high bank of the Harlem River, at the present 169th Street. The premises are now better known as the late Madame Jumel's estate. Adhering to the Crown during the war of the Revolution, his property, including the large estate of his wife, was confiscated by the New York Legislature in 1779. He received from the English government the same amount that Col. Robinson did, £17,000, as *"compensation money."* It appears, however, that, owing to his marriage settlement, the Confiscation Act did not affect the rights of Mrs. Morris' children, and in 1809, they sold to John Jacob Astor their reversionary interest in the estate for £20,000. In 1828, Mr. Astor received from the State of New York, for the rights thus purchased, the sum of $500,000. At the close of the war, Col. Morris went to England, where he died, Sept. 13, 1794, aged 67. His widow died, July 18, 1825, aged 96. The remains of both were deposited near Saviour-gate Church, York.† She and her sister Susanna were remarkable for their longevity, considering the fact that their father died of consumption, and three of their sisters and two brothers in infancy. Col. Roger and Mary (Philipse) Morris, had with other issue Henry Morris, for an account of whom see Burke's Landed Gentry and Sabine's Loyalists.

7. MARGARITA PHILIPSE, bap. Feb. 4, 1733. The sponsors were *Adolf Philipze* and *Margarita de Peyster*. She is supposed to be the *Margaret* named in her father's will as his *youngest* daughter. She died in July, 1752, unmarried.

8. ANTHONY PHILIPSE, bap. July 13, 1735. The sponsors were *David Clarkson* and *Maria Ver Plank, the wife of Henry Brockhols.* Died young.

---

* Sparks' Writings of George Washington, etc., vol. 1, pp. 77–8.
† Burke's Landed Gentry. Sabine's Loyalists.

9. JOANNA PHILIPSE, bap. Sept. 19, 1739. Sponsors, *Stephanus Bayard* and *Miss Anna French.* Died young.

10. ADOLPHUS PHILIPSE, bap. Mar. 10, 1742. Sponsors, *Adolph Philipse* and *Miss Maria Brokholst.* Died young.

II. PAULUS SCHRICK (son of Paulus and Maria (Varleth) Schrick), bap. Sept. 2, 1663, the same date as his sister Susanna Maria. He was born at Hartford, Conn., and joined the Dutch Church, in New York, March 5, 1681. He was a merchant, and engaged in the Virginia trade. He married May 11, 1686, MARIA DE PEYSTER, dau. of Jan (or Johannes) and Cornelia (Lubberts) de Peyster.* She was born Sept. 5, bap. Sept. 7, 1659, and became a communicant of the Dutch Church, June 10, 1682. This lady, whom we regard, by reason of her birth and alliances, as one of the most remarkable women born in New Amsterdam, was thrice married, and it is hazarding little of historical accuracy to say that a complete account of her family connections, by birth and marriage, would include a fuller history of the civil and military affairs of colonial times than the same account of any other person, born during the Dutch possession of Manhattan Island.

PAULUS SCHRICK, her first husband, died Oct. 11, 1685, just five months from the day of his marriage—an event which Dominie Selyns doubtless deemed sufficiently noteworthy, from the high social position of the young couple, to place in the church records. Their dwelling during their brief married life was on the east side of the *Heeren Gracht* (Broad Street.) They had no issue.

She married, second, Aug. 26, 1687, JOHN SPRATT, of Wigton, in Galloway, Scotland, and had three daughters and one son baptized in the Dutch Church, in New York.

---

* JAN (or JOHANNES) DE PEYSTER, the ancestor of a distinguished race of noted public men in the civil and military affairs of New York, was born at Harlem, in Holland, and came to New Amsterdam as early as July, 1649. His ancestors were originally from France, of noble descent, and fled to Holland to escape the persecution of Charles IX. against his Protestant subjects. Possessed of a considerable fortune by inheritance, he engaged in mercantile pursuits upon his arrival here, his trading operations being chiefly with the home country, and soon became in wealth and influence one of the prominent men of New Amsterdam. He was a Schepen in 1655-1657, 1658, and 1662; Alderman, 1666, 1667, and 1669; Burgomaster, 1673; Alderman, 1673 and 1676, and Deputy Mayor in 1677, having declined the Mayoralty in that year, on account of his imperfect acquaintance with the English language. It has been supposed he died prior to 1686, but as no mention of his widow's name (as such), who survived him many years, is found till 1689, it is probable his death occurred near the latter date. He married in the Dutch Church in New Amsterdam, Dec. 17, 1651, CORNELIA LUBBERTS, also from Harlem. She was a near relative of the De La Noys, and probably the sister of Marritie Lubberts, wife of Abraham De La Noy, who was keeper of the City tavern in 1652, and the first of that family in New Amsterdam. She made her will Jan. 19, 1699, with two codicils; the first dated Dec. 22, 1711, and the second ——— 17, 1714. It was admitted to probate Sept. 25, 1725. Supposing that to have been the year of her death, and that she was eighteen years old when married, her death must have occurred at the advanced age of 92 years. Johannes De Peyster and Cornelia Lubberts had nine children baptized in the Dutch Church, in New York, viz.:

1. JOHANNES DE PEYSTER, bap. Aug., 1653: died in infancy.
2. JOHANNES DE PEYSTER, bap. Oct. 7, 1654: died in infancy.
3. ABRAHAM DE PEYSTER, bap. July 8, 1657; m. at Amsterdam, Holland, April 5, 1684, Catharine De Peyster; Mayor of New York in 1691-2, and 1693; died Aug. 8, 1728. His wife was born July 19, 1655. They had issue, thirteen children, of whom eleven were bap. in the Dutch Church, in New York.
4. MARIA DE PEYSTER, born Sept. 5, 1659, and married as noticed in the text.
5. ISAAC DE PEYSTER, bap. April 16, 1662: m. Dec. 27, 1687, Maria Van Balen [Van Baal], dau. of Jan Hendrickse and Helena (Teller) Van Baal, of Albany. They had ten children bap. in the Dutch Church, in New York.
6. JACOB DE PEYSTER, bap. Dec. 23, 1663; d. s. p.
7. JOHANNES DE PEYSTER, b. Sept. 21; bap. Sept. 22, 1666; m. at Albany, Oct. 10, 1688, Anna Bancker, dau. of Garrit and Elizabeth Dirkse (Van Eps) Bancker; Mayor of New York in 1698, and died Sept. 25, 1711. His wife was born April 1, 1670. They had twelve children bap. in the Dutch Church, in New York.
8. CORNELIS DE PEYSTER, bap. Oct. 4, 1673; m., first, Sept. 20, 1694, Maria Bancker, probably dau. of Evert and Elizabeth (Abeel) Bancker, and had seven children bap. in the Dutch Church, in New York. He m., second, July 21, 1711, Cornelia Dishington (or Dissenton), widow of Alexander Stewart, by whom he had five daughters. He made his will Aug. 8, 1729; proved Aug. 22, 1752; names wife Cornelia, daus. Cornelia, Maria, Johanna, Catharina, Margaret, Jane, Elizabeth and Sarah.
9. CORNELIA DE PEYSTER, bap. Dec. 4, 1678; d. s. p.

She married, third, January 28, 169⅔, DAVID PROVOOST, JR., Mayor of New York in 1699, by whom she had no issue.

The following is a copy of entries made in the Spratt family Bible, published in Amsterdam in 1682, for which I am indebted to the courtesy of Mrs. John Rutherfurd, of Newark, N. J. :

1687. John Spratt of wigton in galloway and Maria de peyster * of Neiw yorcke were married on the 26 of August.

1688. upon wednesday the 16 July between 8 & 9 of the clock in the afternoon was born my daughter Cornelia baptized 18 of July 1688.

168⅞⁄₉. ffebruary Saturday betwixt 10 & 11 of the clocke in the forenoon was born my son John, baptized on Sunday being ye 2 of Febebruary.

1693. Monday 17 of april at 12 of the clock in the afternoon was born my daughter Maria baptized 23 of April.

(Then lower down, on the same page, is written :)

Cornelia Spratt, Haar Bybell New York 15 April 1705.
John Spratt, Zyn Bybel den 27 Mart 1716.

(On the next page are these entries in the Dutch language, which are thus translated :)

In the year 169⅔, the 28th of January, I, David Provoost, was lawfully joined in marriage with Maria Depeyster, widow of John Spratt, of blessed memory.

In the year 1659 was born my wife Maria, between the 4th and 5th of September, at 2 o'clock in the night, at New York.

In the year 1701, on the 3[d] of May, died in the Lord my beloved wife Maria, in the afternoon, between 6 and 7 o'clock, aged 41 years, 7 months, and 29 days, of which we lived together 2 years, 3 months, and 3 days, until the Lord separated us. She was buried in Col. Abraham De Peyster's vault, in the churchyard.

(ALTHOUGH only connected by marriage with the Varleth family, it is believed that a further account of JOHN and MARIA (DE PEYSTER) SPRATT and their descendants will not be deemed inappropriate in this place. It is corrected, with some additions, from the author's notice of the family in the Genealogical Notes of the Provoost Family, pages 18 and 25.

JOHN SPRATT[1] was a native of Scotland, from Wigton in Galloway. The first notice found of him is in the ante-nuptial agreement entered into by him and Maria Schrick, widow, August 5, 1687. He was then a merchant in New York. At the time of this agreement, the parties made a joint will, which was proved January 5, 1696-7; this date of course approximates nearly that of his decease. He became a communicant of the Dutch Church in New York February 29, 1688; was an Alderman of the Dock Ward, 1688 and 1689-90; one of the Representatives from the city and county of New York, and Speaker of the Assembly, which convened under Leisler's authority in April, 1690. On the 11th of January, 1690, he was commissioned, with others, to hold a Court of Oyer and Terminer and

---

* MARIA DE PEYSTER, bap. 7th Sept., 1660 [1659] ; espoused, first, PAULUS SCHRICK, &c. (De Peyster Genealogy, pp. 21-2.) It appears that she is not put down as the widow of Paulus Schrick, in the family Bible, but she is so called in the Dutch Church marriage records, and we note in this connection the omission in the Bible of the birth and baptism of CATHARINA SPRATT, her youngest daughter. She was bap. in the Dutch Church, in New York, Oct. 25, 1696, and the sponsors were Cornelis De Peyster and Catharina De Peyster, the wife of Col. Abraham De Peyster.

General Jail Delivery at New York, and was again a member of the General Assembly from 1693 to 1695, inclusive. *Issue :*

i. CORNELIA SPRATT[2], born July 16, bap. July 18, 1688 ; so says the family Bible, while the date of her baptism is recorded in the Dutch Church Register, July 12, 1688. She was living in July, 1711, and died unmarried.

ii. JOHN SPRATT[2], born Feb. 1, bap. Feb. 2, 1690. He resided with his uncle, Col. Abraham De Peyster, after the death of his mother, until May 1717, when he engaged in business for himself. In 1717, he made a journey to London and visited Holland.* From 1722 to 1732–3 and perhaps for a longer period, he was Captain of a Military Company in New York. He died unmarried. In his will, dated Sept. 15, 1743, proved December 18, 1749, he is styled of the City of New York, Gentleman ; names his nephew, John Provoost, and William Alexander ; his brother and sister Alexander ; John Spratt Lawrence ; Charles Le Roux, Jr., and Isaac Governeur, "his god son at Carocoa ;" Lewis Morris, Jr., and Staats Morris, to all of whom he bequeaths a portion of his estate ; makes a bequest to all the children of James Alexander, without naming them, and to the three youngest children of Richard Ashfield, † he gives all his right in the estate of his grandmother, Cornelia De Peyster ; appoints John Provoost and Peter Van Brugh Livingston executors.

iii. MARIA SPRATT, born April 17, bap. April 23, 1693. She m. first, Oct. 15, 1711, SAMUEL PROVOOST, son of David and Tryntje (Laurens) Provoost ; he was bap. Jan. 9, 1687. He was a New York merchant. His will is dated July 21, 1719, with codicil July 31, 1719 ; proved Feb. 10, 1719–20. His widow was his successor in trade, which she conducted in her own name, and for many years after her second marriage with James Alexander, and in which she amassed a fortune. She was long remembered for her "liberality and intelligence, for her mental vigor, as well as her skill and activity in business." She married second, January 1, 1721, JAMES ALEXANDER, ESQ., a native of Scotland, descended from John Alexander, an uncle of the first Earl of Stirling, who came to New York in 1715. He was a distinguished lawyer, politician, statesman and man of science ; for many years a member of the Council and Assembly of

---

* De Peyster Genealogy, page 197.

† RICHARD ASHFIELD, the first of his name in this country, came to America soon after the Duke of York had confirmed, in March, 1682–3, the sale of East Jersey to the proprietors. His father, who bore the same name, was a member of Cromwell's Parliament, and Colonel in the army of the Commonwealth. His mother, Patience Hart, was a sister of Thomas Hart, of Enfield, Middlesex, Eng., merchant, one of the twenty-four East Jersey proprietors. Richard Ashfield married in New York, August 5, 1687, Maria, dau. of Warner and Anna Elizabeth (Masschop) Wesselszen ; she was bap. October 24, 1660. He was a merchant, a member of the Church of England, and on the 19th of March, 1695, with Thomas Clark, Robert Lurting and others, petitioned "for license to purchase a piece of land without the north gate of the city of New York, between the Kings garden and the burying ground, on which to erect a Protestant Episcopal Church." In April, 1701, he applied for the place of Comptroller of Customs in New York, and probably died the same year. He had bap. in the Dutch Church in New York six children, viz. :

1. ANNA ELIZABETH ASHFIELD, bap. May 23, 1688 ; died in infancy.
2. ANNA ELIZABETH ASHFIELD, bap. December 25, 1691.
3. MARIA ASHFIELD, bap. May 27, 1694 ; died in infancy.
4. RICHARD ASHFIELD, bap. Dec. 15, 1695. He is the person noticed in the text. Thomas Hart, above named, dying after 1700, his rights in East Jersey descended to his sister and heir, Patience Ashfield, from whom they descended to her grandson and heir, Richard Ashfield, of whom we now speak. In Sept., 1725, he was appointed Receiver-General of the Board of Proprietors of East Jersey ; was in business as a merchant in New York, in August, 1732 ; appointed Sheriff of the city by Rip Van Dam, Sept. 29, 1736, for the ensuing year, and in 1740 was recommended by Gov. Morris for a seat in the New Jersey Council. He married Isabella, dau. of Gov. Lewis and Isabella (Graham) Morris. His will was proved July 27, 1742 ; names wife Isabella ; children, Lewis Morris Ashfield, Richard Morris Ashfield, and Mary and Isabella Ashfield. In 1745, his brother-in-law, Robert Hunter Morris, held his lands in New Jersey, *in trust* for his children.

5. PATIENCE ASHFIELD, bap. Sept. 4, 1698.
6. MARIA ASHFIELD, bap. Dec. 10, 1701.

New York, and for some time member of the Council of New Jersey. He died April 2, 1756. She died April, 1760.

SAMUEL PROVOOST and MARIA SPRATT[2] had *issue:*

1. MARIA PROVOOST, bap. August 17, 1712; died young.

2. JOHN PROVOOST, bap. Jan. 10, 1714; m. about 1741, EVE, dau. of Harmanus and Catharine (Meyer) RUTGERS. He died Sept. 24, 1767. She died about the year 1788. They had five children, the eldest of whom was the Rt. Rev. Samuel Provoost, D.D., Rector of Trinity Church 1784–1800, and first Bishop of the State of New York.

3. DAVID PROVOOST, bap. June 19, 1715; died in 1741, unmarried.

JAMES ALEXANDER and MARIA SPRATT[2], the widow of Samuel Provoost, had *issue* four daughters and one son, viz. :

1. MARY ALEXANDER, born in 1721; m. Nov. 3, 1739, PETER VAN BRUGH, son of Philip and Catharine (Van Brugh) LIVINGSTON; he was bap. in Albany, Nov. 3, 1710; a prominent merchant in New York, and died in 1793; she died in New York Sept. 24, 1767, and was buried in the family vault in Trinity Church. They had twelve children baptized in the Dutch and Presbyterian Churches in New York; the first five in the former, and the others in the latter, viz. :

    1. PHILIP LIVINGSTON, bap. Nov. 12, 1740.

    2. MARIA LIVINGSTON, bap. May 27, 1742; died in infancy.

    3. CATHARINA LIVINGSTON, bap. October 2, 1743.

    4. JAMES ALEXANDER LIVINGSTON, bap. Oct. 10, 1744; died young.

    5. MARIA LIVINGSTON, bap. Oct. 29, 1746.

    6. PETER VAN BRUGH LIVINGSTON, born March 31, bap. April 5, 1753.

    7. SARAH LIVINGSTON, born April 30, bap. May 18, 1755.

    8. WILLIAM ALEXANDER LIVINGSTON, born Feb. 10, bap. Feb. 20, 1757.

    9. SUSANNA LIVINGSTON, born March 23, bap. April 5, 1759.

    10. ELIZABETH LIVINGSTON, born June 20, bap. June 28, 1761.

    11. JAMES ALEXANDER LIVINGSTON, born July 27, bap. Aug. 14, 1763.

    12. ANN LIVINGSTON, born Sept. 14, bap. Oct. 4, 1767.

2. WILLIAM ALEXANDER, born December 27, 1725; called Earl of Stirling; eminently distinguished for his bravery and patriotism; a Major-General in the Army of the United States during the Revolution. He m. March 1, 1748, SARAH, dau. of Philip and Catherine (Van Brugh) LIVINGSTON; she was bap. in Albany, Nov. 7, 1725, and died in 1804; he died in the U. S. service at Albany, Jan. 15, 1783. They had two daughters bap. in the Dutch Church in New York, viz.: 1. Mary Alexander, bap. April 12, 1749; she was commonly called Lady Mary Alexander; m. Robert, eldest son of John and Ann (De Lancey) Watts; he was born Aug. 23, 1743; grad. King's Col., 1760, and died in Phila., Sept. 16, 1814; was buried in Trinity Churchyard, New York. 2. Catherine Alexander, bap. March 18, 1753; usually called Lady Catherine; m. July 27, 1779, COL. WILLIAM DUER, born in England, March 18, 1747; he came to New York as early as 1768; filled various public offices in the Colony and State; was an active patriot during the war of the Revolution; a delegate to the Continental Congress 1777–8; Secretary of the Treasury Board until the organization of the U. S. Treasury Department in 1789, and Assistant Secre-

tary of the Treasury under Alexander Hamilton until 1790. He died in New York, May 7, 1799.

3. ELIZABETH ALEXANDER; m. JOHN STEVENS, a merchant, in 1756, and prominent citizen of Perth Amboy, N. J. In June, 1763, he was appointed one of the New Jersey Council; he died in Hunterdon Co. in 1792; she died at Clermont, Livingston Manor, in 1800. They had one son and two daughters, viz. :

　　1. JOHN STEVENS, born 1750; he died March 6, 1838, leaving four sons: Edwin A., John C., Robert L., and James H. ; and four daughters :. Elizabeth J., who m. Thomas A. Conover; Harriet, m. Joshua R. Sands; Esther B., and Sophia C. Van Cortlandt.

　　2. ELIZABETH STEVENS, m. Sept. 9, 1770, Chancellor ROBERT R. LIVINGSTON.

　　3. MARY STEVENS.

4. CATHERINE ALEXANDER, third dau. of James and Mary (Spratt) Alexander; m. first ELISHA, son of Hon. John and Janet (Johnstone) PARKER, of Perth Amboy, N. J.; he studied law under James Alexander, Esq., and was licensed to practise May 3, 1745; he died of consumption March 14, 1751, in his 47th year, leaving no issue. His widow m. second, December 21, 1758, MAJOR WALTER RUTHERFURD, of the British Army, who served in the French war in the campaign on Lake Ontario, and in Canada. He settled in New York, from whence he removed to New Jersey. (?) After their marriage they went to housekeeping in "the Broadway," their residence being on the corner of Vesey Street, the present site of the Astor House. His wife died in June, 1801. His will is dated April 18, 1801; proven Jan. 18, 1804; describes himself, "son of Sir John Rutherfurd of that Ilk in Roxburghshire, North Britain, being at present in the 78th year of my age; " names wife Catherine and "Major General Mathew Clarkson, the worthy father of my grand daughter, Mary Rutherfurd Clarkson; " son John and grandson Robert Walter Rutherfurd, and his nephew John Rutherfurd, of Edgerton, son of his elder brother John ; also his nephew John Rutherfurd, of Messburnford. Appoints Mathew Clarkson and his son John executors. *Issue :*

　　1. JOHN RUTHERFURD, born Sept. 21, 1760; grad. Princeton Col. in the class of 1776; m. HELEN, dau. of Gen. Lewis Morris, of Morrisania, and settled in New York City, where he engaged in the practice of law. He subsequently removed to New Jersey, from which State he was a Senator of the United States from 1791 to 1798. "He was the last survivor of the Senators in Congress during the administration of Washington." He died at Edgerton, N. J., Feb. 23, 1840. He had one son and four daughters, viz. : Robert Walter, m. Sabina Morris; Helen Sarah, m. Peter G. Stuyvesant; Mary; Louisa; and Anne, who m. in 1813 Dr. John Watts, son of Robert and Mary (Alexander) Watts. Dr. Watts was born in New York, in Dec., 1785, and became an eminent practitioner of medicine in his native city, where he died, Feb. 4, 1831.

　　2. MARY RUTHERFURD, born Nov. 4, 1761; baptized by Dr. Barclay, the Earl of Stirling godfather, Mrs. Rutherfurd, of

Edgerton, by her daughter Elinor, proxy, and Miss S. Alexander, godmothers. She m. May 24, 1785, GENL. MATHEW CLAKSON (see page 93), and died, July 2, 1786, leaving one dau., Mary Rutherfurd Clarkson, born July 2, 1786 ; she m. July 29, 1807, Peter Augustus Jay, eldest son of Governor John Jay, and died Dec. 24, 1838 ; he was born Jan. 24, 1776 ; grad. at Columbia Coll., 1794 ; studied law in the office of Peter Jay Munro, and became eminent in his profession ; represented the county of New York in the Assembly in 1816 ; Recorder of the city, 1819–20 ; member of the State Constitutional Convention of 1821, and for many years President of the New York Historical Society, and trustee of Columbia College ; he died Feb. 20, 1843. Their children were : John Clarkson Jay, M.D. ; Peter Augustus Jay ; Mary Jay, who m. Frederick Prime ; Sarah Jay, who m. William Dawson ; Catharine Helena Jay, m. Henry A Dubois, M.D. ; Anna Maria Jay, m. Henry E. Pierrepont, Esq., of Brooklyn ; Susan Matilda Jay, m. Mathew Clarkson ; and Elizabeth Clarkson Jay.

5. SUSANNAH ALEXANDER ; m. JOHN REID.

iv. CATHARINA SPRATT, bap. Oct. 25, 1696 ; died young.)

MARIA VARLETH[2], widow of Paulus Schrick, married her third husband, WILLEM TELLER, of Fort Orange (Albany), according to the records of the Ref. Dutch Church of Brooklyn,* May 4, 1664. It would seem from the register of the New York church that they were married April 9, 1664, but this must have been the date of the publication of their marriage banns, as more clearly appears from the time and place at which the following paper was executed :

"In the name of the Lord Amen, be it known that in the year of our Lord Jesus Christ sixteen hundred and sixty-four, the 19th day of April, appeared before me Johannes La Montagne, in the the service of, etc., the honorable Willem Teller, widower of the late Margariet Donckesen, who declares in the presence of the afternamed witnesses, that for God's honor he has contracted a future marriage with Maria Verlet, widow of the late Paulus Schrick, and before the consumation of the same, he, the subscriber, has made up and exhibited for the seven remaining children of Margariet Donckesen (the subscribers late wife), the sum of three thousand five hundred carolus guilders in beaver's price, exclusive of all debts hitherto made, which he undertakes to pay, to be distributed as follows, to wit : to Anderies Teller aged 22 years, Helena Teller 19 years, Martjen ? 16 years, Elysabeth Teller 12 years, Jacob Teller 9 years, Willem Teller 7 years, and Johannes Teller 5 years, being her matrimonial inheritance, and for the payment of the aforesaid sum, the subscriber offers all his estate personal and real, as a pledge and mortgage ; to which end said subscriber appoints, as guardians, the honorable Sander Leendertse Glen † and Pieter Loocker-

---

* Were they married in Brooklyn or New Amsterdam? I think it probable in the latter place, and by Domine Selyns, who was then the minister at Stuyvesant's Bouwery, as well as of the Brooklyn congregation. His performance of the ceremony accounts for the entry of their marriage in the Brooklyn church records.

† Sander Leendertse Glen married Catalva Doncassen or Dongan, sister of Willem Teller's first wife.

mans, uncles of said children; in the meantime the subscriber shall remain holden to bring up the aforesaid children, to wit, the minors, in the fear of the Lord, to teach them to read and write; furthermore, to maintain them in food and clothing, until their majority and marriage, without any diminution of their matrimonial [maternal?] estate; all which the subscriber promises to do, without craft or guile, pledging therefor his person and estate, real and personal, present and future.

"Thus done in the village of Beverwyck, in the presence of the honorable Evert Wendel and Johannes Provoost, as witnesses hereto called, of date *ut supra.*

"WILLEM TELLER.

" *Evert Janse Wendel, as witness.*
" *Johannes Provoost, witness.*
"Acknowledged before me,
"LA MONTAGNE, *Commis.* at Fort Orange." *

WILLIAM TELLER,† born in 1620, came to New Netherland in 1639, and settled at Albany. He was one of the proprietors of Schenectady in 1662, though he probably never resided there. He was engaged in trade in Albany, and removed to New York in 1692, he and his wife Maria becoming members of the Dutch Church there December 1st of that year. In his will, dated March 19, 1698, proved May 23, 1701, he mentions his wife Mary and following named children: Andrew; Helena Rombout; alludes to "the two children of Mary Van Aelen," his deceased daughter, without naming them; Elizabeth Vanderpoel; William and Johannes Teller; Janneke Schuyler, and Susanna Brockholes, his daughter-in-law; Anna Margareta, daughter of his son Jacob Teller, deceased; and speaks of his son Casper Teller, deceased. Appoints his sons Andrew, William, and Johannes, executors.

The will of MARY TELLER [*nee* Maria Varleth²] of the city of New York, relict of William Teller, decᵈ, is dated Nov., 1701, proved Sept. 21, 1702; names children of her eldest daughter, Susanna Brockholst, viz.: Mary, Henry, Judy, Susanna, and Jannetie Brockholst; also the children of her youngest daughter, Jannetie Schuyler, decᵈ, viz.: Margareta, Philip, Mary, and Casparus Schuyler. Appoints as executors her brother-in-law, Col. Nicholas Bayard, and in case of his death, his son, Mr. Samuel Bayard; her son-in-law, Major Anthony Brockholst, and in case of his death, his then widow, Susanna Brockholst; and her son-in-law, Capt. Arent Schuyler, and in case of his death, his brother, Capt. Brant Schuyler.

WILLIAM TELLER, SEN., and his first wife MARGARET DONCKESEN or DUNCES, had *issue,* viz.:

1. ANDRIES TELLER, born 1642; m. May 6, 1671, SOPHIA VAN CORTLANDT, dau. of Olof Stevense and Ann (Loockermans) Van Cortlandt. He was a merchant and magistrate for many years at Albany, where his children were born and baptized. In 1692 he and his wife removed to New York, and became communicants of the Dutch Church here on the 1st of December of that year. He made his will May 18, 1700, proved Nov. 9, 1702, in which he mentions his wife Sophia, eldest son Andries, and dau. Margrieta; his son, Oliver Stephen, who was bap. in Albany Nov. 29, 1685, is not named in the will.

---

* Pearson's Early Records of the City and County of Albany, pp. 345–6.
† See N. Y. G. & B. RECORD, Vol. II., p. 139, and Pearson's First Settlers of Albany.

ANDRIES and SOPHIA (VAN CORTLANDT) TELLER had *issue:*

    i. Andries Teller, who m. about 1699 ANNA VERPLANCK, dau. of Gelyn and Hendrickje (Wessels) Verplanck; she was bap. Sept. 15, 1680; they had bap. in the Dutch Church in New York one son, Andries, Feb. 2, 1701. In his will, dated Sept. 3, 1702, proved Nov. 9, 1702, he is styled merchant; names his only son, Andrew Teller,* his brother, Oliver Stephen, sister Margaret, and his mother, Sophia Teller, widow.

    ii. MARGRIETA TELLER.

    iii. OLIVER STEPHEN TELLER, bap. in Albany Nov. 29, 1685. His second name, Stephen, is dropped in the record of his marriage and baptism of his children. He m. Oct. 12, 1712, CORNELIA DE PEYSTER, dau. of Isaac and Maria (Van Baal) De Peyster; she was bap. Oct. 30, 1690. They had ten children baptized in the Dutch Church in New York, viz.: 1. Margareta, March 18, 1713; 2. Johannes, Aug. 21, 1715; 3. Margareta, Dec. 25, 1716; 4. Cornelia, March 29, 1719; 5. Oliver, Feb. 12, 1721; 6. Isaac, Oct. 21, 1722; 7. Andries, Feb. 21, 1724; 8. Maria, Feb. 17, 1725; 9. Johannes, April 6, 1726; and 10. Sophia, Aug. 20, 1729.

    2. HELENA TELLER, born 1645; m. first CORNELIS BOGARDUS, son of Rev. Everardus and Anneke (Janse) Bogardus; he was bap. Sept. 9, 1640, and died in 1666. His widow married second, JAN HENDRICKSE VAN BAAL [VAN BALEN], free trader, in Beverwyck (Albany), 1661–78. She became a communicant of the Dutch Church in New York August 29, 1683, and was then the widow of Van Baal. She married third, Sept. 26, 1683, FRANCOIS ROMBOUT or ROMBOUTS, Mayor of New York in 1679. He was a merchant and had been married twice before; 1st, on the 31st day of May, 1665, to Aeltje Wessels, and 2d, Aug. 8, 1675, to Anna Elizabeth Masschop, the widow of Warnar Wessels. He died in 1691, his will bearing date Jan. 20, 1690, proved March 3, 1707; names his wife, Helena Teller, and dau. Catharina, "gotten by his said wife," to whom he bequeaths his entire estate, which included a large landed property in the present town of Fishkill, Duchess Co., N. Y. His widow Helena made her will Nov. 20, 1706, proved March 4, 1707, in which she mentions her eldest son, Cornelis Bogardus; her youngest dau., Catharina, wife of Roger Brett; son, *Henry Van Bael;* daughters, Maria, wife of Isaac De Peyster; Margaret, wife of Nicholas Evertsen; Helena wife of Gualtherus Du Bois; Rachel, wife of Petrus Bayard, and "Hannah, who is *non compos mentis.*"

CORNELIS and HELENA (TELLER) BOGARDUS had *issue:*

    i. CORNELIS BOGARDUS, who m. RACHEL DE WITT, dau. of Tjerck Claezen De Witt, of Esopus, and had Jenneken, bap. May 13, 1694, in the Dutch Church in New York. He died Oct. 13, 1707.

JAN HENDRICKSE and HELENA (TELLER) VAN BAAL had *issue:*

    i. HENRY VAN BAAL, who died before 1716, probably without issue.

---

* This is probably the Andrew Teller who m. Sept. 15, 1722, Catharine Vandewater, and had bap. in the Dutch Church in New York, Andries, Nov. 25, 1726, and Catharina, Dec. 4, 1728, and probably settled soon after at Fishkill. N. Y.

ii. MARIA VAN BAAL, m. Dec. 27, 1687, ISAAC DE PEYSTER, and
had *issue* bap. in the Dutch Church in New York, viz.:
1. Cornelia, Oct. 20, 1689; 2. Cornelia, Oct. 30, 1690;
3. Johannes, Jan. 8, 1693; 4. Helena, Jan. 30, 1695; 5.
Isaac, April 11, 1697; 6. Maria, March 19, 1699; 7. Abraham, July 6, 1701; 8. Jacobus, Sept. 5, 1703; 9. Hendricus, Dec. 12, 1705; and 10. Hendricus, Dec. 15, 1706.

iii. MARGARET VAN BAAL, m. 1697, m. l. dated Dec. 13 of that
year, CAPT. NICHOLAS EVERTSEN, mariner, of New York.
She joined the Dutch Church in New York March 1, 1693.
They had two sons baptized there, viz.: Nicolaas, May
29, 1699, and Johannes, Jan. 29, 1701.

iv. HELENA VAN BAAL, m. Jan. 1, 1700. Do. GUALTERUS DU
BOIS, son of Rev. Peter Du Bois, of Amsterdam. She
joined the Dutch Church in New York "upon confession
of faith," Sept. 3, 1696. Her husband survived her many
years. He was called as minister to the Ref. Dutch
Church in New York in 1699, his name appearing upon
the church register October 26, of that year. He ministered here for nearly fifty-two years, preaching for the last
time on the 25th of Sept., 1751. He was taken ill that
evening, and died on the 9th of October following, in
the eighty-first year of his age. His remains were in-
terred in the Old Dutch Church in Garden Street. They
had six children bap. in the New York Dutch Church, viz.:
1. Elizabeth, Nov. 29, 1700; 2. Johannes Petrus, Sept.
20, 1702; 3. Gualterus, July 25, 1705; 4. Johannes, April
11, 1708, m. Oct. 11, 1730, his cousin Helena, dau. of
Peter Bayard; 5. Elizabeth, Oct. 26, 1712; and 6. Isaac,
June 12, 1715. Isaac Du Bois became a physician, and
m. Dec. 10, 1740, Margarita Nicoll, by whom he had one
son and two daughters bap. in the Dutch Church in New
York; their youngest dau., Margareta, bap. Jan. 15, 1746,
was a posthumous child, her father, Dr. Isaac Du Bois,
having died, "a gentleman of a fair character, and univer-
sally lamented," on the 9th of Nov., 1745.

v. RACHEL VAN BAAL, m. first, Oct. 5, 1699, PETRUS BAYARD,
probably the son of Petrus and Blandina (Kierstede) Bayard. They had four sons and one dau. bap. in the Dutch
Church in New York, viz.: 1. Petrus, August 14, 1700;
2. Helena, Dec. 9, 1702; 3. Johannis, Oct. 8, 1704;
4. Samuel, July 14, 1706; and 5. Hendrikus, Feb. 25,
1708. Rachel Van Baal, the widow of Petrus Bayard,
m. second, HENRY WILEMAN, and had bap. in the Dutch
Church in New York one dau., Rachel, Jan. 28, 1719.

vi. HANNAH VAN BAAL, mentioned in her mother's will as *non
compos mentis.*

FRANCIS and HELENA (TELLER) ROMBOUT had *issue :*

i. JANNETIE ROMBOUT, bap. Sept. 5, 1684; d. young.

ii. CATHARINA ROMBOUT, bap. May 25, 1687; m. 1703, m. l.
dated Nov. 25 of that year, ROGER BRETT. They had one
son bap. in the Dutch Church in New York, viz.: **Thomas,**

bap. March 11, 1705. Roger Brett settled at Fishkill, in Duchess County, N. Y., upon lands bequeathed to his wife by her father. He and his wife built the first grist-mill in that county, which was known after his death, far and wide, as "*Madam Brett's Mill*," and which was at that period a point of considerable local importance. He was killed in 1721, on board of a sloop going from New York to Fishkill, by being struck by the boom of the vessel.* His widow Catharina made her will Dec. 13, 1763, proven March 14, 1764, in which she names her eldest son, Francis Brett; her son, Robert, and his five children, viz.: Matthew, Francis, Rombout, Sarah, and Robert; also her two youngest grandsons, Theodorus, son of Francis, and Robert, son of Robert Brett. Appoints her son, Francis Brett, Col. John Brinckerhoff, Capt. Eleazer Dubois, and Peter Dubois, of Rombout Precinct, executors.

iii. JOHANNES ROMBOUT, bap. June 12, 1689; died young.

3. MARIA TELLER, born 1648; m. first PIETER VAN ALEN, trader, of Albany, about 1667. He died January 1674, leaving two sons, Johannes and Willem. His widow m. second (PIETER?) LOOCKERMANS in 1676.

4. ELIZABETH TELLER, born 1652; m. first ABRAHAM VAN TRICHT, of Albany, by whom she had two daus., Magdalena, bap. at Albany Oct. 21, 1683, who m. Nov. 28, 1703, Abraham Lansing; and Helena, bap. at Albany May 30, 1686. There was an Elizabeth Van Tricht who may have been an elder dau., who m. July 28, 1703, in New York, MICHAEL FALLON, and had bap. in the Dutch Church there, Helena, Feb. 6, 1706, and Jacobus, July 27, 1707. On the 29th of June, 1692, at Albany, Elizabeth, widow of Abraham Van Tricht, m. MELGERT WYNANTSE VANDERPOEL, widower of Ariaantje Verplanck, by whom she had bap. at Albany, Willem, March 19, 1693, and Ariaantje, Nov. 17, 1695.

5. JACOB TELLER, born 1655; m. Oct. 24, 1683, CHRISTINA WESSELS, dau. of Warner and Anna Elizabeth (Masschop) Wessels; she was bap. March 5, 1662. They had two children bap. in the Dutch Church in New York; Willem, Dec. 22, 1689, and Anna Margareta, August 1, 1694, who married Sept. 25, 1710, DIRK EGBERTSE, and had three children bap. in New York, viz.: 1. Christina Egbertse, Sept. 23, 1711; 2. Egbert Egbertse, Oct. 14, 1713, and 3. Maria Egbertse, June 6, 1722. Jacob Teller, mariner, made his will Aug. 17, 1696, proved April 23, 1697, in which he mentions wife Christina, dau. Anna Margaret, his brother William Teller, Jr., and brothers-in-law Richard Ashfield and Isaac De Riemer. Appoints his wife executrix. His widow Christina made her will Sept. 17, 1698, proved 1698, in which she speaks of her dau. Anna Margaret Teller; her brother Gerardus Wessels, and sisters Gertruyd Wessels, widow of ——, minister; Maria Wessels, wife of Richard Ashfield, and Aeltie Wessels, wife of Isaac De Riemer.

6. WILLEM TELLER, JR., born 1657; m. in New York, Nov. 19, 1686, RACHEL KIERSTEDE, dau. of Dr. Hans and Sara (Roelofs) Kierstede; she was bap. Sept. 13, 1665. They both joined the Dutch Church in New York, "gekomen van N. Albanien," Sept. 1, 1689. They had bap. in New York eight children, viz.:

* Smith's History of Duchess Co., p. 178.

  i. MARGARETA TELLER, bap. Aug. 17, 1687; died young.
  ii. WILLEM TELLER, bap. Sept. 1, 1689; died young.
  iii. WILLEM TELLER, bap. Dec. 25, 1690; m. MARIA KENNEF
   (KENNICH, KENNIP, VAN TRICHT, ? m. l. dated Jan. 19,
   1706, of William Teller and Maria Van Tricht), and had
   Willem, bap. in New York, March 24, 1714.
  iv. HANS or JOHANNES TELLER, bap. March 12, 1693; m. in
   New York, April 23, 1719, CATHARINA VAN TILBURG, dau.
   of Pieter and Elizabeth (Van Hoogten) Van Tilburg; she
   was bap. July 7, 1700. They had bap. in the Dutch
   Church in New York, Willem, May 26, 1720, and Petrus
   August 24, 1722.
  v. MARGARIET TELLER, bap. Feb. 2, 1696; m. May 25, 1717,
   JACOBUS STOUTENBURG, son of Tobias and Anna (Van
   Rollegom) Stoutenburg; he was bap. June 7, 1696. They
   had bap. in the Dutch Church in New York, Tobias, Feb.
   12, 1718; Rachel, March 16, 1720; Willem, June 3, 1722;
   Anna, Nov. 11, 1724, and Margrietje, April 14, 1734.
  vi. JACOBUS TELLER, bap. Jan. 18, 1699; died young.
  vii. ANDRIES TELLER, bap. Jan. 25, 1702; died young.
  viii. JACOBUS TELLER, bap. August 29, 1703.

  7. JOHANNES TELLER, born 1659; m. Aug. 18, 1686, SUSANNA, dau. of
CAPT. JOHANNES WENDEL, of Albany. He was a farmer at Schenectady,
and at the burning of the village in 1690 was carried away captive by the
French and Indians to Canada. He was much reduced in property by
that event, in consideration of which, his father conveyed to him on the
20th of June, 1700, a house lot, and his lands in Schenectady. He made
his will May 15, 1725, and spoke of sons Johannes, Willem, and Jacob;
and daughters Margareta, wife of Jacob Schermerhorn; Maria, wife of
Abraham Glen; and Annatie, wife of Harmanus Vedder. He died May
28, 1725.*

  WILLIAM TELLER, SEN., and his second wife, MARIA VARETH[2], had *issue*,
viz. :

  8. CASPER TELLER, born at Albany. Certificates dated Sept. 16, 1692,
that he had transported men from Albany to New York, with their ac-
coutrements, etc., are noticed in the Calendar of N. Y. Hist. MSS., English,
from which it may be inferred that he was a skipper on the North River.
He was a sponsor at the bap. in New York, Sept. 18, 1692, of Jenneken,
dau. of Major Anthony Brockholst, and had deceased before March 19,
1698, the date of his father's will.

  9. JANNETIE (JOHANNA) TELLER, m. at Albany Nov. 26, 1684, CAPT.
ARENT SCHUYLER, son of Col. Philip Pieterse and Margarita (Van Schlich-
tenhorst) Schuyler. He was born in 1661, was a trader, and removed
from Albany to New York, as early as 1694, himself and wife joining the
Dutch Church there on the 28th of February of that year. She died June
22, 1700. He married second, m. l. dated Dec. 12, 1702, SWANTIE DYCK-
HUYSE. His third wife was MARIA WALTERS,† of New York, and perhaps
the second dau. of Robert and Catharina (Leisler) Walters.

  In 1696 or 7, Capt. Schuyler having purchased with others, as stated
ante, page 90, a tract of land in what is now known as Pompton Plains,

---

* Pearson's First Settlers of Schenectady, p. 189.
 † MS. Notes by the late S. Alofsen, of Jersey City, in Dr. Rogers' Hist. Discourse, Albany, 1857, now in
possession of Dr. Samuel S. Purple, of New York.

Morris Co., N. J., settled there in company with his brother-in-law, Major Anthony Brockholst. They located themselves, according to Mr. Schenck's statement, near to each other, on the east side of the river, just below the steel-works; Brockholst on the spot where Major William Colfax now resides (1871), and Schuyler, as near as can be ascertained, on the site of the residence of Dr. William Colfax. They were thus, in all probability, the pioneers in the settlement of this region, and the first to open up what was then a wilderness, "unless the tradition that Joost Beam settled at Wynockie as early as 1660 is true."*

How long he remained here is not known, but in April 1710, he had become a resident of New Barbadoes Neck,† in Bergen Co., N. J., where he lived until his death, which probably occurred in the latter part of the year 1730. His will is dated Dec. 17, 1724, with codicil Oct. 30, 1730; proven February 27, 1730-1. He had *issue*, twelve children, six by his first wife, and the mother of the others we are unable to identify.

    1. MARGARETA SCHUYLER, bap. at Albany Sept. 27, 1685.

    2. PHILLIPUS SCHUYLER, bap. at Albany Sept. 11, 1687; m. about 1713, HESTER, dau. of Isaac and Elizabeth KINGSLAND, of New Barbadoes, N. J. Will dated April 9, 1760, proved Jan. 27, 1764. In 1755, a division of part of the land which he inherited from his father, called the "*Upper Pacquanac Patent*," at Pompton, N. J., was made between him and Harry Brockholst (to whom the right had come from his father) and the sons of Samuel Bayard, the son and heir-at-law of Col. Nicholas Bayard. On part of this tract some of his descendants are yet living. He had *issue :* 1. Johanna, born Sept. 2, 1713; m. June 24, 1741, Isaac Kingsland. 2. Arent, born Feb. 23, 1715; m. first, Oct. 1, 1741, Helena, dau. of Gerrit and Annetje (Sip) Van Wagenen, of Acquack-anonck, N. J.; m. second, Rachel ——. 3. Isaac, born April 26, 1716; died in infancy. 4. Philip, born Dec. 23, 1717; married and had sons, Philip and Garret. 5. Isaac, born Sept. 8, 1719; married and had son, Major Schuyler. 6. Elizabeth, born Feb. 22, 1721; m. Rev. Benjamin Van der Linde; marriage bond dated Nov. 9, 1748. 7. Pieter, born June 7, 1723; m. Mary ——, d. s. p. Oct. 18, 1808. 8. Hester, born April 12, bap. at Hackensack, June 29, 1725; m. Teunis Dey. 9. Maria, born Sept. 11, 1727. 10. Jenneke, born Oct. 26, 1728; m. —— Board; resided at Wesel. 11. Johannis, born June 4, 1730; died in infancy; and 12. Casparus, born Dec. 10, 1735; m. and had one dau., Hester, who m. Genl. William Colfax, of Pompton, Captain Commandant of Washington's Life Guard; m. l. dated Sept. 1, 1783; he was the grandfather of Schuyler Colfax, late Vice-President of the United States.

    3. MARIA SCHUYLER, bap. at Albany Oct. 6, 1689.

    4. JUDIK SCHUYLER, bap. at Albany March 13, 1692; died young.

    5. CASPARUS SCHUYLER, bap. in New York May 5, 1695; married and settled in Burlington, N. J. Among his children was Arent, who m. Jane ——.

---

* Schenck's Hist. Discourse at Pompton Plains, 1871. † Winfield's Hist. of Hudson Co., N. J., p. 533

6. WILHELMUS SCHUYLER, bap. in New York June 2, 1700 ; died young.

7. OLIVIA SCHUYLER, mentioned in her father's will, but dead at that time, leaving issue.

8. JOHN SCHUYLER, m. Jan. 1, 1739, ANN VAN RENSSELAER. Will dated Dec. 22, 1772 ; proved Feb. 12, 1773. He received by his father's will his lands on New Barbadoes Neck, and left them to his son Arent J., who was born Oct., 1746, and m. Nov. 2, 1772, his cousin Swan Schuyler ; he died Oct. 28, 1803.

9. PETER SCHUYLER, born about 1710 ; m. MARY, dau. of John WALTER, of New York. Col. Peter Schuyler was one of the prominent men of New Jersey in his day, and a brave soldier who did honor to his country. A sketch of his life and military services will be found in Winfield's History of Hudson Co., N. J., pp. 536–541—in the Schuyler Genealogy—to which we are indebted and the reader is referred. He died March 7, 1762. He had *issue*, a dau., Catharine, who m. ARCHIBALD KENNEDY, Earl of Casselis. She inherited her parents' property, and also that of the grandfather, John Walter, who was a man of great wealth. She was also the heiress of Richard Jones. She died without issue, and Kennedy m. second, Ann, dau. of Hon. John and Ann (De Lancey) Watts, of New York.

10. ADONIJAH SCHUYLER, m. GERTRUDE VAN RENSSELAER. By his father's will he received two tracts of land at Elizabeth-town Point. Will dated May 20, 1761 ; proved May 28, 1762. He had seven children, viz. : 1. Van Rensselaer ; 2. Mary ; 3. Swan, m. Nov. 2, 1772, Arent Schuyler ; she died May 20, 1801, aged 60 years ; 4. John, m. Feb. 16, 1769, Mary Hunter ; 5. Peter ; 6. Adonijah, a Lieut. in the British Navy, m. Susan Shields, of Plymouth, Eng., where he settled ; 7. Philip, d. s. p. in 1795.

11. EVA SCHUYLER, m. PETER BAYARD, and died in 1737.

12. CORNELIA SCHUYLER, born June (?) 26, 1715 ; m. Dec. 19, 1733, PIERRE GUILLIAUME DE PEYSTER, youngest son of Col. Abraham and Catharine De Peyster, of New York. He was born Jan. 15, 1707, and was the ancestor of the De Peyster family of New Jersey. They had *issue*, four sons and two daughters, viz. : 1. Abraham De Peyster, born Feb. 22, 1734-5. 2. Arent Schuyler De Peyster, born July 19, 1736 ; he entered the British Army on the 10th of June, 1755, served in the 8th or *King's Regiment* of Foot, in which he was commissioned a *Lieutenant* in Sept., 1757, and rose in the various grades to the Colonelcy of the regiment in Oct., 1793. 3. Pierre De Peyster, born May 20, 1737 ; died July 28, 1737. 4. Catharine Adriana De Peyster, born Sept. 29, 1738. 5. Swantia De Peyster, born Nov. 15, 1741 ; and 6. Pierre Guilliaume De Peyster, born March 1, 1745-6 ; m. May 29, 1771, BERTHIAH, dau. of Samuel HALL, of Kingston upon Hull, York, Eng.*

* De Peyster Genealogy.

5 iv. CATHARINA VARLETH,² probably the third daughter of Casper Varleth¹ and his wife Judith, was born in Amsterdam, and married, in New Amsterdam, August (?), 1657, FRANCOYS DE BRUYN (BRUYN, BROWNE). It has been supposed by some that this Francoys De Bruyn was identical with Francis Browne, or Frans Bruyn, a soldier at Curaçoa in 1643, and living, in 1647, in New Amsterdam; but they were doubtless different persons, as the latter was from Yorkshire, while the former was a native of Amsterdam. Francoys or Francis De Bruyn was a member of the church in New Amsterdam prior to 1660. He removed to New Utrecht, L. I., as early as 1663—was a Schepen there in 1663–1664, and in August, 1673, was appointed Secretary of the Five Dutch Towns on Long Island, and Auctioneer, *vice* Corteljoú, in January following, which is the last notice found of him. His wife, Catharina Varleth, probably deceased before September, 1662—the date of the death of her father. They had the following-named children baptized in the Church at New Amsterdam, viz.:

1. CASPARUS DE BRUYN, bap. Sept. 14, 1659. The sponsors at his baptism were *Nicholaes Verleth* and *Otto Bagelaer*.
2. AGATHA DE BRUYN, bap. Jan. 26, 1661. The sponsors at her baptism were *Johannes De Peyster* and *Anna Verleth*.
3. JACOB DE BRUYN, bap. March 5, 1662. The sponsors at his baptism were *Anthony De Mill* and *Anna Stuyvesants*.

6 v. JUDITH VARLETH,² born in Amsterdam, was probably the youngest daughter of Casper¹ and Judith Varleth. She resided for some time with her parents at Hartford, Conn., and in 1662 was imprisoned there on a "pretended accusation of witchery." In that year Ann, daughter of John Cole, "who lived near a Dutch family" at Hartford, "was seized in a strange manner with Fits wherein her Tongue was improved by a Demon," &c., who confounded her language, so that she "made Uterances in Dutch of which Language she knew Nothing." * It was probably in this case the accusation of witchery was made against Judith Varleth. Through the interposition of Gov. Stuyvesant she escaped her peril,† and it is related "that as soon as the suspected Witches were executed or fled Mrs. Cole was restored to Health." In happier hour, says the not always prosaic Mr. Savage, Judith Varleth's power of fascination was sufficient to ensure her marriage with NICHOLAS BAYARD, one of the patrician families of the neighboring province of New York. She married May 23, 1666, in New York, Nicholas, son of Samuel Bayard and Anna Stuyvesant, born at Alphen, in Holland, who accompanied his widowed mother and uncle, Gov. Petrus Stuyvesant, to New Netherland in May, 1647. In 1654 he was Clerk in the Secretary's office at New Amsterdam, and possessing, with other scholarly attainments, a knowledge of the English language, was appointed, July 1, 1657, English Secretary, and August 16, 1663, was made Commissary of Imports and Exports, *vice* Jacob Sam, who had returned to Holland. In August, 1673, he was commissioned Secretary of the Province, and, on the 20th of September following, Receiver-General. He was Mayor of New York in 1685, and for many years a prominent member of

* Drake's Annals of Witchcraft in New England, p. 120–122.
† Gov. Stuyvesant sent the Deputy Governor and General Court at Hartford, in October, 1662, the following letter in her behalf: "Honored and worthy Sirs: By this occasion of my brother in law [Nicholas Varleth] being necessitated to make a second voyage to ayd his distressed sister, Judith Varlet, imprisoned, as we are informed, upon pretend accusation of witchery, we realey believe, and, out of her well-known education, life, conversation, and profession of faith, we dare assure that she is innocent of such a horrible *crimen*, and wherefor, I doubt not he will now, as formerly, finde your honour's favor and ayde for the innocent." Gerard's *Old Stadt Huys*, p. 47.

the Legislative Council. As the " Dutch head of the English party," he was among the most active of Leisler's opponents, and was imprisoned in the Fort by Leisler's orders for more than a year. Upon the arrival of Gov. Sloughter in New York, he was foremost in urging Leisler's execution. He was tried and condemned to death for high treason in March, 1701 ; but this judgment was reversed by Act of the Legislature during Lord Cornbury's administration. While ostensibly a brewer by occupation, he was from early youth an office-holder, and essentially a politician, with all the name implies. He died in 1709, leaving a large estate to his widow and only son Samuel ; and it may be regarded as a fitting commentary upon the slackness of genealogical and biographical investigations in New York, that among his numerous and respectable descendants, male and female, the biography of a man who filled so large a space in the early history of the Colony remains unwritten. His will is dated May 9, 1707, in which he styles himself " of the city of New York Merchant," and names only his wife *Judy*, and son *Samuel*, whom he makes executors of his estate.

NICHOLAS and JUDITH (VARLETH) BAYARD had *issue :*

1. SAMUEL BAYARD, bap. Sept. 5, 1669 ; m. March 12, 1696, MARGARITA VAN CORTLANDT, dau. of Stephanus and Geertruyd (Schuyler) Van Cortlandt ; she was bap. July 29, 1674. He was a merchant in New York, and made his will April 10, 1745, probated May 1, 1746, in which he mentions his two grandchildren, Nicholas and Margaret Van Dam, children of his deceased dau. Judith Van Dam ; his dau. Gertrude, wife of Peter Kemble ; dau. Margaret, wife of James Van Horne ; dau. Ann, and his three sons, Stephen, Nicholas, and Samuel, whom he appoints executors. He had *issue* eleven children, all of whom were bap. in the Dutch Church in New York, except his dau. Geertruyd, viz. :

> 1. JUDITH BAYARD, bap. Dec. 13, 1696 ; m. Sept. 18, 1719, RIP VAN DAM, JR., son of Rip Van Dam and Sara Van der Spiegel. He was bap. October 7, 1694. They had bap. in the Dutch Church in New York : 1. Margareta, bap. October 30, 1720 ; the sponsors at her baptism were *Rip Van Dam, Senr*, and *Margareta Bayard.* She m. Dec. 25, 1747, William Cockroft. 2. Nicholas, bap. March 25, 1722 ; the sponsors were *Samuel Bayard* and *Sara Van Dam.* He was prob. the Nicholas Van Dam who m. March 10, 1749, Sophia Van Horne.
>
> 2. NICHOLAS BAYARD, bap. August 28, 1698 ; m. 1st July 3, 1729, ELISABETH RYNDERS, dau. of Barent and Hester (Leisler) Rynders. For a notice of their children see *ante*, Vol. VII., p. 151. He m. 2^d, Dec. 22, 1755, MARGARITA VAN BEVERHOUT, *née* MARGARITA LANGMAT, the widow of JOHANNES GLAŬDISZEN VAN BEVERHOUT, by whom he had *issue*, viz. : 1. Elizabeth, bap. June 17, 1756 ; sponsors, *Samuel Bayard* and *Miss Judith Bayard.* 2. Anna, bap. June 21, 1758 ; sponsors, *William Bayard, Francyntje Moor, his wife,* and *Samuel Bayard.* 3. Stephanus, bap. July 16, 1760 ; sponsors, *Gerhardus Stuyvesant, Geertruy Van Cortland, his wife,* and *Joh^s Renselaar.*

The will of NICHOLAS BAYARD of the City of New York, Merchant, is dated Sept. 18, 1760 ; proved Dec. 30, 1765 ;

names dau. Hester Van Cortlandt; dau. Judith Van Rensselaer; son Nicholas, and children by his "last wife, Elizabeth, Ann, and Stephen." Appoints his son, Nicholas, son-
in-law John Van Cortland, Esq., son-in-law Jeremiah Van
Ransalier, brother Samuel Bayard, and nephew William
Bayard, Esq., executors.

3. STEPHANUS BAYARD, bap. May 31, 1700; m. March 12, 1725.
ALIDA VETCH.* In his will, dated Jan. 31, 1753, with codicil Dec. 17, 1753 (4?), proved Feb. 9, 1757, he styles him-
self of Bergen County, East New Jersey, Yeoman (in the
codicil, Gentleman), and mentions of his children only his
eldest son, William; dau. Margaret, and son, Robert.
Speaks of his father, Samuel Bayard, and mother, Margaret
Bayard. Appoints his son, William, his brother, Nicholas
Bayard, and brother-in-law, Peter Schuyler, "with his said
children as they shall respectively come to age," executors.
He and his wife, Alida Vetch, had ten children bap. in the
Dutch Church in New York, viz.: 1. Samuel, bap. Jan. 16,
1726; the sponsors were *Samuel Bayard* and *Margreta Van
Cortlandt, his wife*. 2. Nicolaas, bap. Oct. 22, 1727; sponsors, *Samuel Vatch* and *Margreta Livenston* [Livingston], *his
wife*. 3. William, bap. June 15, 1729; sponsors, *Nicolaas
Bayard* and *Margareta Vetch*. 4. Stephen, bap. March 5,
1731; sponsors, *Philip Livingston, Robert Livingston*, and
Judith Van Dam. 5. Stephanüs, bap. Oct. 15, 1732; sponsors, *Philip Van Kortland* and *Geertruyd Bayard, the wife
of Pieter Kemble*. 6. Nicolaas, bap. April 16, 1735; sponsors, *Samuel Bayard, Junior*, and *Margriet Harden, the wife
of Robᵗ Livingston*. 7. Vetch, bap. Sept. 15, 1736;
sponsors *Gilbert Livingston* and *Catharina Van Brüg, the
wife of Philippus Livingston*. 8. Nicolaas, bap. April 26,
1738; sponsors, *Peter Camble* [Kemble] and *Miss Maria
Brokholst*. 9. Robert, bap. July 15, 1739; sponsors,
Philip Livingston and *Elisabet Rynders, the wife of Nicolaüs
Bayard*. 10. Margarita, bap. Aug. 30, 1741; sponsors,
James de Lancey and *Margarita Livingston, widow of Saml.
Vetch*.

4. GEERTRUYD BAYARD, bap. in the First Ref. Dutch Church at
Hackensack, N. J., October 4, 1702; m. PETER KEMBLE.†
They had two sons bap. in the Dutch Church in New York,
viz.: 1. Samuel, bap. April 19, 1732; the sponsors at his baptism were *Samuel Bayard* and *Margareta Van Cortland, his
wife*. 2. Richard, bap. Sept. 30, 1733; sponsors, *Stephen
Bayard* and *Judit Bayard, widow of R. V. Dam*.

5. MARGRETA BAYARD, bap. Dec. 4, 1706; died young.
6. MARGRETA BAYARD, bap. Dec. 15, 1708; died young.

---

* STEPHEN BAYARD was probably twice married, his second wife being EVE SCHUYLER, whom he married
prior to November, 1747.
† PETER KEMBLE was a member of the Council in New Jersey, and in 1732-5, probably longer, was a
resident of New Brunswick. His eldest son, Samuel, according to the statement in Stevens' *Chamber
of Commerce Records*, p. 139, was born at New Brunswick, though it appears by the records he was bap.
in New York. His dau. Margaret, born about 1734-5, married Dec. 8, 1758, General Gage, who succeeded, in 1763, Genl. Amherst, as Commander-in-Chief of the British forces in America.

7. SAMUEL BAYARD, }
8. JACOBUS BAYARD, } twins, bap. July 1, 1711.
9. SAMUEL BAYARD, bap. July 24, 1715.
10. MARGARETA BAYARD, bap. May 24, 1719 ; m. Dec. 16, 1742, JAMES VAN HORNE. They had three sons bap. in the Dutch Church in New York, viz. : 1. Johannes, bap. Oct. 12, 1743 ; the sponsors at his baptism were *Samuel Bayard* and *his wife Margritje Van Cortland.* 2. Samuel, bap. April 22, 1746 ; sponsors, *John McEvers* and *Catharina Van Horne, his wife.* 3. James, bap. Nov. 15, 1747 ; sponsors, *Stephen Bayard* and *Aafje Schuyler, his wife.*
11. ANNA BAYARD, bap. August 7, 1720.

DITELOFSZEN.—DIEDELOOS.—DOREN. (?)

THIS name (not given in the following list of *aliases*) provokes inquiry, from the different forms in which it appears in the New York Dutch Church Baptismal Register, whether CLAES DITELOFSZEN or DIEDELOOS may not have been the ancestor of the DOREN family. Let us examine the record :-

CLAES DITELOFSZEN and his wife Aeltie Samsons had a son Ditelof, bap. Feb. 1, 1662 ; their next child, daughter Catharyn, was bap. Dec. 31, 1664 ; at her baptism his name is recorded CLAES DUDLOOS ; on the 13th Feb., 1667, their second son Samson was baptized, the father's name being registered CLAES DIEDELOOS. At each of these baptisms, Rutger Willemszen was a sponsor. On the 12th of January, 1681, DIDLOF DOORN (called DOREN in the Baptismal Register), married Elsje Jeuriaens, both living in the city suburbs. I suspect that this *Didlof Doren* was the eldest son of CLAES DITELOFSZEN, who was bap. Feb. 1, 1662. His first child, Diedlof (I follow the orthography of the record), was bap. May 25, 1681, Rutger Willemszen being present as one of the sponsors. DIEDLOF DOREN's other children were, Claes, bap. Feb. 7, 1683 ; Catharina, bap. May 4, 1684 ; Cornelis, bap. Nov. 1, 1685 ; and Jeuriaen, bap. Sept. 14, 1687.

To those interested in this family I suggest that it is not improbable that CLAES DITLO, or DIDLO, was identically the CLAES DITELOFSZEN above mentioned, and that he had a second wife AELTJE RUTGERS, but when and where married I am uninformed.

CLAES DITLO and his wife AELTJE RUTS, or RUTGERS (who was probably the dau. of Rutger Willemszen), had the following named children bap. in the Dutch Church, viz. :

1. GYSBERTIE, bap. Nov. 6, 1675 ; sponsors, *Ruthger Willemszen* and *Magdalena.*
2. GEERTRUYD, bap. Oct. 10, 1677 ; sponsors, *Joris Walgraef* [George Walgrave, of London], *Geertie Jans,* and *Magdaleentie Rutgers.*
3. HANS, bap. Oct. 30, 1680 ; sponsors, *Willem Wessels* and *Geertie Siecken.*

DUTCH ALIASES.

THE following list gives all, or nearly all, the *aliases* of males that appear in the Baptismal Records of the Reformed Dutch Church in the city of New York, from 1639 to 1756. The dates at the end of each name denote the years in which the baptism of the children of the person mentioned is recorded, and in which his two first names, or his first and *surname*, are given. Considerable care has been taken in making up the list, and it is offered as a *help* to those engaged in tracing the pedigrees of the early Dutch Families of New York.

ABRAHAMSZEN.

Hendrick Abrahamszen Kermer, 1680–1694
Hendrick Abrahamszen Rycke, 1681–1692
Isaac Abrahamszen Van Deürsen, or Van
Deusen, 1659–1670
Jacob Abrahamszen Van Deürsen, 1665.
Jacob Abrahamszen Santvoort, 1667–1678
Pieter Abrahamszen Van Deürsen, 1667–
1684

ADAMSZEN.

Jan Adamszen Metselaer, 1658–1676

ADOLPHSZEN.

Dirk Adolphszen De Groof, 1694–1707

ADRIANSZEN.

Ide Adrianszen Van Schaick, 1686–1692
Jan Adrianszen Sip or Zip, 1684–1708
Jan Adrianszen Van Duyvelant, 1658–1664

ALBERTSZEN.

Adriaen Albertszen Roos, 1678
Leendert Albertszen De Graw, 1685–1703
Hendrick Albertszen Bosch, 1661–1666

ARENTSZEN.

Claes Arentszen Toürs, 1685–1694
Evert Arentszen Van Hoeck, 1687–1700
Harmen Arentszen De Graw, 1686–1690
(to 1704 ?)
Isaac Arentszen Van Hoeck, 1687–1692
Leendert Arentszen De Graw, 1699–1701

BARENTSZEN.

Cornelis Barentszen Van der Cüyl, 1655–
1665
Cornelis Barentszen Van Wyck, 1677
Jacob Barentszen Cool, 1668–1673

CASPARSZEN.

Pieter Casparszen Van Naerden, 1652–1662

CLAESZEN.

Claes Claeszen Bording, 1650–1673
Cornelis Claeszen Van den Berg, 1696–1697

Cornelis Claeszen Switzart, 1641–1655
Dirck Claeszen Draeck, 1657–1659
Hendrick Claeszen Vechten, 1691–1704

CORNELISZEN.

Dirck Corneliszen Hooglant, 1666–1692
Gerrit Corneliszen Van Westveen, or Van
Veen, 1681–1683
Ide Corneliszen Van Vorst, 1653–1662
Jacob Corneliszen Stille, 1672–1692
Jan Corneliszen Nieukerk, or Van Nieu-
kerk, 1710–1727
Jan Corneliszen Ryck, or De Ryck, 1658–
1666
Jan Corneliszen Van Texel, 1676–1678
Jan Corneliszen Damen, of Boswyck, 1676–
1680
Laürens Corneliszen Koeck, or Cock, 1677–
1702

CORSZEN.

Cornelis Corszen Vroom, 1690

DIRCKSZEN.

Cornelis Dirckszen Hoyer, 1690–1706
Jan Dirckszen Meyer, 1652–1663
Jan Dirckszen Stratemaecker, 1671–1685
Jan Dirckszen Van Aernam, 1664–1680
Jan Dirckszen Woertman (*Brooklyn Ch.
Rec.*), 1691–1698

ELBERTSZEN.

Gysbert Elbertszen Van Loenen, 1661–1678

EVERTSZEN.

Arent Evertszen Keteltas, 1661–1674
Jan Evertszen Carseboom, or Kerseboom,
1665–1682
Jan Evertszen Keteltas, 1670–1683

FRANSZEN.

Dirck Franszen Van Dyck, 1675–1689
Jacobus Franszen Van Dyck, 1678–1697
Jan Franszen Van Huysen, 1640
Thymen Franszen Van Dyck, 1682–1704
Wessel Franszen Wessels, 1707–1721

FREDRICKSZEN.

Salomon Fredrickszen Boog; 1691–1694

GERRITSZEN.

Claes Gerritszen Ravenstein, 1682–1703
Cornelis Gerritszen Van Horne, 1724–1739
Gysbert Gerritszen Van Brakel, 1672
Hendrick Claeszen Gerritszen Vechten, 1691–1704
Huybert Gerritszen Van den Berg, 1695–1714
Jan Gerritszen Van Boxtel, 1656–1659
Stoffel Gerritszen Van Laer, 1662–1682
Willem Gerritszen Van Coüwenhoven, 1662

GILLISZEN. See JILLISZEN.

GYSBERTSZEN.

Teunis Gysbertszen Bogaert, 1655–1668
Woüter Gysbertszen Verschure, 1667–1688

HENDRICKSZEN.

Arie Hendrickszen Sip. 1657–1662
Evert Hendrickszen Bras, 1686–1703
Folkert Hendrickszen Bries (*Brooklyn Ch. Rec.*), 1696–1701
Fredrick Hendrickszen Boog, 1658–1683
Hendrick Hendrickszen Obee, 1658–1659
Jan Hendrickszen Brevoort, 1669–1679
Jan Hendrickszen Van Bommel, 1658–1680
Jan Hendrickszen Van Günst, 1670–1683
Martin Hendrickszen Wiltson (*Brooklyn Ch. Rec.*, 1693), 1695

HERBERT.

Johannes Herbert Cool, 1748–1753

HUYBERTSZEN.

Lambert Huybertszen Moll, 1642–1648

HUYGENS.

Gerrit Huygens Cleyn, 1671
Leendert Huygens De Kleyn, 1684–1698

IDENSZEN.

Cornelis Idenszen Van Vorst, 1687–1694

ISAACKSZEN.

Abraham Isaackszen Planck, 1641–1651
Arent Isaackszen Van Hoeck, 1687–1692
Denys Isaackszen Van Hartvelt, 1660–1667
Jacobus Isaackszen Van Deûrsen, 1691–1702
William Isaackszen Vredenburg, or Van Vredenburg, 1665–1682

JACOBSZEN.

Barent Jacobszen Cool, 1640–1657
Cornelis Jacobszen Quick, 1682–1704
Cornelis Jacobszen Stille, 1643–1672
Cornelis Jacobszen Woertendyk, 1711–1714
Fredrick Jacobszen Somerendyk and Fredrick Woertendyk, 1709–1722

Hans Jacobszen Harberding, 1670–1685
Isaac Jacobszen Kip, 1721–1728
Jacob Jacobszen Van Winckel, 1676–1686
Pieter Jacobszen De Groot, 1685–1695
Willem Jacobszen Hellaken, 1683–1702

JANSZEN.

Abraham Janszen Van Aernem (*Van Alen* and *Van Aren*), 1696–1705
Abraham Janszen Van der Heûl, 1660, 1676
Abraham Janszen Van Gelder, 1724–1731
Achyas Janszen Van Dyck, 1674–1688.
Andries Janszen Meyer, 1672–1689
Barent Janszen Bosch, 1691–1703
Claes Janszen Van Heyningen,* 1668–1695
Cornelis Janszen Scher, or Seeñn, 1677 ; or Cornelis Janszen De Zeeüw of Boswyck (*Brooklyn Ch. Rec.*), 1679–1682
Cornelis Janszen Van Hoorn, 1660–1681
Dirck Janszen Smith, 1662–1669
Dirck Janszen Woertman, or Veerman, 1669–1677
Evert Janszen Van den Enden [Van Embden], 1645–1650
Frans Janszen Bloedtgoet, 1660–1675
Frans Janszen Van Hoogten, 1659–1665
Gerrit Janszen Roos, 1653–1667
Gerrit Janszen Van Oldenburg, 1640–1646
Hendrick Janszen Rûyter, or Van Utrecht, 1650–1662
Hendrick Janszen Spiering, 1655–1667
Hendrick Janszen Van Feûrden, 1661–1678
Hendrick Janszen Van Gerwen, 1656
Hendrick Janszen Van Schalckwyck, 1653–1657
Herman Janszen Van Houten, 1667–1669
Huybert Janszen Van Blerkum, 1704–1710
Jacob Janszen Blaeck, 1666–1668
Jan Janszen Moll, 1677–1692
Jan Janszen Romans, 1661–1686
Jan Janszen Schepmoes, 1642–1654
Jan Janszen Slot, 1672–1687
Jan Janszen Van den Ham, 1653–1662
Jan Janszen Van Harlingen, 1680–1682
Jan Janszen Van Langestraeten, 1661–1686
Johannes Janszen Van Tilburg, 1686–1703
Johannes Janszen Van Quisthout, 1685–1695
Joris Janszen Van Hoorn, 1667–1683
Matthys Janszen Boeckhout, 1679–1688
Mangel Janszen Rol, 1694–1711
Pieter Janszen Bogert, 1687–1695
Pieter Janszen Haring, 1688–1706
Pieter Janszen Mesier, 1659–1681
Pieter Janszen Rommen, 1658–1668
Pieter Janszen Van Tilburg, 1686–1703
Pieter Janszen Van Langendyk, 1689–1698
Pieter Janszen Wit, 1652–1654
Philip Janszen Ringo, 1648–1658
Philip Janszen Vos, 1673

* In 1683 and 1684 his name appears in the Register Claes Janszen Tüynier.

Roelof Janszen Van Meppelen, 1653–1667
Staets Janszen De Groot, 1676–1688
Teunis Janszen Coevers (*Brooklyn Ch. Rec.*),
1661–1663
Thomas Janszen Minsar, 1660–1662
Theunis Janszen Van Pelt, 1691–1715
William Janszen Romen, 1712–1735
William Janszen [Isaackszen] Vredenburg,
1665

JEÜRIANSZEN.

Arent Jeurianszen Lantsman, 1661–1671

JILLISZEN, or GILLISZEN.

Hendrick Jilliszen Maniviel [Mandeviel],
1681–1682
Hendrick Jilliszen Meyer, 1672–1692
Jan Jilliszen Cock, 1658–1664

JOHANNESZEN.

Johannes Johanneszen Burger, 1725–1746
Johannes Johanneszen Montagne, 1726–
1736

JORISZEN.

Burger Joriszen (Burger), 1640–1664
Jan Joriszen Van Hoorn, 1703–1713
Jeronymus Joriszen Rappelje, 1671–1690

JOOSTEN.

Jan Joosten Van Rollegom, 1660–1676

JOSEPHS.

Daniel Josephs Waldron, 1674–1689

LAMBERTSZEN.

Abraham Lambertszen Moll, 1664–1685

LAURENSZEN.

Wessel Laurenszen Wessels, 1715–1741

LEENDERTSZEN.

Arent Leendertszen De Graw, 1661–1684
Jacob Leendertszen Van der Grist, 1649–
1667
Paulus Leendertszen Van der Grist, 1649–
1658

LÜCASZEN.

Johannes Lucaszen Schoŭten, 1662–1674

MARIŬS.

Jacob Marius Groen, 1702–1716

MARTENSZEN.

Claes Martenszen Van Rosenvelt, or Rosenvelt, 1650–1658
Hendrick Martenszen Wiltse, or Wiltson,
1669–1676
Joris Martenszen, *alias* Joris Reyerszen,
1692–1706

MICHIELSZEN.

Enoch Michielszen Vreeland, 1671–1687,
and 1705–1717.

PAŬLŬSZEN.

Michiel Pauluszen Van der Voort, 1642–
1658

PIETERSZEN.

Abraham Pieterszen Molenaer, 1642–1644
Adolf Pieterszen Van der Groest, 1657–
1669
Albert Pieterszen De Bruyn, 1649–1651
Daniel Pieterszen Coolman, 1702–1707
Frans Pieterszen De Vries, 1713–1732
Jan Pieterszen Bant, 1672–1693
Jan Pieterszen Bosch, 1664–1678
Jan Pieterszen De Wit, 1730–1735
Jan Pieterszen Haring, 1667–1681
Jan Pieterszen Meet, or Meeck, or Meed,
1689–1702
Jan Pieterszen Van Husen, 1640–1653
Pieter Pieterszen Menist, or Van Nest, 1653–
1678
Reynier Pieterszen Quackenbos, 1693–1705
Wessel Pieterszen Van Norden, 1694–1714
Willem Pieterszen De Groot, 1650–1660
Willem Pieterszen Romen, or Roome, 1714–
1738

RESOLVERT.

Willem Resolvert Waldron, 1672–1694

REYERSZEN.

Joris Reyerszen, *alias* Joris Martenszen,
1692–1706

THEUNISZEN.

Aart Theuniszen Middag, 1660–1661
Dirck Theuniszen Quick, 1673–1680
Jacob Theuniszen De Key, 1659–1686
Jacobus Theuniszen Quick, 1718–1737
Jan Theuniszen Van Tilburg, 1670–1676
Nicolaas Theuniszen Somerendyk, 1709–
1724
Wouter Theuniszen Van Pelt (*Brooklyn
Ch. Rec.*), 1687–1690

THOMASZEN.

Gabriel Thomaszen Studles, 1693–1696
Jan Thomaszen Schouten, 1720–1731
Theunis Thomaszen Metselaer, 1640–1648

WESSELSZEN.

Hendrick Wesselszen Ten Broeck, 1671–
1690
Johannes Wesselszen Van Norden, or Van
Orden, 1721–1751

WILLEMSZEN.

Andries Willemszen Soppe, or Hoppe, 1651–
1658
Floris Willemszen Crom, or Krom, 1681–
1694

Jan Willemszen Romen, 1685–1695
Jan Willemszen Van Yselsteyn, or Van Iselsteyn, or Van Leyden, 1650–1669
Pieter Willemszen Romen, or Room, 1685–1705

Pieter Willemszen Van der Schueren, 1688–1705
Thomas Willemszen Koeck, or Cock, 1681–1689

FROM the same source as the preceding is appended a list of such names as are spelt in two or more ways, together with a few other miscellaneous *aliases.*

AALSTEYN, Mattheus, *see* Mattheus Van Aalsteyn, 1736–1752
a, Brakele Steven, *see* Steven Brakel, or Van Brakel, 1706–1711
Aken, or Ekes, or Eckens, Jan Thomaszen, *see* Jan Thomaszen, 1692–1708, p. 23
Albady, Jochem, *see* Jochem Van Albady, 1720–1727
Alderon, Jan, *see* Jan Badron and John Haldron, 1708–1711
Axceen, John, *see* John Exceen, 1743–1751

BADRON, Jan, *see* John Alderon and John Haldron, 1708–1711
Bloedtgoet, Frans, *see* Frans Goedbloedt, 1660–1675
Boekenhoven, Stephanis, *see* Stephanis Van Boekenhoven, 1697–1717
Boog, Isaac, *see* Isaac Van den Boog, 1703–1705
Borkens, Robert, *see* Robert Darkens, 1677–1695
Brevoort, Hendrick, *see* Hendrick Van Brevoort, 1700–1717

CANDREY, Cambrick, and Camrik, Richard, *see* Richard Kendrik, 1716–1727
Casjoŭ, Jacques, *see* Jacob Casar, 1665–1671
Chahaan, Samuel, *see* Samuel Sjahaan, Shahaan, and Thahaan, 1700–1717
Chardevine, Isaac, *see* Isaac Sharduvyn, 1728–1750
Charther, William, *see* William Sester, 1678–1690
Cheklen, Robert, *see* Robert Sjeklen, 1715–1716
Chirurgyn, Paulus, *see* Paulus Van der Beeck, 1645–1656
Cise, James, *see* James Sise, or Seys, 1720–1730
Cornel, Pieter, *see* Pieter Kernel, 1749–1753
Crocker, Charles, *see* Charles Tockker, or Tucker, 1695–1702

DARKENS, or DERKENS, Robert, *see* Robert Borkens, 1677–1695
De Four, David, *see* David De Foreest, 1658–1662
De La Montagne, *see* Montagne, 1684–1756
De Trieux, Jacob, *see* Jacob Truer, 1675–1683
De Voor Daniel, *see* Daniel In de Voor, 1696–1713

De Wendel, Gerrit, *see* Gerrit Wendel, 1712–1725
Dorsou, Looys, *alias* Jan Martyn, 1650–1658

ECKERSON, or Eckes, or Aken, Jan Thomaszen, *see* Jan Thomaszen, 1692–1708, p. 23
Eldes, Benjamin, *see* Benj. Oldes, 1705–1713
Elsworth, *see* Elswaert, Elsenwaert, Elzewaart, Elsward, and Yde Waert.
Exceen, Jan, *see* Jan Axceen, 1743–1751

FALING, Michael, *see* Michael Valey, 1706–1707
Fardon, Jacob, *see* Jacob Verdon, 1721–1727
Fardon, Thomas, Jr., *see* Thomas Verdon, Jr., 1741–1754
Fell, Simon, *see* Simon Sel, or Vel, 1656–1667
Fenix, Alexander, *see* Alexander Phenix, 1713–1737
Filips, Charles, *see* Charles Philips, 1714–1727
Folleman, Cornelis, *see* Cornelis Volleman, 1726–1744

GAYWOOD, William, *see* William Haywood, 1719–1727
Goedbloedt, Frans, *see* Frans Bloedtgoet, 1660–1675
Guet, Rendel, *see* Rendel Huwits, 1651–1653

HALDRON, John, *see* Jan Alderon and Jan Badron, 1708–1711
Hanszen, Hans, *see* Hans Noorman,[*] 1640–1653
Haywood, William, see William Gaywood, 1719–1727
Hoboken, Harmen, *see* Harmen Van Hoboken, 1655–1664
Hoed, or Hood, Jasper, *see* Jasper Woed, 1697–1711
Hoeder, Jeams, *see* Jeams Woeder, 1668–1686
Hues, Hendri, *see* Henry Ives, 1699–1703
Huwits, Rendel, *see* Rendel Guet, 1651–1653

IN DE VOOR Daniel, *see* Daniel De Voor, 1696–1713
IVES, Henry, *see* Hendri Hues, 1699–1703

JAKSON, Willem, *see* Willem Yackson and Sjeckson, 1694–1709
Jansen, Thomas, *see* Thomas Johnson, 1710–1723

[*] Ancestor of the Bergen family.

Jay, Augustus, *see* Augustus Sjee, 1698–1707

Jeats, Abraham, *see* Abraham Yeads, 1727–1728

KENDRIK, Richard, *see* Richard Candrey, Cambrick, and Camrik, 1716–1727

Kernel, Pieter, *see* Pieter Cornel, 1749–1753

Kwik, *see* Quick.

LANGENDYK, Pieter Janszen, *see* Pieter Van Langendyk, 1689–1698

Langestraat, *see* Van Langestraat, 1661–1686, and 1691–1712

MANNY, Francis, *see* Francis Onanrie, 1734–1747

Martyn, Jan, *see* Looys Dorsoŭ, 1650–1658

Merberg, Johannes Adolphus, *see* Johannes Adolphus Otterberg, 1741–1748

Modder, Jeams, *see* Jeams Woeder, 1668–1686

Monckebaen, Adam, *see* Adam Onckelbaen, 1663–1670

Montagne, *see* De La Montagne, 1684–1756

Muyt, Willem, *see* Willem Wyten, Wyt, and Wydt, 1671–1682

NINSTER, Pieter, *see* Pieter Winster, 1664–1677

Noorman, Hans, *see* Hans Hanszen, 1640–1653

OBLINUS, *see* Van Oblinus, 1672–1685, and 1693–1698

Oldes, Benjamin, *see* Benj. Eldes, 1705–1713

Onckelbaen, Adam, *see* Adam Monckebaen, 1663–1670

Onanrie, Francis, *see* Francis Manny, 1734–1747

Otterberg, Johannes Adolphus, *see* Johannes Adolphus Merberg, 1741–1748

PHENIX, Alexander, *see* Alexander Fenix, 1713–1737

Philips, Charles, *see* Charles Filips, 1714–1727

Philips Fredrick, *see* Fredrick Philipse, 1720–1742

Pitt, Jacob, *see* Jacob Piet, or Pet, 1751–1755

Post, Elias, *see* Elias Pos, 1672–1689

QUAAK, Jan Stevens, *see* Jan Stevens, 1693–1711

RASENBURG, Willem, *see* Willem Van Rasenburg, 1661–1664

Richt, Jonathan, *see* Jonathan Wright, 1694–1699

Roeder, Jeams, *see* Jeams Woeder, 1668–1686

Romans, Jan Janszen, *see* Jan Janszen Langestraat, 1661–1686

Romen, Johannes, *see* Johannes Langestraat, 1691–1712

Romen, Johannes, *see* Johannes Van Romen, 1691–1712

Ruyter, Jeams, *alias* Jeams Woodart, or Woeder, 1668–1686

Rycke, Rycken, or De Rycke, Abraham, *see* Abraham Wycke, 1682–1702

SEL, Simon, *see* Simon Fell, Vale, or Vel, 1656–1667

Sester, William, *see* William Charther, or Churger, 1678–1690

Sharduvyn, Isaac, *see* Isaac Chardevine, 1728–1750

Simons, Joseph, *see* Joseph Zeeman, 1748–1755

Sise, Seys, or Sys, James, *see* James Cise, 1720–1730

Sipkins, Jan, *see* Jan Tsipkins, 1675–1695

Sjahaan, Thahaan, or Shahaan, Samuel, *see* Samuel Chahaan, 1700–1717

Sjee, Augustus, *see* Augustus Jay, 1698–1707

Sjeckson, Willem, *see* Willem Jakson and Yackson, 1694–1709

Sjeklen, Robert, *see* Robert Cheklen, 1715–1716

Stevens, Jan, *see* Jan Stevens Quaak, 1693–1711

TANNER, Benjamin, *see* Benjamin Tenner, 1746–1754

Thahaan, Samuel, *see* Samuel Chahaan, 1700–1717

Tienhoven, Lucas, *see* Lucas Van Tienhoven, 1671–1693

Truer, Jacob, *see* Jacob De Trieux, 1675–1683

Tsipkins, Jan, *see* Jan Sipkins, 1675–1695

Tucker, Charles, *see* Charles Crocker, 1695–1702

Tŭynier, Claes Janszen, *see* Claes Janszen Van Heyningen, 1668–1695

VAN ALBADY, Jochem, *see* Jochem Albady, 1720–1727

Van Boekenhoven, Stephanis, *see* Stephanis Boekenhoven, 1697–1717

Van Brakel, Steven, *see* Steven a, Brakele, 1706–1711

Van Brevoort, Hendrick, *see* Hendrick Brevoort, 1700–1711

Van den Boog, Isaac, *see* Isaac Boog, 1703–1705

Van der Beeck, Paulus, *see* Paulus Chirurgyn, 1645–1656

Van Langendyk, *see* Langendyk, 1689–1698

Van Langestraat, *see* Langestraat, 1661–1686, and 1691–1712

Van Oblinus, *see* Oblinus, 1672–1685, and 1693–1698

Van Rasenburg, Willem, *see* Willem Rasenburg, 1661–1664

Van Romen, Johannes, *see* Johannes Romen, 1691–1712

Van St. Cubis, Jan Janszen, *see* Jan Wanshaer, 1649–1666

Van Thuyl, Jacob, *see* Jacob Theuniszen De Key, 1659–1686

Valey, Michiel, *see* Michiel Faling, 1706–1707

Verdon, Jacob, *see* Jacob Fardon, 1721–1727

Volleman, Cornelis, *see* Cornelis Folleman, 1726–1744

WANSHAER, Jan, *see* Jan Janszen Van St. Cubis, Van St. Ubus, Van St. Obyn, Jan Van Sara, and Jan St. Benen, 1649–1666

Wendel, Gerrit, *see* Gerrit De Wendel, 1712–1725

Wessels, Willem, *see* Willem Welchem, 1674–1676

Winster, Pieter, *see* Pieter Ninster, 1664–1667

Woed, Jasper, *see* Jasper Hoed or Hood, 1697–1711

Woeder, Jeams, *see* Jeams Hoeder, Modder, and Roeder, 1668–1686

Wycke, Abraham, *see* Abraham Rycke, 1682–1702

Wyd, or Weyt, Pieter, *see* Pieter White, 1738–1754

Wyten, Wyt, or Wydt, Willem, *see* Willem Muyt, 1671–1682

YACKSON, Willem, *see* Willem Sjeckson, 1694–1709

Yde Waert, Christoffel, *see* Christoffel Elswaert, 1655–1670

Yeads, Abraham, *see* Abraham Jeats, 1727–1728

ZEEMAN, Joseph, *see* Joseph Simons, 1748–1755

GOUVERNEUR.

We are under many obligations to Thos. H. Montgomery, Esq., of Philadelphia, for genealogical favors, among which are the following, which he has copied and arranged from a family Bible in possession of his sister-in-law. By referring *ante* page 20, it will be seen that the fifth child of Isaac Gouverneur (the names of whose children are there given) was Alida. This

ALIDA, dau. of Isaac and Sara (Staats) Gouverneur, m. 12th May, 1737, John Broughton. *Issue :*

1. ISAAC, b. 14th September, 1740.
2. SAMPSON SHELTON, b. 19th February, 1741.
3. JOHN, b. 8th November, 1743.
4. SARAH, b. 16th March, 1746.
5. Mary, b. 6th April, 1748 ; m. 5th July, 1769, Herman Gouverneur, b. August, 1745, son of —— Gouverneur. . *Issue :*
   i. MARY MATILDA GOUVERNEUR, b. 22d May, 1771.
   ii. ALIDA GOUVERNEUR, b. 1st October, 1772 ; m. 7th July, 1795, Isaac Gouverneur (b. 10th March, 1757 ; d. 28th February, 1800). *Issue :* (1) JULIANA MATILDA GOUVERNEUR, b. 18 July, 1796 ; m. 5th April, 1826, Francis Rawle Wharton, of Philadelphia. (2) ADELAIDE GOUVERNEUR, b. 18th July, 1798 ; m. 24th February, 1825, John S. Brinton, of Philadelphia ; d. 9th August, 1825, s.p. He died 18 August, 1825. (3) ISAAC HERMAN GOUVERNEUR, b. 23d August, 1800 ; d. 21st June, 1820.

ALIDA GOUVERNEUR, m. secondly, 10th December, Gilbert Robertson, of New York, who was afterwards British Consul in Philadelphia from June, 1817, to his death in 1837.

MARY (BROUGHTON) GOUVERNEUR, m. secondly, 11th April, 1782, William H. Ludlow, of Claverack. *Issue :* (1) Henry Corbett, b. 8th January, 1785. (2) William Broughton, b. 20th March, 1788. (3) Maria Matilda, b. 17th January, 1790. (4) Gabriel, b. 14th May, 1791.

KIP'S OF KINGSTON AND RHINEBECK, N. Y.*

We are greatly indebted to Mr. Gerrit H. Van Wagenen for the following account of the descendants of Hendrick and Jacobus Kip, sons of Isaac Hendrickszen Kip, noticed *ante* pages 50 and 51. Mr. Van Wagenan has, as will be seen, kindly favored us with an emended copy of his paper published in the NEW YORK GENEALOGICAL AND BIOGRAPHICAL RECORD, Vol. XII., p. 29, containing many additions to his article as there printed. The materials comprised in the following account were gathered by him mainly from the records of the Dutch churches of Kingston and Rhinebeck, N. Y.

9. HENDRICK KIP, oldest son of ISAAC HENDRICKSZEN KIP, and Catalyntje Hendrick Snyers (Snyder), was baptized February 8, 1654. He settled at Kingston. N. Y., at an early date. He purchased from the Indians, July 28, 1686, a tract of land on the east side of the Hudson River, opposite Rondout Creek. This deed mentions no boundaries, and does not appear on record in Ulster County, but the original deed is in the possession of Wm. Bergh Kip, Esq., of Rhinebeck. This tract, and a tract of land adjoining it, purchased from the Indians by Gerrit Artsen, Arie Rosa and Jan Elton (Elting), June 8, 1686, the deed for which is recorded at Kingston, are covered by a patent granted by Governor Dongan, June 2, 1688, to Gerrit Artsen, Arie Rosa, Jan Elton, Jacob Kip, and Hendrick Kip. This patent is recorded at Albany in Book 6, page 328, of Patents. The original patent is in the possession of the family of the late William Kelly of Rhinebeck, whose lands are all within the territory covered by the Indian deed to Artsen, Rosa, and Elting. Hendrick Kip, whose wife's name appears in the baptismal records of Kingston to have been Annetje Jans (Van Putten), had only three children of whom I find any record, viz. :

61. JAN, bap. at Kingston, March 31, 1678 ; married, at Kingston, Sept. 28, 1703, Lysbet Van Kleeck. Their children were : 1. Henricus, bap. Sept. 3, 1704. 2. Baltus, bap. Mar. 17, 1706. 3. Baltus, bap. May 23, 1707. 4. Matthew, Oct. 31, 1708. 5. Tryntje, May 7, 1710. 6. Barent, Jan. 27, 1712. 7. Annetje, Jan. 24, 1714. 8. Baltus, Sept. 4, 1715. 9. Jacob, Jan. 12, 1718.

62. HENDRICK, bap. at Kingston, July 7, 1688 ; married, at Kingston, Sept. 28, 1715, Jacomynte Newkerk. Had one child, named Jannetje, bap. at Kingston Sept. 23, 1716. A deed from Hendrick Kip and Jacomynte his wife, dated April 16, 1719, assigns to Matthys Sleight, Jr., his brother-in-law, "The one just half of two-thirds of the lands of Hendrick Kip, late of Dutchess County, father of the said Hendrick, which land was conveyed to said Hendrick and Catholynte his sister, by their eldest brother, John Kip, eldest son of Hendrick Kip, deceased."

63. CATHOLYNTIE, whose birth I find no record of at Kingston, married Matthys Sleight, Jr. Their children were : 1. Matthew, bap. April 29, 1711. 2. Anna, Oct. 12, 1712. 3. Hendrikus, Nov. 15, 1713. 4. Maria, July 24, 1715. 5. Hendrikus, June 9, 1717. 6. Maria, Oct. 16, 1720. 7. Johannes, Aug. 26, 1724. 8. Cornelis, April 23, 1727. 9. Tryntje, June 15, 1729.

* (Continuation of pages 50 and 51.)

14. JACOB KIP, son of Isaac Hendricksen Kip, and one of the five partners in the Arie Rosa & Co. patent, was born, as stated by Mr. Purple, Aug. 25, 1666, and died Feb. 28, 1753. He married at Albany, Rachel Swartwout (whose birth Mr. Holgate gives as April 10, 1669), daughter of Roeloff Swartwout, first Sheriff of Wiltwyck, at the Esopus, and Eva, daughter of Albert Andrieszen Bradt, and widow of Anthony De Hooges. Issue :

64. ISAAC, born Jan. 8, 1696, bap. at Kingston, Feb. 9, 1696 ; married, Jan. 7, 1720, Cornelia, dau. of Leonard and Elizabeth (Hardenburg) Lewis, born Nov. 9, 1692 ; died, July 10, 1772. He died July 2, 1762. Their children were : 1. Elizabeth, bap. in N. Y., April 9, 1721. 2. Jacob, bap. in N. Y., Oct. 17, 1722. 3. LEONARD bap. in N. Y. June 27, 1725; m. April 11, 1763, Elizabeth, dau. of Francis and Anneke (Lynsen) Marschalk, of New York. 4. Rachel, bap. in N. Y. Oct. 2, 1726. 5. Elizabeth, bap. in N. Y. Aug. 28, 1728. 6. Isaac, born 1732. 7. Abraham, bap. at Rhinebeck, Aug. 3, 1735. 8. Abraham, bap. at Kingston, Feb. 6, 1737 ; m., Jan. 6, 1768, Dorothea Remsen.

LEONARD, the third child of Isaac Kip and Cornelia Lewis, m. April 11, 1763, Elizabeth, dau. of Francis Marshalk, of New York He d. 1804. She d. 1818. Issue : 1. Anne, b. 1764 ; d. unm. 1796 2. Isaac Lewis, b. 1767 ; m. Sarah, dau. of Jeremiah Smith, of Elizabethtown, N. J. 3. Leonard, b. 1774; m. Dec. 12, 1809, Maria, dau. of Duncan Ingraham, Esq., of Greenvale near Poughkeepsie, N. Y. Issue : 1. WILLIAM INGRAHAM. 2. Elizabeth. 3. Sophia. 4. Mary. 5. Leonard.

WILLIAM INGRAHAM KIP, eldest child of Leonard Kip and Maria Ingraham, was b. in New York, October 3, 1811, ordained Deacon in the Protestant Episcopal Church, July 1, 1835, and Priest in November following. Has been successively Rector of St. Peter's Church, Morristown, N. J. ; Assistant Minister of Grace Church, N. Y., and Rector St. Paul's Church, Albany, N. Y. Elected Missionary Bishop of California, Oct. 23, 1853. Diocesan Bishop of California, in April, 1857. He m. July 1, 1835, Maria Elizabeth, dau. of Isaac Lawrence, Esq., of N. York. Issue : 1. Lawrence, b. Sept. 17, 1836, Lieut. Colonel (by Brevet) U. S. Army; m. April 23, 1867, Eva, daug. of Peter Lorillard, Esq., of N. Y. Issue : Eva Maria and Edith. 2. William Ingraham, b. Jan. 15, 1840 ; m. Feb. 28, 1865, Elizabeth Clementina, dau. of Hon. Wm. B. Kinney. Issue : Wm. Ingraham, and Lawrence.*

RIGHT REV. WM. INGRAHAM KIP—the distinguished prelate—is author of many important works, and has contributed numerous interesting articles to the leading magazines of the day, not the least entertaining of which are those that relate to the genealogical history of the Olden Time in New York.

65. ROELOFF, 2d son of Jacob Kip, bap. at Kingston, Oct. 31, 1697 ; m., Feb. 9, 1721, Sara, daughter of John Baptist Dumond and Neeltje Van Vegten. Their children were :

* Historical Notes of the Kip Family. 1871.

1. Grietjen, bap. Dec. 24, 1721. 2. Jacob, May 19, 1723. 3. John Baptist, Feb. 28, 1725, m. June 25, 1757, Catharine Heermans. 4. Rachel, bap. Sept. 8, 1728. 5. Neeltje, Jan. 25, 1730. 6. Neeltje, March 25, 1732. 7. Sarah, bap. at Rhinebeck, Sept. 16, 1733. 8. Igness, Oct. 17, 1738.

66. JACOBUS, bap. at Kingston, Nov. 26, 1699 ; m., Feb. 17, 1733, Klaartje (Clara), daughter of Evert Van Wagenen and Marytje Van Heyningen, bap. April 22, 1711. Their children were : 1. Marytje, bap. Aug. 11, 1734 ; m. Jacob, son of Roeloff Kip. 2. Rachel, bap. Sept. 7, 1735. 3. Sara, bap. April 24, 1737 ; died Sept. 1, 1785 ; m., April 10, 1761, William Radcliff. 4. Rachel, Feb. 11, 1739 ; m. Isaac Kip. 5. Jenneke, bap. Jan. 13, 1741 ; m. Nicholas Heermans, April, 1761. 6. Jacobus, bap. Dec. 5, 1742 ; m. Claartje Heermans. 7. Evert, bap. May 8, 1745.

67. RACHEL KIP, bap. Nov. 26, 1699 ; m., Feb. 16, 1720, Gerardus Lewis. Their children were : 1. Rachel, bap. Jan. 15, 1721. 2. Gerardus, Dec. 25, 1724. 3. Johannes, Feb. 8, 1730. 4. Abraham, March 17, 1734 ; m., Aug. 18, 1759, Marytje, daughter of Aart and Rebecka Van Wagenen ; bap. June 1, 1735. 5. Elizabeth, bap. May 2, 1736.

68. JOHANNES, bap. May 3, 1702 ; m. Margriet Van Etten. Their children were : 1. Jacob, bap. Jan. 5, 1724. 2. Petrus, bap. Feb. 28, 1725. 3. Rachel, bap. Sept. 25, 1726. 4. Eva, bap. Sept. 1, 1728. 5. Benjamin, bap. June 25, 1732. 6. Abraham, bap. Aug. 11, 1734. 7. Johannes, bap. Jan. 9, 1737. 8. Isaac, bap. Nov. 7, 1738. 9. Anna, bap. Feb. 15, 1741. 10. Samuel, June 20, 1743. 11. Catharine, Aug. 18, 1745. 12. Elizabeth, Oct. 12, 1747.

69. CATALYNTIE, bap. Feb. 18, 1705, at Albany ; m. William Van Vredenburgh. Their children were : 1. Wilhelmus, bap. Sept. 10, 1727. 2. Jacob, bap. April 6, 1729. 3. Isaac, bap. Oct. 5, 1732. 4. Isaac, bap. Dec. 9, 1733. 5. Johannes, bap. May 11, 1740.

70. EVA, bap. April 15, 1707 ; m., Dec. 9, 1733, Gerrit, son of Barent Van Wagenen and Lea Schepmoes, born Sept. 26, 1707. Their children were : 1. Barent, bap. Oct. 23, 1737. 2. Rachel, bap. Feb. 15, 1742 ; m. Jacobus Van Etten, had dau. Eva, bap. March 13, 1774.

71. MARIA, bap. Feb. 18, 1709 ; m. Jan Van Benthuysen, bap. Feb. 6, 1704, son of Barent Van Benthuysen and Jannetje Van Wagenen. Their children were : 1. Jacob, bap. Feb. 6. 1737. 2. Barent, bap. April 29, 1739. 3. Jannetje, bap. Dec. 25, 1744.

72. ABRAHAM, bap. Jan. 24, 1714 ; m. Elsie Pruyn. Their children were : 1. Johannes, bap. April 14, 1745. 2. Amelia, bap. Aug. 24, 1746. 3. Jacob, bap. Oct. 12, 1747. 4. Jacob, bap. Sept. 26, 1748.

65. ROELOFF KIP, 2d son of Jacob Kip, m. Feb. 9, 1721, SARAH DUMOND. Their children were :

73. GRIETJEN, bap. Dec. 24, 1721, m. May 19, 1742, at Rhinebeck. Philip Van Ness, of Albany, had one child bap. Aug. 26, 1744, named Cattahynte.

74. JACOB, bap. May 19, 1723, m. Marytje, daughter of Jacobus
Kip and Klaartje Van Wagenen. Their children were : 1.
Roeloff, bap. Nov. 13, 1753. 2. Abraham, bap. Jan. 18,
1756. 3. Annetje, bap. June 10, 1759. 4. Ignas, bap. Apr.
12, 1760, died April 12, 1795. 5. Claartje, bap. Jan. 1762.
6. Johannes, bap. May 27, 1764. 7. Sara, bap. June 29, 1766.
8. Rachel, bap. Sept. 11, 1768. 9. Isaac, bap. Oct. 25, 1772.

75. JOHN BAPTIST, bap. Feb. 28, 1725, m. June 25, 1757, Catharine Heermans. Their children were : 1. Roeloff, bap.
April 25, 1758. 2. Neeltje, bap. Nov. 12, 1759, died July
23, 1830; m. Feb. 8, 1785, Gerrit, son of Johannes and Annetje Van Wagenen, bap. Sept. 6, 1758, died March 31, 1830.
3. Andrew, —— 1761, died June 24, 1843 ; m. Sara, daughter
of Jacobus Kip and Claartje Heermans, born Aug. 31, 1772,
died June 27, 1833. 4. Sarah, bap. Nov. 10, 1765. 5. Gerrit.
bap. July 12, 1767, died Jan. 13, 1841 ; m. Clarissa, daughter
of Jacobus Kip and Claartje Heermans, bap. May 26, 1776.
6. Claartje, bap. Sept. 2, 1770. 7. John, bap. June 19, 1774.

76. ISAAC, bap. Jan. 22, 1727.
77. RACHEL, bap. Sept. 8, 1728.
78. NEELTJE, bap. Jan. 25, 1730.
79. NEELTJE, bap. March 25, 1732.
80. SARAH, bap. Sept. 16, 1733.
81. IGNAS, bap. Oct 17, 1736.
82. ABRAHAM, bap. Oct. 22, 1738, died Feb. 11, 1830 ; m. Helena
Tremper, who died March 24, 1827, aged 86. Their children were : 1. Roeloff, bap. Aug. 31, 1761. 2. Hans For-
gen, bap. April 15, 1764. 3. Abraham, bap. July 13, 1776.
4. Lena, bap. Aug. 14, 1768. 5. Harmanus, bap. Aug. 5,
1770. 6. Sara, bap. Feb. 28, 1773. 7. Catrina, bap. Aug.
30, 1777. 8. Sara, Jan. 30, 1780.

66. JACOBUS KIP, 3d son of Jacob Kip and Sara Dumond, m. Feb. 17,
1733, KLAARTJE VAN WAGENEN, daug. of Evert Van Wagenen. Their
children were :
83. MARYTJE, m. Jacobus, son of Roeloff Kip.
84. RACHEL.
85. SARA, m. William Radcliff. Their children were : 1. Hilletje,
bap. April 2, 1762. 2. Jacob, bap. April 29, 1764. 3.
Klaartje, bap. May 18, 1766. 4. Willem, bap. Jan. 9, 1768.
5. Klaartje, bap. May 13, 1770. 6. John, bap. June 7, 1772.
7. Petrus, bap. July 3, 1774. 8. Evert, bap. Sept. 9, 1777.
86. RACHEL, bap. Feb. 11, 1739, died June 10, 1796 ; m. Isaac,
son of Isaac Kip and Cornelia Lewis, born 1732. 1. Cornelia, bap. April 15, 1764. 2. Klaartje, bap. Sept. 1, 1771.
3. Elizabeth, bap. July 3, 1774.
87. JENNETEE, m. Nicholas Heermans. 1. Andries, bap. March
17, 1765. 2. Klaartje, bap. Oct. 18, 1767. 3. Jacob, bap.
March 4, 1770. 4. Neeltje, bap. Aug. 16, 1772. 5. Sara,
bap. Jan. 29, 1775. 6. Evert, bap. April 1, 1784.
88. JACOBUS, m. Klaartje Heermans. 1. Sara, bap. Aug. 31,
1772. 2. Klaartje, bap. May 26, 1776.
89. EVERT, bap. May 8, 1745.

CORRECTIONS AND ADDITIONS.

After "Frans bap. Feb. 1, 1727," insert, Johannes bap. March 19, 1732, in the 14th line of page 8.

For "He m. 2ᵈ Amerentia ———," read, He m. 2ᵈ Amerentia Stout, in the 7th line of page 9.

After "Jacquemyntie bap. Nov. 29, 1727," insert, Isaac bap. Dec. 19, 1731, and Coenraad bap. June 12, 1734, in the 16th line of page 9.

For "Aug. 3, 1718," read, Aug. 31, 1718, in the last line of page 12, and add the following : *Margreta Howarding*, wife of Robert Livingston, Jr., was the dau. of Thomas Howarding, an English merchant in New York, and his wife Catharina Bedlo; she was bap. July 30, 1693. Her father's will is dated Dec. 12, 1700 ; proven Feb. 17, 1703. Her mother was the dau. of Isaac and Elizabeth (de Potter) Bedlo, and became the second wife of Dr. Samuel Staats. At the baptism, Aug. 31, 1718, of Robert, son of Robert Jr. and Margaret (Howarding) Livingston, the sponsors were Robert Livingston and Catharina Staats, widow, the grandparents, without doubt, of the infant.

For "Rachel Monjour," read Rachel Defour (De Foreest ?) in the 10th line of page 13. The authority for this correction can be seen under date of Aug. 18, 1647, when Johannes de La Montagne, "widower of Rachel Defour" (De Foreest), married Agnietie Jillis, widow of Arendt Corszens Stam. *See* Marriage Records of Dutch Church, page 14, and published in the NEW YORK GENEALOGICAL AND BIOGRAPHICAL RECORD for 1875, vol. vi. page 37.

Add to 25th line, page 13, the Flatbush, L. I., records give the date of this marriage Feb. 16, 1687.

For "Jacobus Van Varick and Anna Maria Brestede," read, Abraham Varick and Anna Bertholf, in the 21st line of page 14.

For "Schont" read, Schout, in the 3d line of page 17.

For "Catharine ———," read, Catharine Smith, in the 3d line of page 18. Catharine Smith, widow of Huybert de Riemer, m. June 28, 1688, John Silkwood, from Wigby, in England.

For "1723," read, 1728, in 45th line of page 19.

After "Jan. 14, 1786," insert, aged 71 years and 3 months, in the 27th line of page 20.

For "vol. vii. p. 23," read, vol. vi. p. 23, in the 41st line of page 22.

After "July 20, 1726," insert, and Jan bap. Sept. 27, 1732, in 16th line of page 26.

After "July 4, 1657," insert, Anthony Wanshaer m. at Flatbush, L. I., Jan. 8, 1682, Maretje Herberts or Harperts, in the 45th line of page 26.

After "Sept. 17, 1662," insert, 9. Jan, bap. Dec. 5, 1663, and 10. Carel, bap. July 4, 1666, in 2d line of page 27.

After "August, 1683," insert, their marriage license is dated June 24, 1687, in 44th line of page 30.

After "Pieter Wessels" insert, and died at Shrewsbury, Jan. 18, 1816, in the 21st line of page 32.

After " 1749," insert, Jacobus, bap. July 3, 1751, and Johanna, bap. Feb. 20, 1754, in the 2d line of page 35.

For "having survived his wife about a year," read, his wife died May 14, 1684, in the 15th line of page 37.

For " RECORD, vol. vii. page 148, foot-note," read, see page 31, foot-note, in the 15th line of page 42.

After "latter place," add, and had son Livingston born Feb. 24, 1785, in the last line of page 43.

Strike out " unmarried," in 42d line of page 44, and see note on page 45.

After " Midwout," insert, Sarah Roelofs made her Will July 29, 1693, with Codicil dated August 7, 1693; proved October 21, 1693, in the 13th line of 3d foot-note on page 53.

After " will," insert, one of her name m. April 25, 1700, Johannes Veet from Brisack, in Sweden, in 13th line of page 72.

After " died there " insert, his will is dated Jan. 10, 1704; proved May 22, 1712; names wife Catrina, and children Nicolaes, Lidia wife of Andries Dow, Anneke, Catrina, and Deborah, in the 42d line of page 74.

After " 1704," insert, his will was made Feb. 17, 1703; proved November 4, 1709; names wife Agnes and her two children Henry and Lydia de Meyer, to whom he gives his estate, in the 35th line of page 76.

INDEX TO NAMES AND FAMILIES.

RECOMMENDED READING
from NEHGS

New York Essays
Resources for the Genealogist in New York State
Outside New York City
By Marian S. Henry
NEHGS • 6 x 9 pbk, 334 pp. • $17.95

New York State Probate Records
A Genealogist's Guide to Testate and Intestate Records
SECOND EDITION
By Gordon L. Remington, FUGA, FASG
NEHGS • 7 x 10 pbk, 224 pp. • $24.95

The Expansion of New England
The Spread of New England Settlement and Institutions
to the Mississippi River, 1620–1865
By Lois Kimball Mathews, Foreword by Ralph J. Crandall
NEHGS • 6 x 9 pbk, 318 pp. • $17.95

For a summary of methods and key sources now available for
researching "Ancient Families of New Amsterdam and New
York," see "New Netherland Connections and Researching
New York Dutch Families," by Henry B. Hoff,
in *American Ancestors* 13:1 (Winter 2012):52–54.